PHOTOGRAPHERS

in ARIZONA

1850~1920

A History & Directory

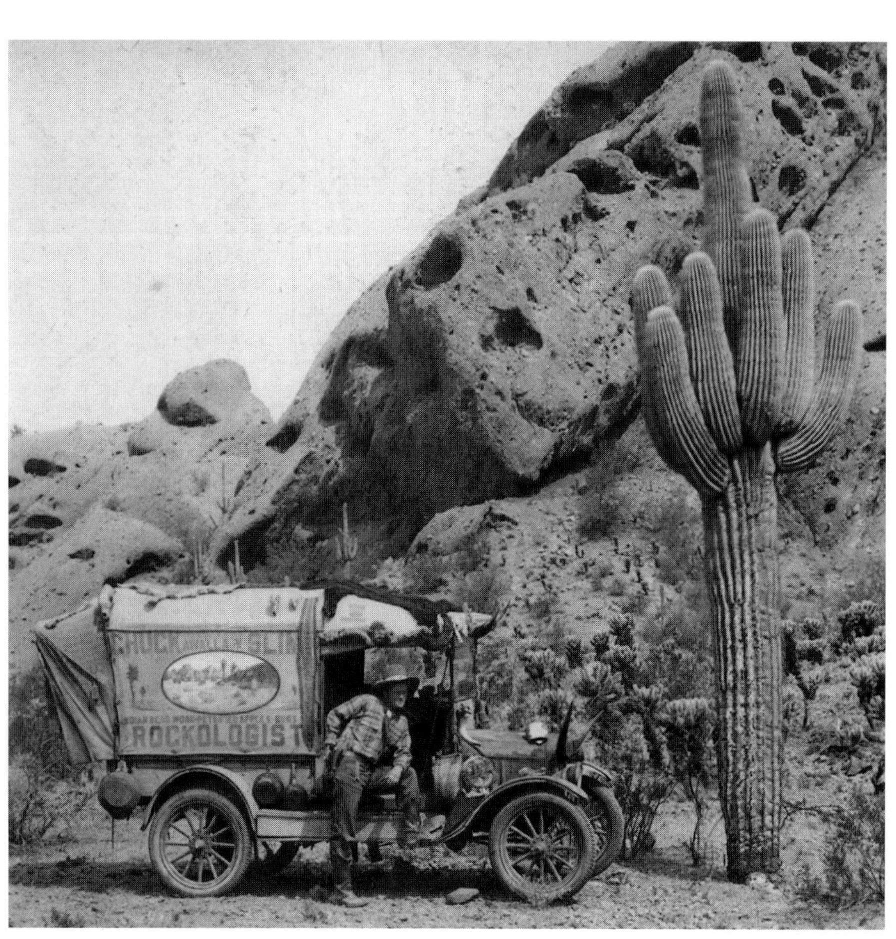
CHUCK AWALLA SLIM
ROCKOLOGIST

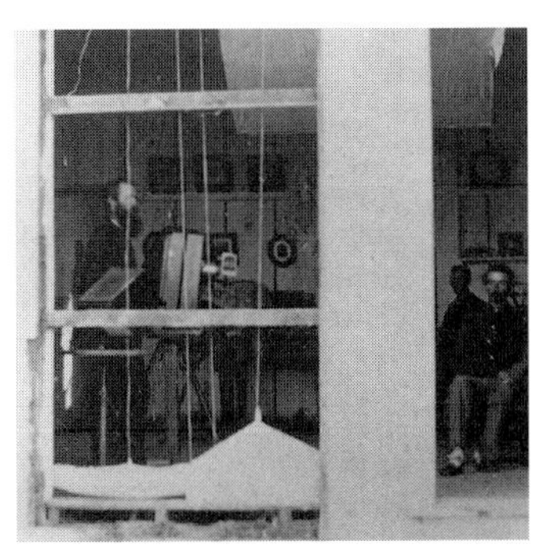

1850~1920

PHOTOGRAPHERS
in ARIZONA
A History & Directory

CARL MAUTZ PUBLISHING
NEVADA CITY 1997

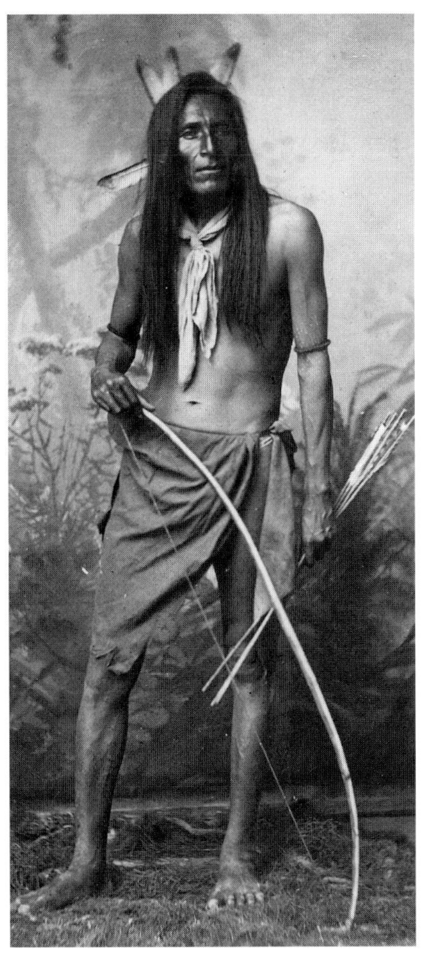

JEREMY ROWE

COPYRIGHT 1997 CARL MAUTZ PUBLISHING
TEXT COPYRIGHT 1997 JEREMY ROWE
ALL RIGHTS RESERVED IN ALL COUNTRIES

FIRST EDITION

FRONTISPIECE: *"Chuckawall Slim, the Rockologist" at what is now Papago Park in Phoenix. Detail of real photo postcard, photographer unknown, c. 1920. Collection of the author.*

TITLE PAGE PHOTOGRAPHS:
TOP. *A photographer at work in the Hole in the Wall Art Gallery, Camp Verde, Arizona Territory. Detail of stereograph by Daniel F. Mitchell. Courtesy of Sharlot Hall Museum.*
BOTTOM. *Unidentified studio portrait of Apache, Phoenix, Arizona Territory. Detail of cabinet card by F. A. Hartwell. Collection of the author.*

DESIGN BY RICHARD D. MOORE
COMPOSED IN MONOTYPE CENTAUR & ARRIGHI TYPEFACES
PRINTED IN THE UNITED STATES OF AMERICA

LIBRARY OF CONGRESS CATALOG CARD NUMBER: 94-077985
LIBRARY OF CONGRESS CATALOGING IN PUBLICATION DATA
Rowe, Jeremy S.
    Photographers in Arizona, 1850–1920 : a history & directory/
by Jeremy Rowe
    p. cm.
    Includes bibliographical references and index.
    ISBN: 1-887694-05-6

    1. Photography—Arizona—History–To 1912. 2. Photography—
Arizona—History–1912–1950. 3. Photography—Arizona—To 1912—
Directories. 4. Photographers—Arizona–1912–1950—Directories.
I. Title

TR24.A6R69 1996   770.9'791
                    QB196-40088

CARL MAUTZ PUBLISHING
228 COMMERCIAL STREET, NO. 522
NEVADA CITY, CALIFORNIA 95959
TELEPHONE 916 478-1610 FAX 916 478-0466

Contents

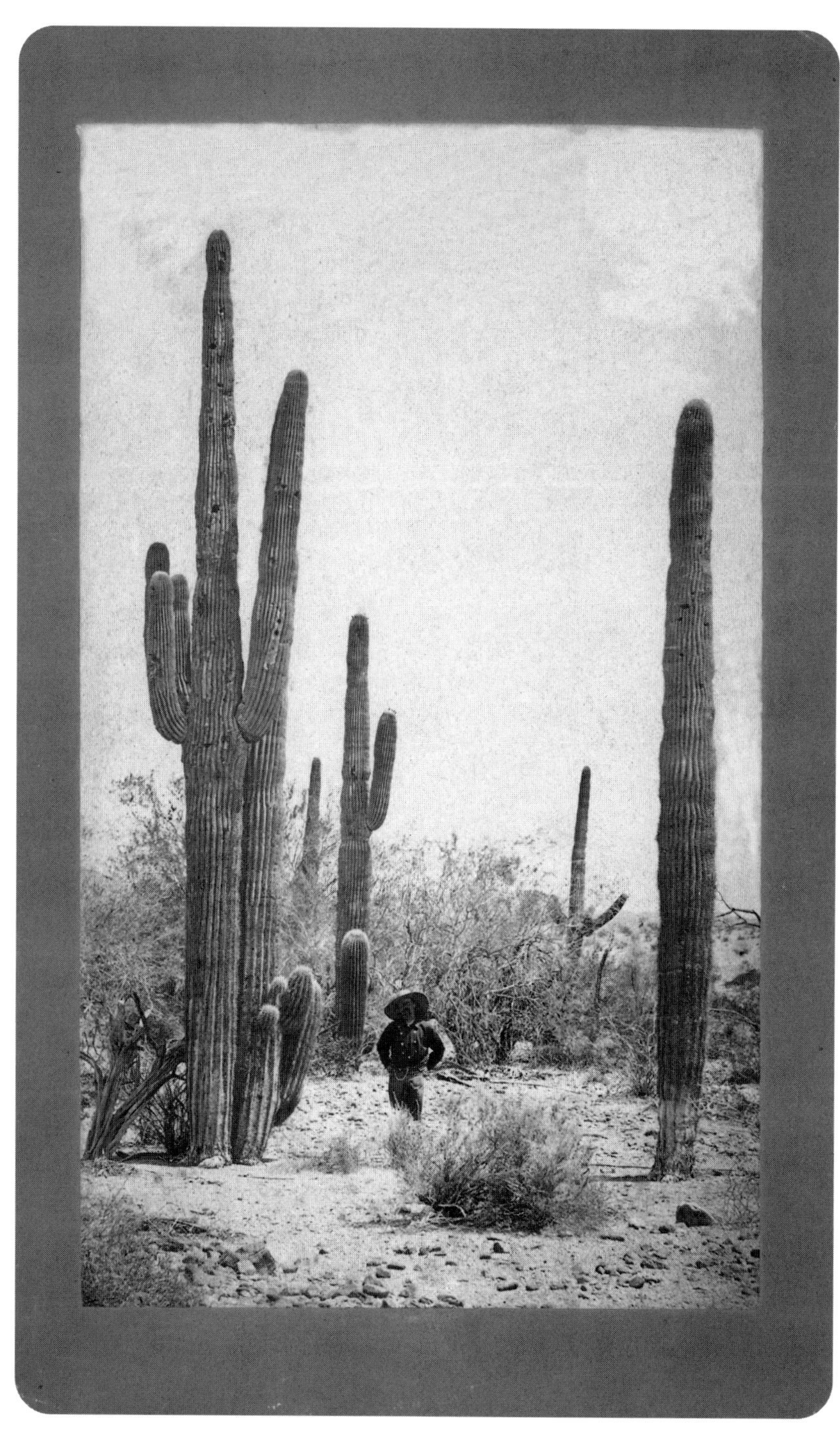

Unidentified man with a 35 foot Saguaro cactus, a popular Arizona subject. Location and photographer unknown, boudoir card, c. 1890. Collection of the author.

Introduction

Something magical happened when I held my first daguerreotype, and for the past 20 years, photography has been a major passion in my life. The magic has followed my path from that first daguerreotype to stereographs, cabinet cards, and finally, to photographic postcards. In about 1980, I narrowed my focus and began to look closely at Arizona-related items. A few years later, my scope narrowed further to a full scale search for historic images of Arizona.

The images of Arizona's past led me to questions about the photographers who made the images—who were they? How did they live? What brought them to the locations photographed or drew customers to their studios? And most pertinent to me as a collector—what became of the rest of their work?

I began making notes about photographs I came across at trade shows, in catalogs, in private collections, and at museums and archives. Lists of photographers and image titles soon formed, leading me to look deeper into the lives of early photographers.

Another catalyst fueling my investigation was the discovery of relationships between groups of images in different collections. New trails to research opened before me.

When I first began this research, photography received little attention in most public collections and images were rarely identified by photographer or format. As the understanding of photography as an historic tool has grown, many collections have begun to identify, catalog and organize their images to enhance their utility.

The directory in this book identifies many of the photographers who lived and worked in Arizona from its early history as a Territory of the United States through the first two decades of this century.

Included are brief notes regarding the dates, addresses, areas of activity and partnerships for each photographer. Dates and areas of activity have been conservatively identified and are based on citations and physical evidence examined to date. For some photographers the ranges of active dates of operation noted may be expanded by future research. Also, variant spellings noted in some sources have been maintained unless a definitive indication of the photographer's name has been found.

It is not possible to identify every photographer who operated in early Arizona, but this listing will provide researchers, historians, and collectors with a useful resource for identification and dating of photographs.

This is a work in progress and includes materials from primary and secondary sources including:

1. Mount imprints and photographic credits from private and public collections.
2. Governmental documents and publications.
3. City and business directories.
4. Newspapers and periodicals.
5. Contemporary listings and biographies of photographers.

I wish to thank all of the collectors, curators, dealers, and others whom I have met in the course of my research and who have helped me in my research efforts.

I encourage additions and corrections and I plan to issue subsequent editions of the directory as additional information becomes available. Please address correspondence to:

Jeremy Rowe
P.O. Box 40577
Mesa, AZ 85274

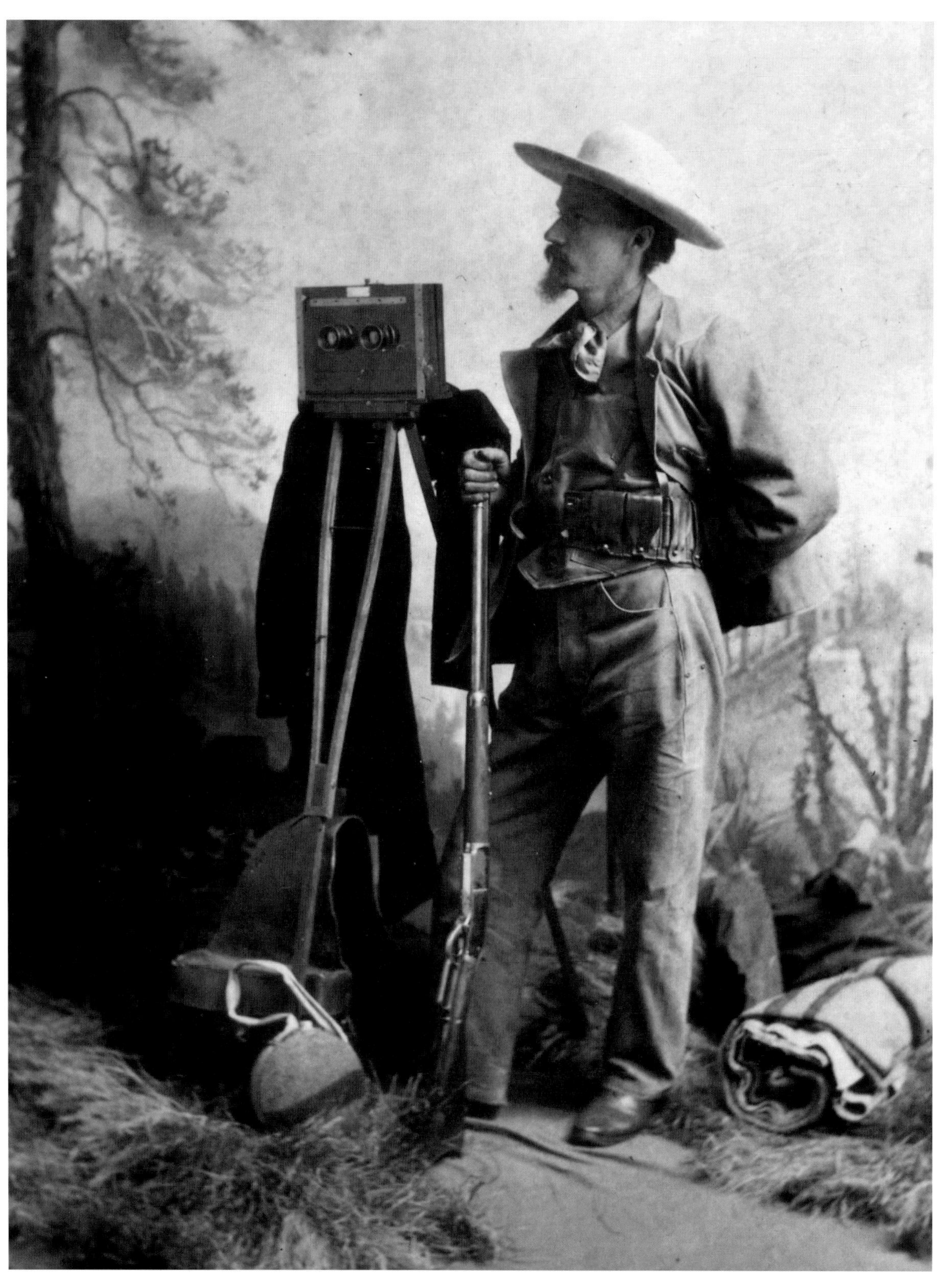

Portrait of Prescott photographer Erwin Baer with his stereo camera. Studio location and photographer unknown, cabinet card, c. 1890. Collection of the author.

ARIZONA IMAGES

FRONTIER PHOTOGRAPHERS OF THE WILD WEST

"But I reckon I got to light out for the Territory ahead
of the rest, because Aunt Sally she's going to adopt me
and civilize me, and I can't stand it. I been there before."
—*Adventures of Huckleberry Finn*, MARK TWAIN, 1884.

LIKE HUCKLEBERRY FINN, adventurous souls and free spirits felt the call of America's western frontier from the beginning of the 18th century. As the heartland of the untamed West, Arizona offered spectacular photo opportunities for the photographer with a taste for adventure and an eye for history. Legendary events such as the capture of Geronimo, the gunfight at the O. K. Corral, the Pleasant Valley War, and Pancho Villa's raids took place against the backdrop of Arizona's mountains and deserts. It was here that photographers found not only the Grand Canyon, the Lucky Cuss Mine, Fort Apache, and mining boomtowns, but such cultural icons as Cochise, Kit Carson, Wyatt Earp, Doc Holiday, and the Clanton gang. It was a land of promise and fable, and photographers packed up their cameras and lit out for the Territory in droves to capture the unfolding story.

Arizona's wild and colorful past was documented by hundreds of adventurous photographers. Some who created collections of photographs identified their work, while others left only anonymous images and albums as their legacy. Compared with other western states, and despite the importance of the personalities and events that occurred there, the number of Arizona images is relatively small. Unfortunately, for reasons that may include the rough frontier lifestyle and the itinerant nature of much of their business, few of Arizona's pioneer photographers left much information about their own lives and experiences.

Many images of frontier Arizona portray the individuals, scenes and events of life in the forts, military outposts, wild mining towns, and growing communities of the West. The sparse, decentralized population kept the scale of photographic operations relatively small, with itinerant photographers far outnumbering established studios until the 1890s. Early Arizona drew many of the nation's finest photographers and many lesser talents, to feed the demand for images of Native Americans, cacti, the Grand Canyon, and the prosperous mining operations in the last 19th century frontier.

This book is a collection of rarely seen images of Arizona, presented in the historical context of its development from a territory to a state. Photo historians will find it a useful reference tool in identifying photographs taken in the state before 1920. This text includes:

❖ A brief overview of the history of photography in Arizona from its beginning in the 1850s to its maturation in the decade after statehood in 1912.

❖ A directory of photographers active in Arizona between roughly 1850 and 1920, including approximate years of operation, partnerships formed, and studio locations.

❖ A selection of images of Arizona demonstrating the range and diversity of photographic subjects, and providing a feel for life in Arizona during this historically rich time.

Legends of treasure drew the first Spanish explorers into what is now Arizona. Though Cabeza de Vaca and Marcos de Niza never found the seven cities of gold, Spanish settlers did find gold, silver, and copper and operated mines in the 18th and early 19th centuries. Missions San Xavier del Bac and San Cayetano del Tumacacori were established in 1700–01, and Tucson, adjacent to Mission San Xavier, followed a few decades later.

American trappers first visited the Colorado, Gila, and other rivers of the region in the 1820s. Kit Carson first explored along the Gila in 1827, returning time and again over the next 25 years. Bill Williams explored the lands above the 35th parallel, and French trapper Pauline Weaver visited Pima Villages in 1832. By the early 1840s, trappers and explorers reached the Hopi villages in the north and had criss-crossed the Territory with trails that would become crucial trade routes opening the West.

The Mexican War of 1846–1848 focused the attention of the nation on America's southern border. Many of the trappers and early explorers became guides for American troops. Kit Carson returned to Arizona and served as a guide for the expeditions of Generals Kearny and Fremont. The Mormon Battalion formed under Kearny in Leavenworth, Kansas, was charged with capturing the area that is now Arizona, New Mexico, and part of California for the United States. The Battalion reached southern Arizona in the winter of 1846 and soon took Tucson, which had been evacuated by the Mexicans. The group continued north to Pima and Maricopa Villages and the Salt River Valley, continuing to explore Arizona as they traveled west into California.

The treaty of Guadelupe Hildago at the end of the Mexican War in 1848 established the Gila River as the southern boundary of the United States. The New Mexico Territory, which included Arizona, was established in 1850 with the Gila River as its southern boundary. The Gadsen Purchase in 1853 extended the border, creating the outline of the United States that we know today.

The lure of California gold brought thousands across the Territory on the mail coaches and trails that had been pioneered by the trappers, military expeditions and surveys. It has been estimated that at least 60,000 travelers crossed Arizona through Apache Pass, Sonoita, and Tucson, crossing the Colorado River at Yuma on their way to the California gold fields.

Throughout the rest of the nation, photography had been firmly established as a business and art in which millions of images were being produced each year. During the early 1850s, the "mirror with a memory," the daguerreotype, was the photographic format of choice and was practiced by thousands of full- and part-time operators. Despite the volume of traffic across the Territory and the existence of daguerreotypes of California, New Mexico and the other surrounding states, no daguerreotypes which can be documented as having been made in the Arizona portion of the New Mexico Territory have been located to date.

Early images of Arizona came from sketches and illustrations by travelers or explorers, apparently made without the benefit of the camera. The personnel involved in the Bartlett survey of 1852–53 included an artist, Henry Cheever Pratt, who recorded the progress of the expedition along the little-known border with Mexico in his small (2¾″ x 5¼″) personal sketchbooks. The first sketchbook included approximately 60 images of the trip down the coast from San Francisco to San Diego, across to Yuma, and up the Gila River to Casa Grande and the Maricopa Villages. Pratt included ethnographic sketches of the Pima and Maricopa, botanical sketches and several pages of notes and impressions of the expedition. Initially, illustrations from the sketchbooks were published in reports of the expedition, and years later, Pratt synthesized elements included in the sketches into a series of paintings of the West.

Relations with Native Americans were volatile, shifting from neutral acceptance to hostility as their territories were encroached. The Navajo were involved in many early conflicts and the first military post in the Territory, Fort Defiance, was built by Col. Sumner in 1852 on the Navajo reservation. Other tribes, most notably the Apache, Mohave, and Yuma, were involved in conflicts, many in response to abuse and

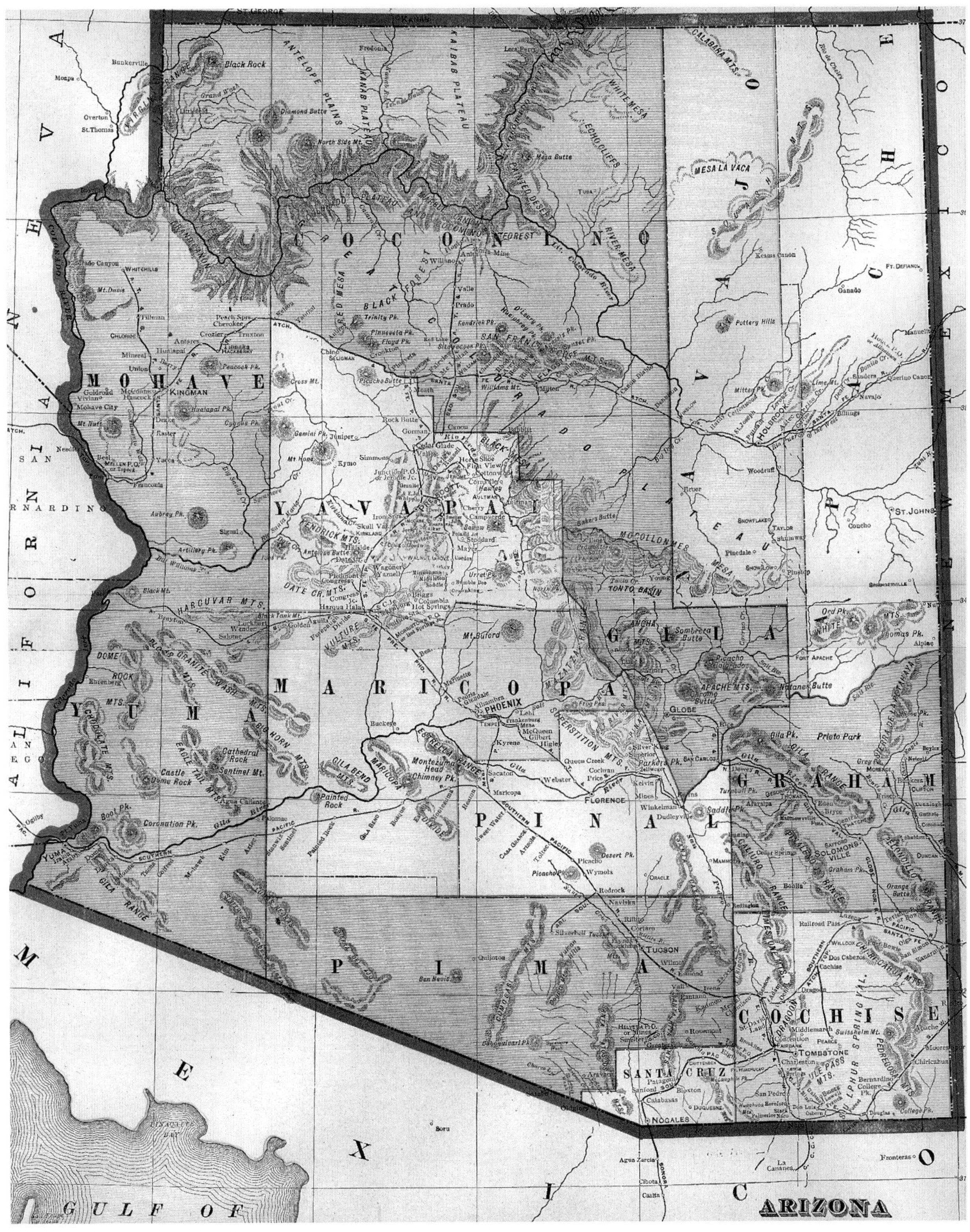

FIGURE 1. *Map of Arizona Territory showing its development. George F. Cram, publisher, c. 1905. Collection of the author.*

encroachment by the early settlers. The rest of the nation followed the events in Arizona with keen interest.

Word of rich mineral deposits in the area ceded by Mexico in the Gadsen Purchase drew commercial interest in Arizona. The Arizona Mining and Trading Company was formed in San Francisco in 1854 to explore and develop mines in the Territory. Rich copper ore was found in the southwest portion near the old Spanish mines close to present day Ajo. Ore was hauled to San Francisco and shipped to Swansea, Wales, for refining. The ore was rich enough to turn a profit for the investors despite the high shipping costs.

Though thousands were traveling through Arizona in the 1850s, few called it their home. By 1856, the largest settlement was at Tubac, with about 800 residents, while Tucson boasted a population of about 500. The first census of the area, the descennial census of 1860, gave the aggregate population of the Territory as 6,482, identified as 2,421 white (including 132 from Fort Yuma, California), 21 free colored, and 4,040 Indians. The bulk of the population consisted of military staff of Forts Arivaipa, Buchanan, Defiance and Mohave. Tucson boasted the largest population of 521, with 109 persons living in a settlement around San Xavier Mission a few miles South of Tucson.

Lt. Joseph Christmas Ives was one of the earliest persons to acknowledge making photographs in Arizona. Ives piloted the riverboat, *U. S. Explorer*, to chart the course of the Colorado River for the U. S. Army Corps of Topographical Engineers survey of 1857–1858. The Ives expedition marked a number of first related to Arizona history. On his northernmost travels along the Colorado River, Ives was likely the first white man to reach the bottom of the Grand Canyon. Photographs attributed to Ives and the expedition are some of the earliest photographic images of Arizona located to date.

Popular interest in Arizona reached an early peak when *Captivity of the Oatman Girls,* by R. B. Stratton, was published in 1857. Six years earlier, en route to California on the Santa Fe trail, the Oatman family had been attacked by Apaches. Daughters Olive and Ann had been abducted and held captive. Their brother Lorenzo Oatman recovered from his wounds and began to search western Arizona for his sisters. Ann died in captivity soon after the attack, but in 1856, after living with several Arizona tribes, Olive was rescued by Lorenzo near Yuma.

The story of the trials of Olive received national distribution and the book sold through several editions. An engraved image of Olive after her rescue and return to civilization was used as the frontispiece of the book and was taken from an ambrotype. At least two ambrotypes and a number of carte-de-visite portraits of Olive Oatman exist today, with her chin bearing the traditional tatoos of a Mohave woman. Though these images of Ms. Oatman were likely taken after her return to civilization, they focused significant attention and interest on the potential danger faced by travelers and settlers in Arizona.

Arizona was recognized as a Territory in 1862 by both the Union and Confederate governments. After the Civil War, Arizona became part of the Military District of California under General Irwin McDowell. Throughout the rest of the century, Civil War military figures such as Generals Orlando Willcox, Nelson Miles, George Stoneman, George Crook, and Colonels A. Katz and Crittenden played important roles in shaping the Territory.

The first military camp in Arizona was Fort Defiance, established in northeastern Arizona in 1849. Fort Buchanan was established in southern Arizona in 1857 to protect the wagon and stage routes. Fort Mohave followed about a year later in the northwestern part of Arizona on the Colorado River. Another important early post, Fort McDowell in central Arizona, was established in 1865, completing a loose network of military protection for the Territory.

As California continued to develop and news of gold discoveries in Arizona drew miners to the Territory, travel increased, and additional forts were established. Fort Bowie (1862) was located in Apache Pass on the southern route, in the heart of the Apache lands at the eastern end of the stage route. Fort Whipple (1863–64) joined Fort McDowell in the central part of the state to protect Prescott and the rapidly developing Bradshaw mining districts.

The web of forts across the Territory continued to develop as word of new strikes spread, or relations with local tribes became strained. Other camps which evolved into more established bases of operation included Camp Lincoln (later Fort Verde) in 1864–66, and Camp McPherson (later Camp Date Creek) in 1866. Fort Apache (1869) in the west-central part of the Territory completed the basic framework of military protection for travelers and the growing number of miners and settlers calling Arizona their home.

The first official Territorial census taken in 1864, listed two persons as photographers: Francis A. Cook and Charles Rogers. Little is known about the activities of these two men during this time. Rogers left no record of his activities, while Mr. Cook became an important figure in Arizona photography later in the decade.

J. C. Gaige was licensed as a photographer in New Mexico in 1863 and was active in the Military District of New Mexico in 1865 and at Fort Sumner in 1866. Gaige later traveled in Arizona and was one of the first to advertise his services, billing himself simply as "the photographer" in the Tucson *Weekly Arizonan*. Gaige died at Camp Goodwin in July, 1869.

French occupation of northern Mexico raised nationalistic concerns as the West developed after the Mexican War and the Gadsen Purchase. Just after the Civil War, concern about potential Continental intervention in southern Arizona may have been stimulated by a Frenchman with a camera. A French survey, including a photographer tentatively identified as Rudolph D'Heureuse, was active in Mexico and southern Arizona about this time. A small body of stereoscopic photographs c. 1865–68 begins in Mazatlan and traces a route up the Baja coast into southern Arizona. Images include overviews of the ports and towns, as well as mining works at Yuma and Fort Mohave, and other as yet unidentified fortifications.

The first photographic gallery identified to date in the Arizona Territory appears to have opened in Prescott around 1868–69. Francis A. Cook arrived in Prescott, c. 1864. No documentation has been located indicating whether Cook operated as an itinerant or in a more formal studio. A notice in the January 1868, *Arizona Weekly Miner* indicates that Carlos Gentile rented a room and was photographing Prescott, its people, and the vicinity.

Charles (Carlos) Gentile had arrived in Victoria, British Columbia, in 1862, opening a dry goods store and later a photography gallery under the Occidental Billiard Saloon on Fort Street producing cartes-de-visite. Gentile triggered the Leach River gold rush in British Columbia in 1864, when he discovered particles of gold adhering to the photographic plates he was washing in a stream.

Gentile left British Columbia for California, opening a gallery in San Francisco in 1867. Later that year, the *Arizona Miner* noted that Gentile would be making photographs of Arizona for an unnamed San Francisco publisher. After producing photographs of the area, and offering portraits to the local population in 1868, Gentile decided to return to California in January, 1869, selling his camera to Cook and Nathan P. Pierce who planned to operate a gallery in Prescott.

The Cook/Pierce gallery became an important fixture in the visual history of the state, being subsequently owned or used by many photographers during the next 20 years. They include E. M. Jennings, William McKenna, Daniel Mitchell, the operators working for William Williscraft, and traveling photographers such as Dudley Flanders. A stereograph c. 1875 on a Williscraft mount captures the gallery with its skylight, a trap door on the south side of the building, and the optics of a solar enlarger open to sunlight. Several other images of the gallery show the building as it existed into the mid–1880s.

As they had in the 1840s and 1850s, surveys continued to focus the interest of the country on Arizona. Alexander Gardner and William Bell, renowned for their studio work and photographic documentation of the Civil War, accompanied the Union Pacific Railroad Eastern Division survey in 1867 and 1868. The photographs from this effort, also known as the Kansas Pacific Railway Survey, were primarily scenic documentation of the proposed route across northern Arizona, and had little commercial potential beyond the survey report published in 1869.

The photographers associated with the Powell and Wheeler surveys of the Colorado Plateau during the 1870s were an entirely different matter, producing hundreds of images documenting the geography of the canyons of the Colorado River and of the Native Americans of Arizona. The images from these surveys were used to support requests for each annual extension of funds from Congress, and competition between the photographers associated with the survey parties was fierce. Sets of stereoviews, some in elaborate blue flocked boxes with embossed titles, as well as handsome presentation albums of photographs, were produced to support the lobbying efforts, and thousands of copies of the stereoviews and large format images of the West taken by photographers including Timothy O'Sullivan, James Fennemore, John Hillers, William Bell and E. O. Beaman were sold throughout the world.

The photographs from the Wheeler and Powell surveys made images of the life of tribes such as the Pai-ute, Apache, Navajo and Hopi, available to the world. The previously little-known Grand Canyon joined Yosemite and the other natural wonders of the West as international curiosities. The interest in Arizona grew dramatically throughout the next decades and drew photographers to the Territory to supply images for the rapidly expanding markets.

The newspapers and periodicals of the time responded to the keen interest in the Wild West during the 1870s. Arizona was a microcosm of the mining strikes, conflicts with the Apache, and the outlaws and personalities that characterized the West. The Territory quickly established the reputation, which was actively promoted in fact and fiction, as a wild outpost of civilization. The demand for images of Arizona was filled by woodcuts and illustrations in print and supplemented by cartes-de-visite, cabinet cards and stereoviews, sold by photographers who visited Arizona, or by unscrupulous operators who freely copied and distributed interesting images that fell into their hands, a practice known as "pirating."

The rough lifestyle and arduous travel made photography difficult. Photographers used the wet-plate process, requiring them to carry glass plates, chemicals to sensitize and process their negatives, and a dark tent, in addition to their cameras. Enlargement was difficult, so typically a photographer would carry

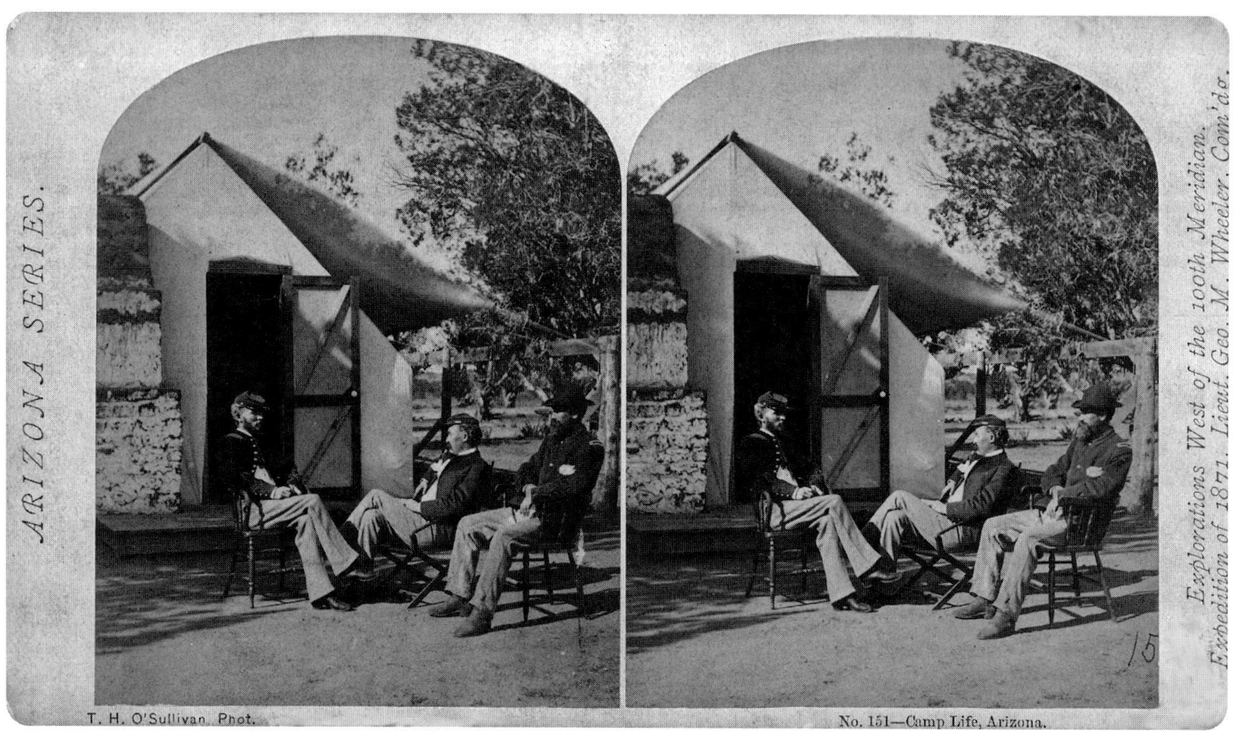

FIGURE 2. *Unidentified soldiers of the 8th Cavalry at Camp Hualapai on the road between Prescott and Fort Mohave, north of Prescott, Arizona Territory, taken in conjunction with the Wheeler Survey. Stereograph by Timothy O'Sullivan, 1871. Collection of the author.*

a camera for each size image that was to be produced. An exception was the stereo camera, which could produce both stereos and the popular cabinet cards by changing lenses and septum. The convenience and small size of the stereo camera, which permitted short exposures and relatively great depth of focus, made stereo the format of choice for many early Arizona photographers.

Carlos Gentile returned to Arizona from California, serving as a member of a prospecting party in the Pinal Mountains with Governor Anson P. Safford in 1871. Gentile stayed to operate a gallery in Adamsville, a small town of about 400 known for Birchard's Mill, which supplied flour to the forts in Arizona, and for its saloon. The gallery produced paper prints and ambrotypes, and received an award for images of Arizona at the 8th Industrial Exposition in California in 1871. The titles of the images for which Gentile received an Honorable Mention and was awarded a diploma at the exhibition included:

1023. Ambrotype. *Belles of Arivaipas.*
1024. Ambrotype. *South Wind Indian Belle.*
1025. Ambrotype. *Indian Group.*
1026. Ambrotype. *Bobtail, Indian Youth.*
1027. Ambrotype. *Old Rye, Indian Chief.*
1028. Ambrotype. *Indian Group.*
1029. Ambrotype. *Laughing Eyes, Indian Maiden.*
1030. Ambrotype. *Daisy, Indian Maiden.*
1031. Ambrotype. *Sunlight, Indian Maiden.*
1032. Ambrotype. *Springtime, Indian Maiden.*
1033. Ambrotype. *Male and Female Musician.*
1034. Ambrotype. *New Pie, Indian Chief.*
1035. Twenty Photographs of Indian Scenery.
1036. Five Photographs of Arizona Squaws.
1037. Photographs. *Group of Cueopa Indians.*
1038. *Irataba, Chief of the Mohaves.*

Unfortunately, none of these images, nor any reproductions which can be attributed to them, have been located to date.

Gentile was also involved in the planning, if not the realization, of an illustrated text about the Territory. In March of 1872, the *San Diego Union* carried a story about Mr. Charles Gentile's intent to publish a volume entitled, "Arizona As It Is," to be illustrated by photographs:

"Mr Gentile has just returned from a two year tour through the Territory and has placed his notes in the hands of Mr. John Melville who will write them up. The work will embrace a minute description of the military stations, with views of the most important of them. It will likewise describe the various towns and villages, both ancient and modern, scattered over the country. The descriptive portion will include a narrow and sterile border of the Territory that encloses an area of wonderful fertility; the southern chains of mountains and the extinct volcanos of the north; the great rocks that rise abruptly out of the earth, both in the green valley and the desert plain. All of these will be treated separately and profusely illustrated. The mineral wealth of the country will receive especial attention, and views of the principal mines and mining districts will illustrate the text. The ethnological department will consist of personal descriptions of every Indian tribe, and of the portion of the Territory they inhabit, together with portraits of members of each tribe taken from life. The work is dedicated by permission to General Halleck and will be issued in monthly installments."

An interesting side note is that a strikingly similar book, *Arizona As It Is, or the Coming Country, Compiled from Notes of Travel During the Years 1874, 1875, and 1876,* by Hiram C. Hodge was published by Hurd and Houghton of New York in 1877. The content of Hodge's book is similar to that outlined by Gentile and Melville, but without the photographic illustrations.

Another early effort to capitalize on the interest in Arizona involved Dudley Flanders and Henri Penlon, a pair of entrepreneurs from Los Angeles. Flanders and Penlon traveled the northern route to Arizona through Fort Mohave, following the stage route to Prescott in November 1873. Penlon died in Prescott a few months later, but Flanders continued his photographic tour, working with other assistants,

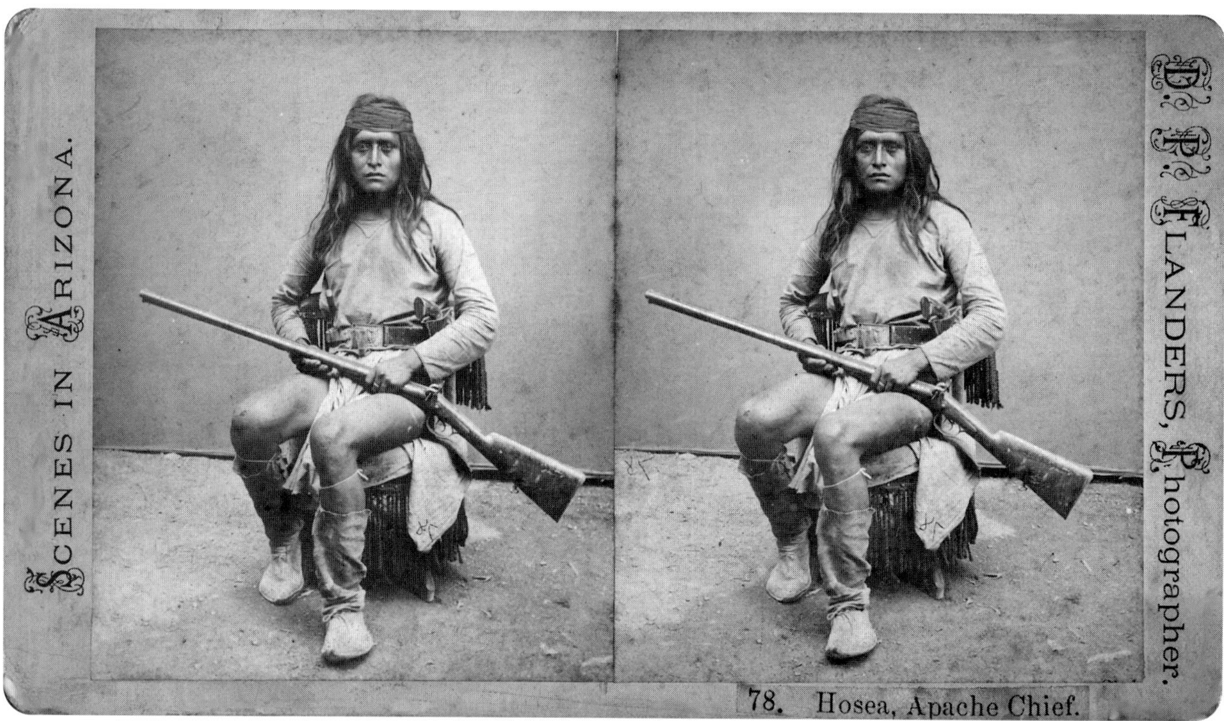

FIGURE 3. *Portrait of Apache Chief Hosea taken at the San Carlos reservation. Stereograph by Dudley Flanders, summer, 1874. Collection of the author.*

until he returned to Los Angeles in November 1874. Producing stereoviews and life–sized portraits (using the solar enlarger at Cook's gallery), Flanders made views in Prescott and the Verde Valley. In April 1874, Flanders and an assistant, Mr. Scott, presented a lantern slide lecture illustrated with his images of Arizona. This event is the earliest record of the presentation of projected photographs in Arizona identified to date. A review in the *Arizona Miner* stated:

"By invitation we visited Mr. Flanders' stereopticon presentation rehearsal last evening and were positively gratified at what we saw. His foreign views are simply splendid, and the views of camps and Indians here in the Territory are all that could be wished. We would suggest this entertainment as instructive and, we believe, will provide more than the money's worth to anyone who may choose to attend. His performance will continue for four evenings. Mr. Scott, assistant to Mr. Flanders, is an excellent hand in this line of business, and has done much credit to himself in the part he has performed in the preparation of these views."

Flanders headed south from Prescott after the show, stopping at stage stations in Wickenberg and Maricopa Wells en route to Tucson, where he repeated his stereopticon lectures at Levin's garden.

In July 1874, Flanders traveled from Tucson with a local photographer named Adolpho Rodrigo, visiting military forts such as Fort Bowie and Camp Grant, and the San Carlos Indian Reservation. They photographed the Indian agents, chiefs and General George Crook, the Apache fighter and military head of Arizona. The result of the effort was a series of over 120 stereoviews of the stage stops, forts, reservation, missions, towns and personalities of the Territory marketed as "A Photographic Album of a Trip Through Arizona by Flanders and Penlon" and "Scenes of Arizona."

Adolpho Rodrigo opened his gallery in Tucson at the corner of Courthouse and Maiden Lane in the summer of 1874. Like the Cook/Pierce gallery in Prescott, the Rodrigo gallery supported other photographers operating in Tucson, such as Henry Buehman, and itinerants like Flanders, who were active in the southern part of the Territory. Whether due to the local water, processing anomalies, heat or other causes, many images attributed to this gallery (those by Buehman and Flanders in particular) unfortunately suffered significant fading and deterioration, today providing only weak approximations of the original images.

The latter half of the 1870s saw a continued increase in photographic activity in the Territory. General Crook and the initial containment of the Apaches on reservations received tremendous national attention. As the surface mineral wealth diminished and placer mining began to taper off, miners looked further underground and made rich strikes in gold, silver and copper. Word of the continuing discoveries of mineral deposits in the Territory spread quickly. Photographers were needed to document the mines and towns for potential development, to make images of the events and activities of the native population, and to support the growing population's desire for portraits.

Itinerant photographers worked throughout Arizona, and while some left little evidence of their work, others stayed on to become successful gallery owners, marketing images to local merchants and by mail. During the 1870s, photographers typically established their presence in a town, traveled to create image inventories, and developed partnerships or contracted with distributors to extend their markets.

In Yuma, a gallery was established on Main Street in 1874 by a father and son team, Joseph and Francis Parker, previously of San Diego. Joseph Parker moved back to California a few years later, opening a gallery in Los Angeles in 1877. He returned to Arizona in the late 1880s with the Atlantic and Pacific Railway, working in Flagstaff, Winslow, and later in Tucson, as an itinerant during the next 20 years.

Henry Buehman arrived from California in 1874, purchasing Rodrigo's gallery in 1875 and beginning a family dynasty that would serve Tucson for several generations. Buehman traveled extensively throughout Arizona and New Mexico making images, promoting his work in local papers, and building his business selling frames, moldings, prints, and photographs including cartes-de-visite, cabinet cards, stereoviews, and large format images of Arizona and the West.

Buehman offered several series of stereoviews marketed as "Arizona Scenery" and "Scenes in Arizona," including hundreds of images of Tucson, the Silver King, Toltec and Picket Post mines, personalities

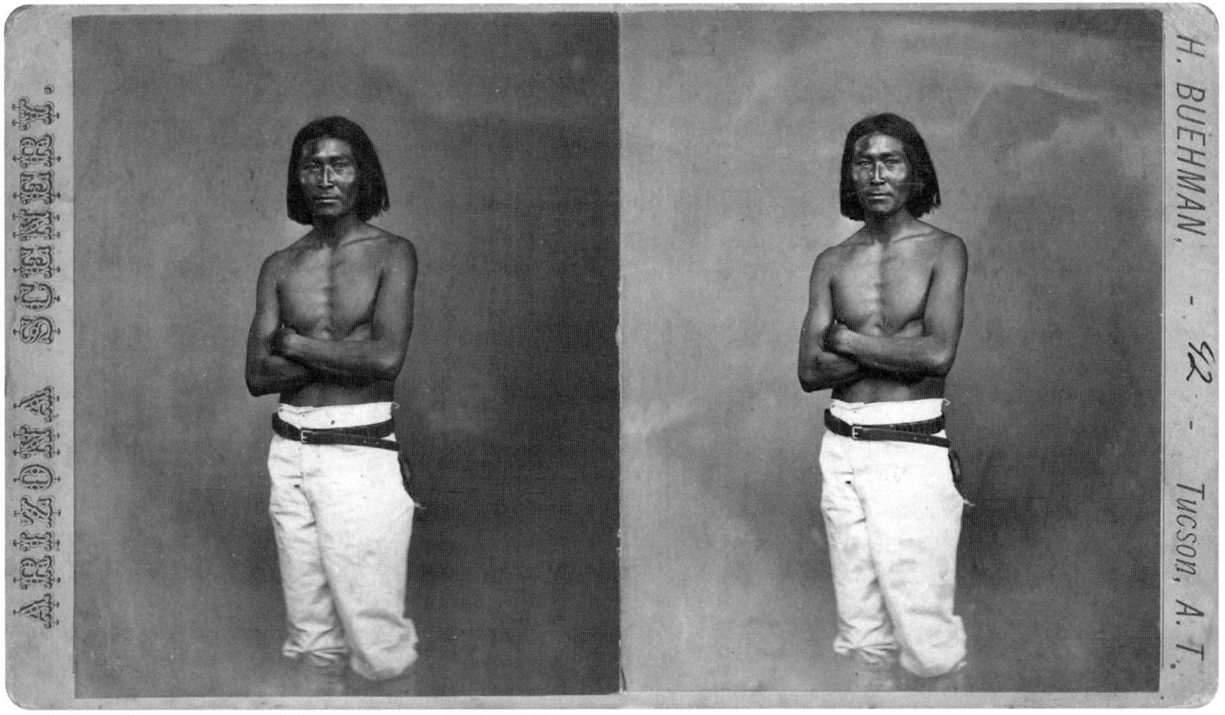

Figure 4. *Studio Portrait of Don Dee, location unknown. Stereograph by Henry Buehman, c. 1878. Collection of the author.*

such as John Clum, Diablo, Eskiminzin, Apache police and scouts at the San Carlos reservation, and studio still life views of Arizona cacti and reptiles.

During the 1870s, the Cook/Pierce gallery in Prescott saw several new owners. William McKenna acquired the gallery in August 1874, and operated it for a year before selling it to a local boot and shoe-maker, William Williscraft. Various assistants were hired to operate the gallery as Williscraft apparently had little or no photographic training. The gallery produced tintypes and stereoviews, distributed on mounts with a Williscraft & Company imprint. In 1876, an assistant, Schroeder, helped to create a trav-eling photographic gallery on wheels that made it at least as far as Camp Verde. Unfortunately, the quality of the operators and assistants was at best, poor, fre-quently producing images of historically valuable subjects veiled by fogging or softly focused.

Daniel Francis Mitchell came to Prescott from San Francisco in 1877, soon taking over the Willis-craft gallery on Cortez Street. Renaming his studio the Capital Art Gallery, Mitchell produced high quality photographs of Prescott and northern Ari-zona. Mitchell operated the gallery into the 1880s, forming partnerships or business arrangements with other Arizona photographers, including Erwin Baer.

George Rothrock arrived in Arizona from Bakers-field, California, as an itinerant photographer in 1875. In 1876, Rothrock and a partner named Young, estab-lished a tent gallery on Main Street in Yuma selling ambrotypes, cartes-de-visite, cabinet cards and stere-oviews. The partners also presented magic lantern exhibitions at the Yuma courthouse and at Fort Yuma. Later that year, Rothrock and Young operated in a small but growing farming community estab-lished in central Arizona to provide hay for the troops at Fort McDowell, forty miles from the present site of Phoenix.

After another year of traveling across Arizona, Rothrock established a studio on Montezuma Street in Prescott, offering a catalog of his stereographic views of Arizona scenery. Rothrock returned to Phoenix in April 1878, and opened a studio at the News Depot, and later at Loring's Bazaar on Wash-ington Street. Like previous photographic entrepre-

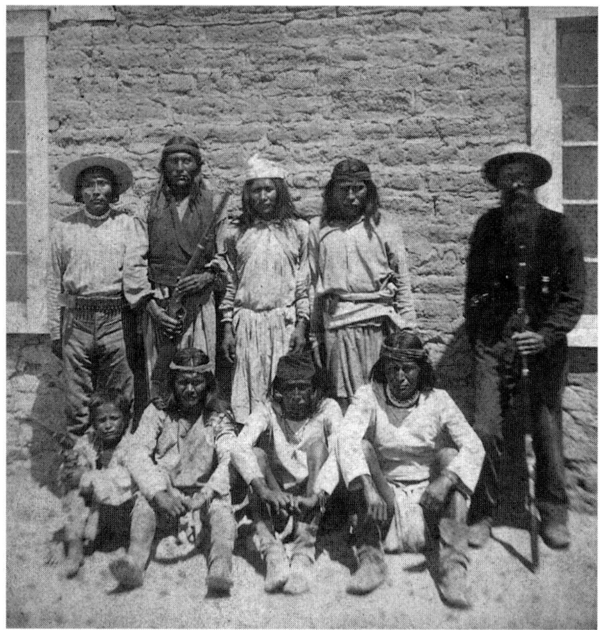

FIGURE 5. *Scout and Apaches at San Carlos. Stereograph by George Rothrock, c. 1878. Collection of the author.*

neurs, such as Dudley Flanders, Rothrock used magic lantern exhibitions as a promotional tool.

Rothrock continued to travel extensively through-out Arizona into the 1890s, opening an additional gallery in Tempe in 1893. Based on travels through the Territory, Rothrock singlehandedly created an exten-sive record of an exciting period of growth and devel-opment. His artistry, technical skill and emphasis on quality resulted in particularly impressive images.

Travel in central Arizona was by horse, wagon or stagecoach. Mines were developed along the Colorado and Gila Rivers only because of steamboats that had the capacity to carry heavy equipment and ore. Though horsepower and steamboats supported the initial growth of the territory, the arrival of the railroad in the 1870s was the watershed event for the explosive development of Arizona. The Southern Pacific extend-ed its rails east from San Diego, reaching Yuma in 1877 and Tucson in March, 1880. The Atlantic & Pacific provided travelers and developers with a rail route across northern Arizona by the end of 1883.

Enoch Conklin, working as a stereographer for the Continent Stereoscopic Company, was in Arizona in 1877 making images for commercial distribution. Conklin was in Yuma in September to document the completion of the railway bridge across the Colorado River and the arrival of the first locomotive in Arizona. Continent produced a series of at least half a dozen stereoviews of this event. In addition to the images of Yuma and Ehrenberg along the Colorado, Conklin traveled throughout the Territory making images of mining in the Santa Rita mountains, explorers on the Gila River, the towns of Tucson and Prescott, and views of the Hopi.

Conklin apparently also acquired negatives or copied work from other Arizona photographers, including Flanders and Buehman, whose uncredited work appears on Continent mount stereoviews. A chronicle of his trip, illustrated with engravings credited to the Continent Stereoscopic Company, was published by the Mining Record Printing Establishment as *Picturesque Arizona: Being the Result of Travels and Observations in Arizona During the Fall and Winter of 1877*.

Camilius Sidney Fly, previously of San Francisco, opened his first Arizona gallery on Fremont Street in Tombstone in 1878. Fly and his wife Mary produced

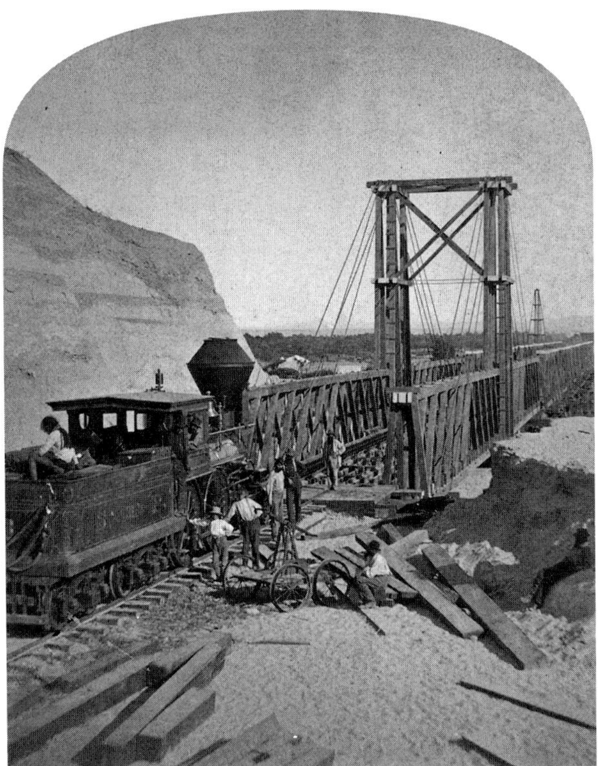

FIGURE 6. *First locomotive en route from California and about to cross the newly constructed railway bridge at Yuma, Arizona Territory. Stereograph published by Continent Stereoscopic Company, photographer Enoch Conklin, c. 1877. Collection of the author.*

a significant body of work, including images of the settlers and visitors to the growing mining and cultural center of the Southwest. Though no images were apparently made of Tombstone's most publicized event, the gunfight at the O. K. Corral, the gallery did make photographs of many of the West's most notable figures, including Geronimo, General Crook, Mickey Free, the Earp brothers, Doc Holliday and others.

The richness of the mineral strikes brought increasing notoriety. Tombstone grew from a boom camp with a population of about 100 in 1879 to a city of 15,000 rivaling San Francisco as a cultural center by the time of the Earp/Clanton shootout a few years later. Ironically, despite the dry climate, too much water ultimately proved to be the demise of Tombstone. Mine shafts reached down to an underground aquifer and pumps were required to control the water seepage. When the pumps burned in 1886 and 1887, the flooding that resulted was never controlled. Tombstone and its mines faded as a commercial center. Local Tombstone photographers like Mr. and Mrs. Fly, Feldman, and Kemp expanded their economic bases by opening new galleries in emerging communities across the Territory.

National attention focused on Geronimo's escape from the San Carlos Reservation in 1885, and his subsequent campaign of terror in New Mexico and eastern Arizona. Sentiment against the Apache and Native Americans in general ran strong. Retaliation against the peaceful individuals for the actions of the renegades was a serious concern of the Territorial government and the Indian Rights Association. The fears were well founded, as evidenced by a $250 bounty offered in February 1886 for the scalp of each renegade Apache presented to the Grant County, New Mexico Board of Commissioners.

General George Crook led the campaign to track Geronimo and his band. Crook and Geronimo held a parley near Nacozari, Mexico in March 1886, where the ultimatum given by the U. S. Government—two years imprisonment in the East, then return to the reservation in Arizona—was accepted by Geronimo. The meeting was documented by C. S. Fly, who accompanied the party and made additional images of the famous Apache warrior and his band.

After another escape and brief rampage through southern Arizona, Geronimo and Natchez surrendered in August 1886 and were sent to Forts Pickens and Marion in Florida. Eventually, Geronimo and the Apache were sent to Fort Sill. Trading on his fame, or exploited by promoters, depending on the point of view, Geronimo traveled extensively selling photographs and autographs at events such as the St. Louis World's Fair in 1904. Geronimo died on the reservation near Ft. Sill in 1909, never returning to his home in Southern Arizona.

Fly's name was immortalized for his images of General Crook's parlay with Geronimo, and the images of his band. The series of photographs of Geronimo were reproduced in *Harper's Weekly* in 1886 and copies were sold widely. Despite Fly's attempt to protect the images with prominent copyright notices on each image, they were actively pirated and sold by other photographers.

To broaden their market beyond Tombstone, the Flys opened a second gallery on Washington Street in Phoenix in 1892, and expanded to Bisbee in 1897.

After the death of Camilius in 1901, Mary continued the business, marketing photographs and printed images of Arizona, such as postcards. Unfortunately, virtually all of the negatives produced by the Flys were destroyed in a studio fire in 1912. The only extant Fly negatives located to date, including several images of Geronimo, the Crook parlay in Mexico, and the hanging of John Heath outside of Tombstone, were apparently purchased from Mrs. Fly by Arizona historian Shallot Hall in 1911 and later donated to an institutional collection.

Through the 1870s and into the 1880s, itinerant photographers operated photographic galleries in primitive outposts throughout Arizona. Charles Farciot, a clockmaker and engineer, operated a tiny adobe gallery in Pima Villages about 1879 and was actively documenting the mines and businesses of Charleston outside of Tombstone in the early 1880s. Farciot traveled as far north as Silver King, Globe and McMillenville making images of mines. Extant prints include stereoviews and full plate photographs of the developing mines and town of Charleston.

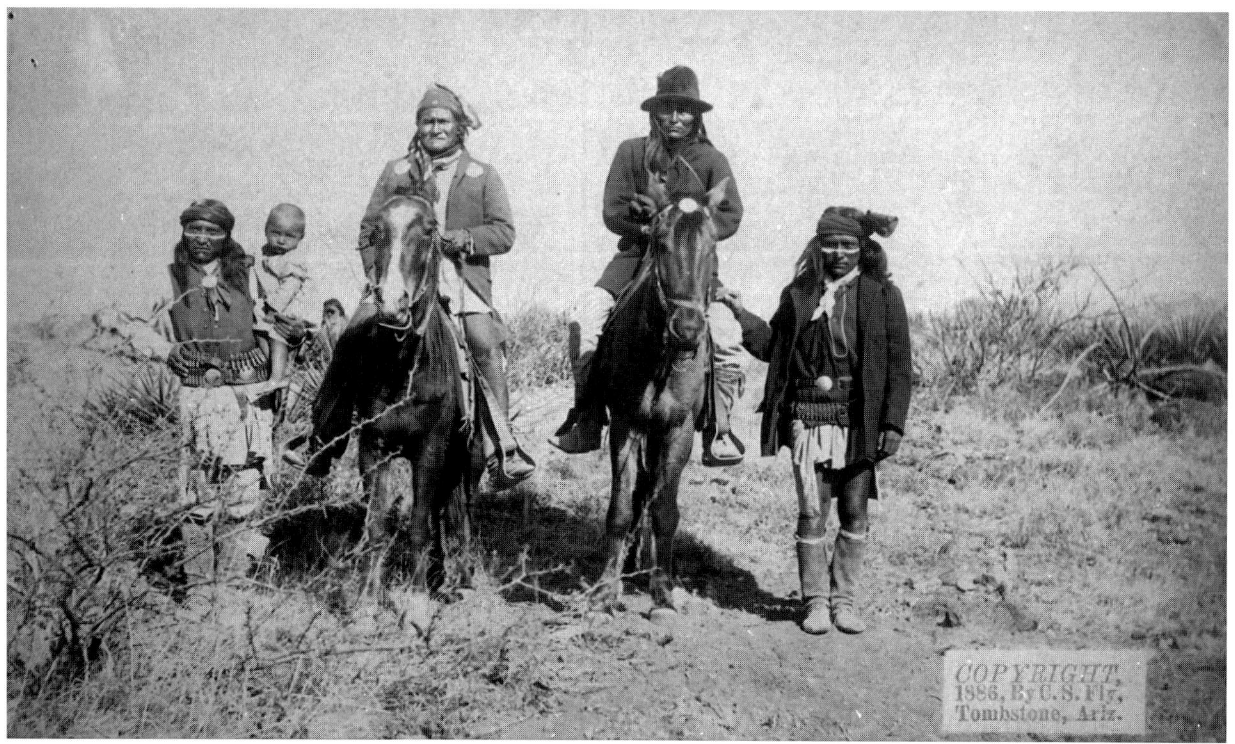

FIGURE 7. *Geronimo and members of his band, taken after leaving the reservation during negotiations with General George Crook for their surrender. Left to right: White Horse holding Nahi's child, Geronimo, Naiche (Natchez), and one of Geronimo's bravest warriors, Fun. Boudoir card by Camilius Fly, c. 1886. Collection of author.*

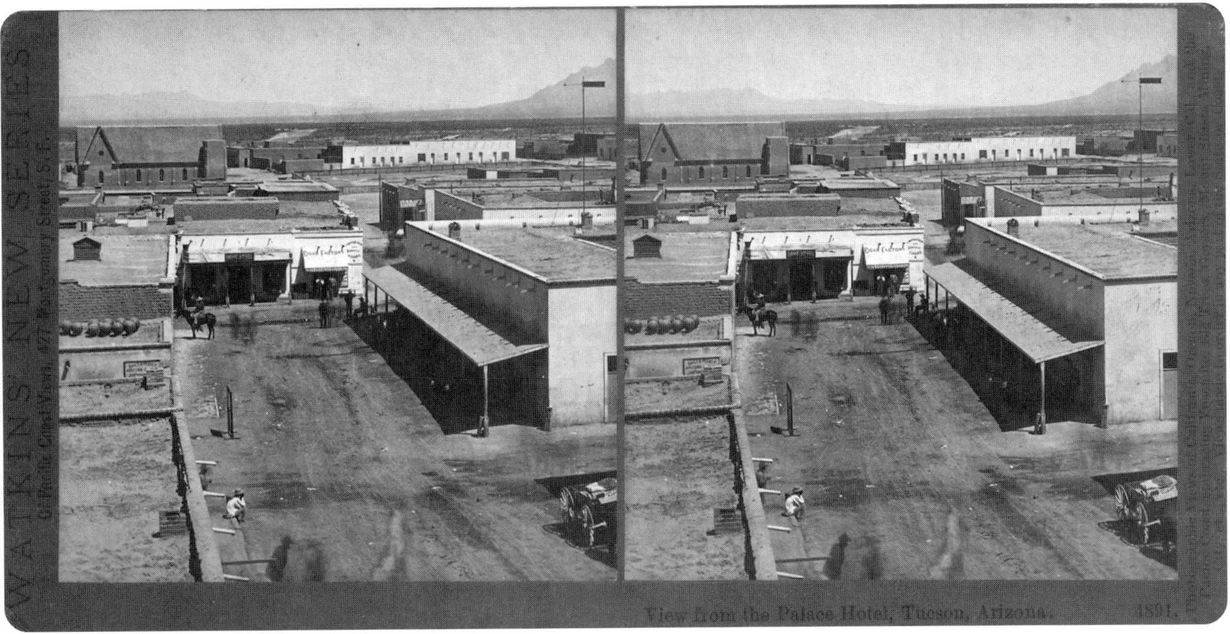

FIGURE 8. *View looking East over Tucson from the Palace Hotel taken for the Southern Pacific Railroad. Stereograph by Carleton Watkins, number 4891, Watkin's New Series, April or May, 1880. Collection of the author.*

A letter by Farciot indicates that at least one purpose for his travels was scouting potential investments, sending images of promising properties to clients in the East. The correspondence indicates that Farciot was working with "very influential Gents from Philadelphia" in an attempt to acquire some of the new mines that were being opened during Arizona's silver boom of the late 1870s. Farciot further indicated that "a great many mines are dayly (sic) being discovered, & mostly by men with but little money, or given to drinking, & by watching chances, very good purchases can be made."

Farciot left Arizona with Ed Schiefflin, the founder of the Lucky Cuss mine, and several other residents of Tombstone on an early commercial expedition to Alaska. En route, Farciot left the stereographic negatives with his brother-in-law, Alexander Edouart, in San Francisco. Under the imprint of Edouart & Cobb, he marketed the stereoviews of Arizona by Farciot as "Arizona Views."

In April 1880, the Southern Pacific Railroad brought Carleton Watkins, California's most famous photographer, to Arizona. Though his stay lasted only a little over a month, Watkins produced a significant body of extremely high quality images of the

Territory. He made images of Yuma and vicinity, traveling along the Gila towards Tucson, then south to Millville and the emerging town of Tombstone, which appears to have been his primary destination. After his return to San Francisco, Watkins included over 80 images of Arizona in his "Watkins' New Series" of stereoviews.

In 1880, Arizona saw the arrival of another giant of 19th century photography, Ben Wittick, one of the first to photograph the Hopi snake dance ceremony. As photographer for the Atlantic and Pacific Railroad, Wittick traveled between his gallery in Santa Fe and Arizona, photographing the Grand Canyon and the construction of the railroad, actively documenting the Native American population until his death at Fort Wingate, New Mexico in 1903, ironically from the bite of a rattlesnake he was taking to the Hopi.

J. C. Burge worked the northern part of the Territory beginning in the early 1880s, operating in Old Town Flagstaff. Burge traveled frequently, making images and eventually moving his gallery to Globe City in 1883, where he produced images of the area and the San Carlos reservation. Burge and a new partner, itinerant photographer James Hildreth from Utah, returned to Flagstaff, opening a gallery in New Town in June, 1884. Hildreth and Burge separated soon after, with Hildreth continuing as a traveling photographer, and Burge moving his operations to Kingman.

Burge formed a temporary partnership with Ben Wittick photographing the Moqui (Hopi) snake dance and offering views of Arizona and New Mexico at a temporary gallery in Flagstaff in 1885. Burge moved on to Kingston, New Mexico in 1885, operating galleries in New Mexico and Texas over the next 12 years.

Elias Bonine of Los Angeles opened a gallery in Yuma in 1881. Bonine produced an extremely fine series of boudoir cabinet cards of southern Arizona. Included were portraits of the Yuma and Mohave Indians, and the town of Yuma as it developed after the arrival of the railroad. Bonine traveled to the booming mines of Silver King and produced images of Pinal, Queen Creek and Pickett Post in the center of the Territory. Elias' cousin, Robert K. Bonine, was also a photographer, operating in Tyrone, Pennsylvania. R. K. Bonine offered a series of curved mount stereoviews of Ehrenberg, Yuma, and the mines of Pinal County. Whether he traveled west and made the images, or only marketed photographs made by Elias, is not known. After a few years of operation Bonine left Yuma, moving his gallery to Pasadena.

A. Frank Randall operated out of Willcox as an itinerant beginning about 1883. Randall is primarily known for his work documenting the Navajo, Hopi and Apache. Randall and Ben Wittick were involved in the creation of one of the finest groups of images of Native Americans of the West, a series of about 100 boudoir cabinet portraits, produced at and around Fort Apache from about 1883 to 1885.

The studio backgrounds for the photographs are similar, and props such as cactus, blankets and rifles appear repeatedly in many of these images. Most are also rich with props such as baskets, pottery, jewelry and crafts. Some images in the series are credited to Randall in rubber stamped or printed labels on the reverse of the mount. Others have a Wittick credit inscribed in the emulsion of the negative, or are on Wittick imprinted mounts. Some are uncredited, and individual images have been found with credits which differ.

Determining which photographer made a given image has become a significant mystery. One portrait of Wittick with Peaches and two armed Apache, was obviously taken by Randall or an assistant. Though there are many theories and hypotheses, the relationship between Randall and Wittick in producing these incredible images has yet to be uncovered. Details about whether the images were jointly produced, if Randall and Wittick duplicated and exchanged some of the negatives, or if this work resulted from the shared use of a common studio space, may never be known.

The photographs in this series depict the Navajo, Apache, Mohave and Hopi of Arizona and New Mexico. Subjects include chiefs such as Geronimo, Nana, Natchez, Mangas and Peaches as individual portraits, in small groups, and with their wives and families. Additional images depict the runners, medicine men, scouts, individuals living in the area, and exterior views of Fort Apache and its surroundings. Images of Albuquerque and vicinity on similar mounts with Wittick imprints further deepen the mystery. It is unfortunate that so little detail has survived about the making of these historical images, and the confusion about credits compounds the enigma.

The Arizona Territory was a wild and colorful place, and the photographers of the period were often colorful characters in their own right. A photographer named Kinney, operating in Prescott, was hung near Grapevine Station in 1878. Cicero Grime, operator of the Cicero Grime Photographic Gallery, producing stereoviews and tintypes in Globe City and Pinal, narrowly escaped Kinney's fate after his arrest for robbing a stagecoach in 1882. Grime's partners were lynched, but he was saved from the gallows by the local sheriff, and was later convicted and sentenced to serve his term in the Yuma Territorial Prison.

Andrew Miller, who came from Silver City, New Mexico to Globe in 1886 to photograph the Apache, operated a gallery in Bisbee briefly in 1897. Ironically, after photographing the end of the wild Apache, Miller was killed by the Yaqui in Sonora, Mexico, two years later, in 1899.

The 1880s saw widespread change wrought by the completion of the railroad across Arizona. Whether

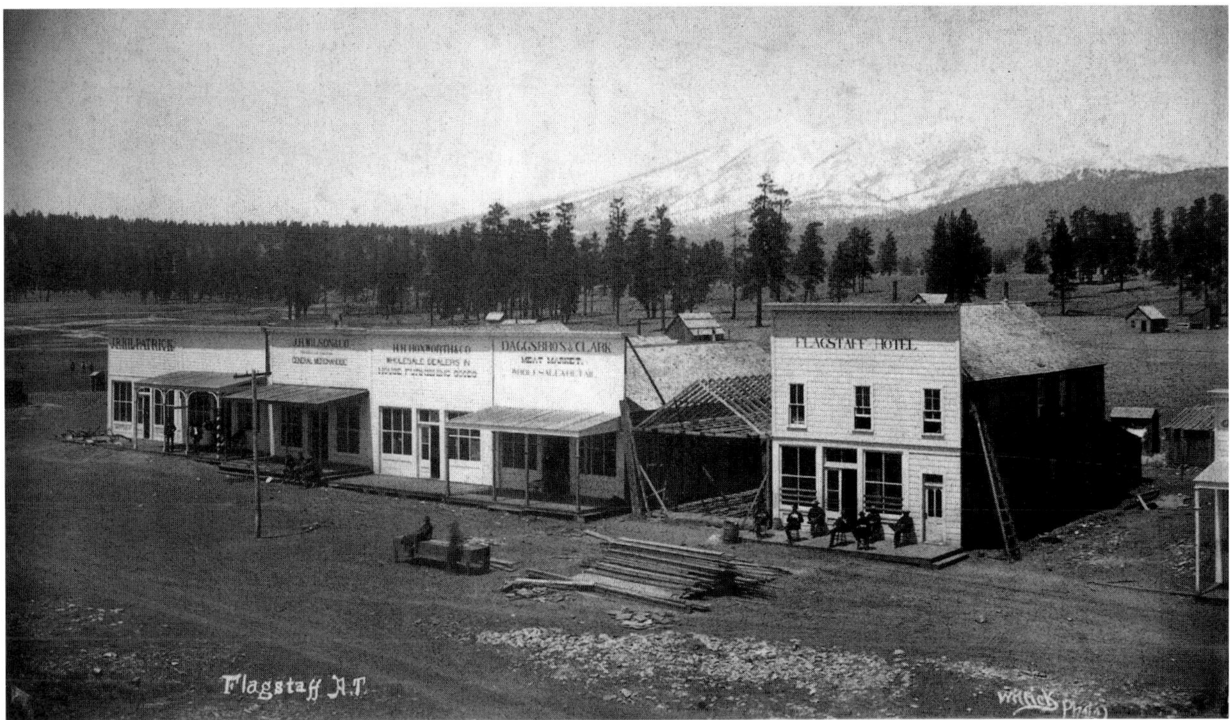

FIGURE 9. *Construction of the business district in "New Town," Flagstaff. The town was moved and buildings rebuilt to accommodate the railroad which inadvertently bypassed the original townsite. Boudoir card by Ben Wittick, c. 1881. Collection of the author.*

by nurturing the businesses in major towns such as Yuma and Tucson, creating new towns like Flagstaff along the route, or providing the means to develop rich but previously remote mines, the railroad spurred the development of Arizona, and the demand for photographs of the booming Territory.

As California became more civilized, Arizona retained its position as the heart of the Old West. Even so, the state continued to mature. As the number of settlers increased, so did the businesses that served them. Farming and tourism began to join mining as primary forces fueling the growth and development of the Territory. Public schools were established in the 1870s and a Normal School and University followed in 1885.

The end of the 1880s saw the growth of communities based increasingly on agriculture, finance and service industries, which joined ranching and mining as the economic foundations of the Territory. Photo studios were established in emerging towns such as Casa Grande (Everett), Clifton (Lucas), Hackberry (Phillips), Hayden (Barnett), Holbrook (Rose), Mesa (Barnett), Willcox (Bright), and Winslow (Rose).

During the late 1880s and into the 1890s, photography began to mature as a business and expand its influence as advances in camera and film design made amateur photography accessible to the general public. The development of roll film further simplified the photographic process, making hand-held snapshot photography possible and creating a major amateur market for the first time. The Eastman Kodak box camera, which became available in 1889, and other inexpensive, lightweight, portable cameras further fueled the boom in amateur photography. Affordable cameras and film permitting instantaneous daylight exposures allowed travelers to make photographs to share the sights they saw while visiting Arizona with friends and acquaintances back home.

Well-to-do locals could now document the events of their daily lives and build family albums that included more than just formal studio portraits. By freeing photographers from the need to carry and change plate holders for each image, the roll film cameras permitted images to be made in relatively rapid sequences, changing forever the way events like parades, fires and ceremonies were documented.

Arizona was promoted as a land of opportunity, a potentially abundant rich farmland waiting for irrigation water to flourish. The canal system of the Hohokam provided proof of the fertility of the Salt River Valley in central Arizona. The mild winters offered the possibility of additional growing seasons and productivity year round. Views of growing towns and healthy citrus orchards combined with images of the Native Americans, cowboys and mining in portraying the history and development of the Territory.

The 1890s also saw the emergence of Arizona and its dry warm climate as a potential cure for ailments, from tuberculosis and consumption, to rheumatism. Claims were even made that the heat sterilized the air. The health benefits of the Arizona climate were touted world-wide, and sanatoriums and retreats became new business opportunities. Some, like Castle Hot Springs, became popular photographic subjects which continued to receive international attention well into the 20th century.

As the Territory continued to develop, so did the photographic business. Partnerships grew as businesses became established and competition increased. Photographic imprints document collaborations during this period between Hildreth and Burge, Rothrock and Catton, Buehman and Hartwell, and Mitchell and Baer, among others.

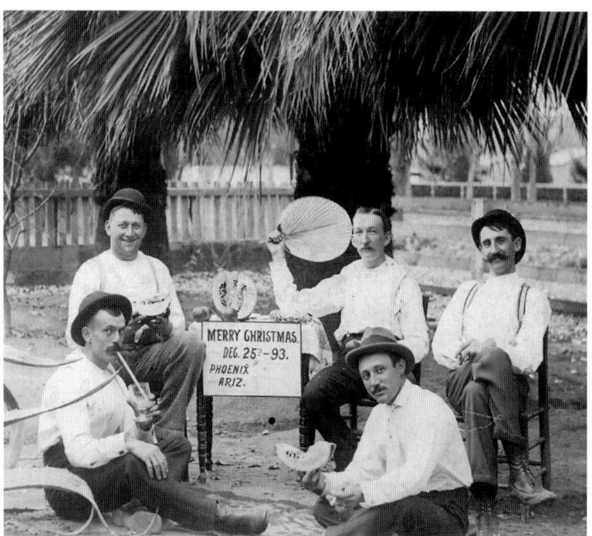

FIGURE 10. *Group of men celebrating Christmas eating watermelon under the palm trees in Phoenix, Arizona Territory. Detail of boudoir card by F. A. Hartwell, 1893. Collection of the author.*

As photography evolved (or in the eyes of many, regressed) from an art to a business with the advent of roll film and affordable cameras, the industry required different skills. The itinerant's endurance and physical strength required to carry the heavy equipment into the remote areas of the Territory gave way to the interpersonal skills, marketing and management ability needed to run a studio emphasizing portrait and commercial work. The investment required grew from the camera and darkroom equipment of the itinerant to the more significant investment of a studio building, props, reception and display area, and the other necessities of a retail business.

Excitement and adventure were replaced by the repetitive work of portraiture, retouching and framing. Even photo finishing for the amateur market, which had provided some revenue for many studios, began to be undercut. Businesses such as drug and stationery stores cut into a primary market (and previous monopoly) for local studios by offering cameras, film, processing and printing in competition with the community photographers.

The freewheeling nature of the itinerant gave way to concerns of market share and maintaining a client base, as studio territories became as important as the quality of the images that were produced. Arizona continued to draw itinerant and talented amateur photographers, but the established studios provided a stable framework for making and marketing photographs of Arizona.

Phoenix became the capital of the Territory in 1889, developing rapidly as irrigation supported raising hay and grain. By 1894, Phoenix boasted electric streetcars, street lights, waterworks, a telephone system, sewage system, and a steam powered fire department. Photographers throughout the Territory moved to the new capital, or opened branch galleries there. Directories and advertisements for photographic services included the Elite Gallery, Sunbeam Studio, New York Gallery and the New York Photo Studio, whose names played on the urban aspirations of the growing capital city.

A. F. Messinger and his partner William Altenburgh, operated a gallery at 243 W. Madison Street in Phoenix beginning about 1897. Their card-mounted photographs carried an elaborate logo, an image of the two photographers with tripod mounted cameras posed proudly in front of their studio. Messinger, apparently independent of Altenburgh, was active until 1901 producing over 400 images predominantly of Phoenix, but including Castle Hot Springs, Flagstaff, Tucson and Jerome. Images of Phoenix include a series of the Phoenix Indian school, including classroom interiors, portraits and architectural views. Other Phoenix views included a series of images of the Phoenix Winter Carnival of 1899 complete with views of parade floats, as well as portraits, ethnographic views, and documentation of commercial growth in the capital of the Territory.

Boomtowns continued to follow the path of mineral development. Eventually, the saloons and entertainment establishments gave way to more sedate businesses. Studios were established in the emerging communities such as Mesa, Casa Grande, and Fort Huachucha. Most developing mining communities in Arizona had their own studios. Jerome was the home of M. F. Brennan, who produced portraits and images of the United Verde mine and works in the Verde Valley in the center of the state. In the Southeast, Morenci's Arthur Davidson produced stereoviews; O. A. Risdon documented life in Clifton and Metcalf.

Regulation of photography became an issue as amateur photography continued to reach broader markets and competition between photographers for the shrinking professional marketplace became fierce. As photographers vied for the opportunity to build photographic businesses in the developing towns, competition by scores of itinerants became an issue. Several established photographers began to lobby for some form of control to protect their businesses. Photographic licenses were instituted in Arizona around 1895, requiring a fee of $10 for a license in Phoenix and Tucson. However, this had little impact on limiting the number of itinerant and amateur photographers who were competing with the established studios.

Bisbee supplanted Tombstone as the cultural center of Arizona in the 1890s. Like its predecessor, Bisbee gave San Francisco a significant challenge for the largest and most cultured city in the West. Opera houses, fine restaurants and hotels supplemented

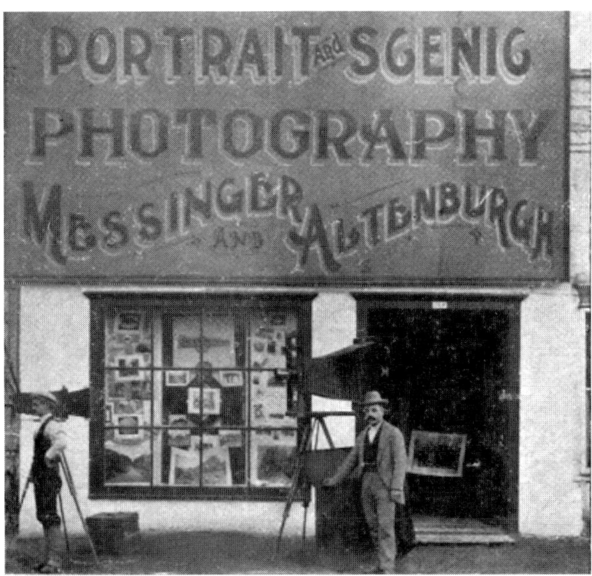

FIGURE 11. *Advertisement showing studio facade with a photographic display of Arizona images in the window. Photographers Messinger & Altenburgh (left to right) with their cameras in Phoenix, Arizona Territory, c. 1899. Imprint on verso of boudoir card. Collection of the author.*

Brewery Gulch and the town's more risque businesses. In 1893, Bisbee demonstrated its wealth by sending a ten-foot copper nugget from the Copper Queen Mine to the Columbian Exposition in Chicago. Copper was increasingly in demand to supply electricity, and Bisbee was one of the richest copper producers in the world. At some point during its heyday, most of the major photographers in the Territory operated at least a branch gallery in Bisbee.

Bisbee also became an operating base for many photographers from other states. Wilfred Humphries rode the railroad between his studios in Bisbee and El Paso, producing photographs and postcards of Cochise County. Olaf P. Larson, of Moscow, Idaho, also operated out of Bisbee, traveling throughout the state producing stereoscopic photographs of the mines in Jerome and events in Nogales and Phoenix. Larson's mounts include both manuscript and printed captions which indicate that he made several trips to Arizona early in the century and likely marketed his catalog of images from both of his studios.

The Indian ceremonies became the primary focus of Native American documentation in the 1890s. The Hopi drew photographers such as A. C. Vroman and Charles Lummis of California, Ben Wittick of New Mexico, and contract photographers for publishers including Continent, Detroit Publishing Co., Underwood and Keystone, as well as hundreds of amateur photographers.

After the turn of the century, E. S. Curtis, Joseph Mora, Kate Coury and many others, continued to build on the work of their predecessors in documenting the Hopi ceremonies and making more romantic images of the Navajo, Apache, and other Arizona tribes. The images, albums and stereoviews that resulted provide a significant cultural record of the time. Later, the burgeoning numbers of photographers and the resulting intrusion led to the banning of cameras at these ceremonies in the mid-teens.

As the West was tamed, images of renegade Indians were replaced by cowboys and ranches, and main streets of the new towns. Renowned artists such as Charles Russell and Frederick Remington visited Arizona, creating romanticized images of the rapidly passing Wild West. In print, Zane Gray and many other popular authors wove thrilling stories of life in

Arizona. Photography played an important role in providing reference materials for work in other media, and built on the interest in the West that resulted from their success.

The Grand Canyon had captivated the world through the survey images of the 1870s, and now became a major tourist attraction. Mining in the canyon gave way to tourism as the primary economic base. Initially tourists came by stagecoach from Flagstaff and Williams to stay in tents on the south rim of the canyon, above Bright Angel Creek. The spectacular scenery continued to entice photographers, who made stereoviews which were offered individually or in sets by publishers like Continent, White, Underwood, and Keystone.

The construction of the El Tovar Lodge in 1904 and of a rail link to the south rim of the canyon simplified access, increased tourist capacity and created posh accommodations which firmly established the Grand Canyon as one of the wonders of the

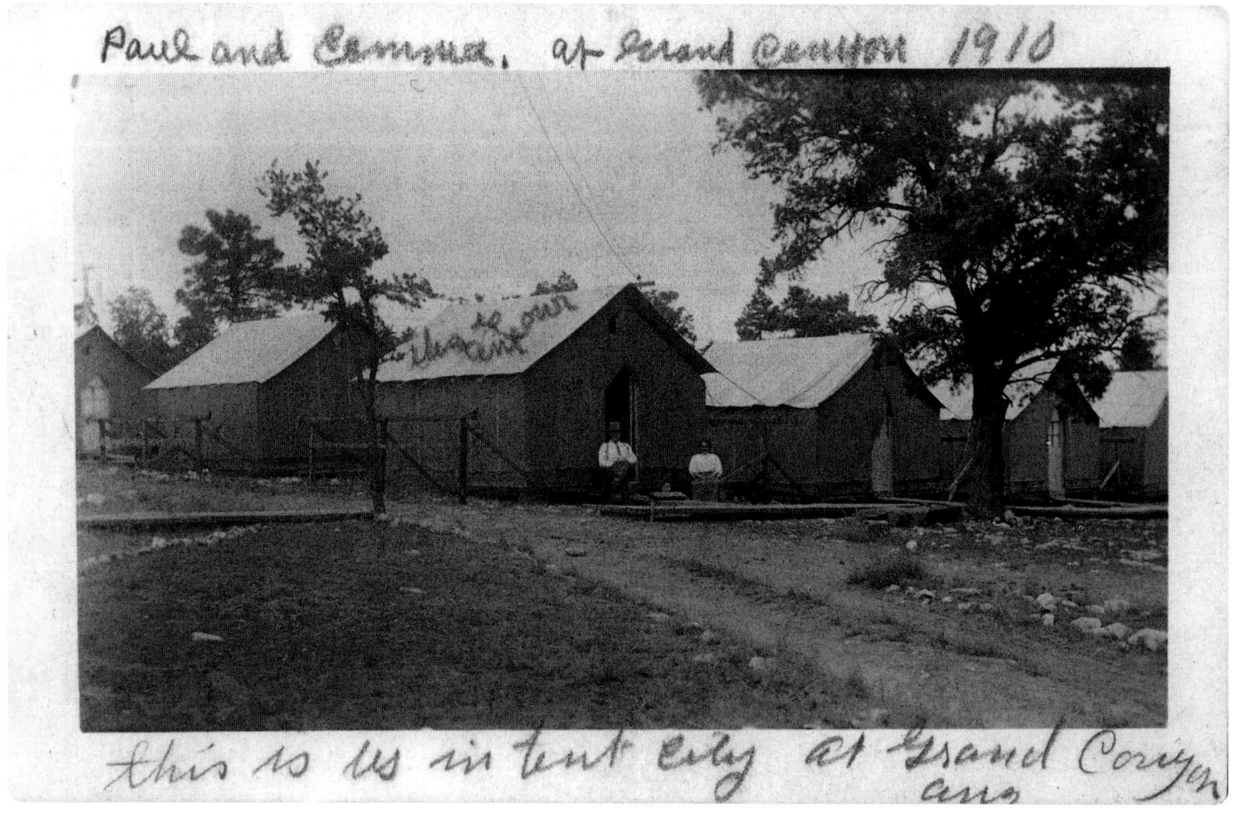

FIGURE 12. *Paul and Emma at the tourist hotel on the South Rim of the Grand Canyon, Arizona Territory. Real photo postcard, photographer unknown, c. 1910. Collection of the author.*

world. Ellsworth and Emery Kolb established a gallery on the rim and spent decades photographing the Grand Canyon. Their studio extended across the trail and was ideally situated for photographing visitors en route to the canyon. The Kolbs traveled the Colorado and throughout the canyon for the rest of their lives, making still and motion pictures.

Though postal cards had been authorized by the U.S. Post Office in 1873, they were technically limited to written communication and holiday greetings. The Columbian Exposition in 1893 spawned thousands of printed postal card images of the fair, increasing public interest in using and collecting the cards. In 1898, the Post Office further fueled public interest by standardizing the cost of sending government issues and authorized privately printed cards displaying the label, "Private Mailing Cards," at one cent each if the phrase, "Authorized by Act of Congress, May 19, 1898," was printed on the card.

An unprecedented boom in collecting and using the penny cards began in 1901, when the Post Office allowed the cumbersome printed label to be replaced with the simple term, "Post Card." High quality printed cards, initially from Germany and later from domestic presses, flooded the market and launched a popular trend of using and collecting postcards.

The availability of roll film and inexpensive 3½″ x 5½″ cameras offered by Kodak and other manufacturers beginning about 1902, plus inexpensive photographic processing, and double weight postcard printing paper, were all factors leading to the popularity of the photographic postcard. The completion of the Rural Free Delivery system, which provided virtually universal daily mail delivery, was the final component that set the stage for the burst of interest in using and collecting postcards in the first decade of the 20th century. It was estimated that by 1908, about 680 million postcards were sent annually, with the volume increasing to almost one billion cards a year by 1913.

Reproduction of photographs in print continued to evolve from illustrations and engravings loosely based on photographs, to recognizable photographic representations. Halftone reproduction became more refined and less expensive, with even local papers and printers able to reproduce photographs. Larger newspapers were able to reproduce photographs of events rather than relying on artist's illustrations. Photomechanical reproduction created significant new opportunities, dramatically increasing the market for images.

The popular press provided a significant market for photographers, both for reproduction of images, and as a forum for advertising their services. Some newspapers employed contract photographers, and all acquired images from whatever source was available: studio photographers, itinerants, and amateurs. Commercial brochures to entice investors, promote land sales, and encourage migration to the Territory formed another significant new market for photographs. In addition to the revenue from the original sale to the newspaper or promoter, there was a market for reproductions of photographs of the personalities and events on postcards for sale to the public.

Motion picture photography, pioneered by animated stereopticon slides, and the multiple camera animal locomotion images made by Edweard Muybridge, began to develop in the late 1880s. Edison and other inventors built on Muybridge's work and a variety of inventions and formats evolved to capture and project "moving pictures." By the mid 1890s, Edison's Kinescope competed with a number of other models for the growing motion picture market.

Motion picture cameras documented the Snake Dance at Walpi as early as 1899, when Oscar Depue visited the Hopi pueblo. Depue presented one of the first motion picture shows in the Territory at a trading post in Canyon Diablo during his second trip to the area in 1900. Apparently responding to competition and interest in western subjects, the Edison Company sent an unidentified camera operator to photograph the ceremonies in 1901.

Bisbee, befitting its role as a cultural center of the West, was also host to early presentations of the Lumiere brothers motion picture process. Warren built an "airdome," a precursor of the drive-in, for presentation of outdoor motion pictures by about 1908. The first primitive theater buildings in communities like Yuma, were soon joined by opulent motion picture palaces in Phoenix, Prescott, Tucson, and most established towns by the mid-teens.

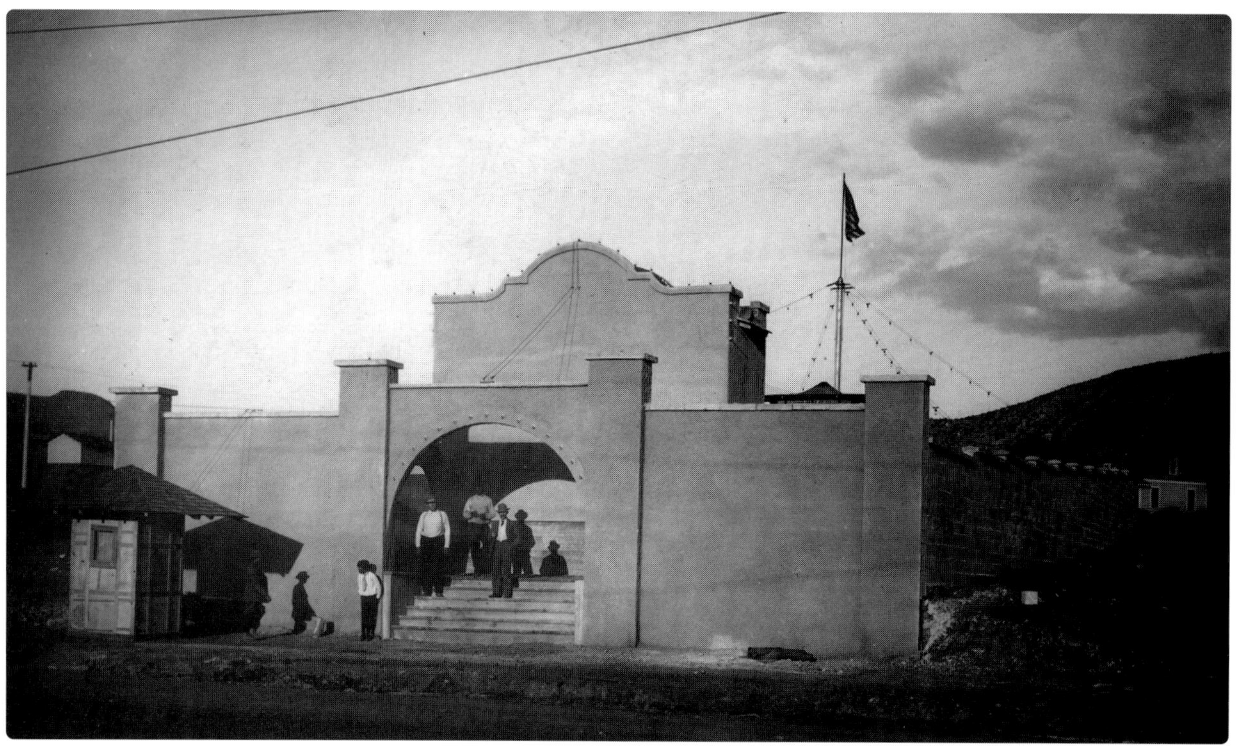

FIGURE 13. *Open air motion picture theater, or "Airdome," with ticket booth left of entrance, in Warren, near Bisbee, Arizona Territory. Real photo postcard, photographer unknown, c. 1907. Collection of the author.*

Images of the grand new buildings, whether in Phoenix or other new communities developing throughout the Territory, became a mainstay of many photographers. Images of parades and community events were taken by "camera fiends" or purchased and sent to friends and relatives across the nation to show how towns like Courtland, Miami, Admana, Paradise and Warren had become civilized.

Development was an important activity in Arizona, whether selling the Territory as an escape from foul weather, for its healthy climate, or as a potential site for productive farms and real estate speculation. Building on the tradition of the promotional books of the 1860s and 1870s, photographers produced images for flyers, brochures, books and postcards to make and support the claims. The Territorial Commissioner for Immigration attempted to change early misconceptions about the climate, hoping to draw good people to Arizona. In addition to tourism and domestic potential, sanatoriums for tuberculosis and the benefits of Castle and Indian Hot Springs and other desert resorts, were touted in photographs and print.

Another commercial enterprise which impacted the early development of the Territory began in 1888 when three young ostriches were brought to Salt River Valley from California. By 1913, Phoenix boasted flocks of over 6,000 birds on ostrich farms producing ostrich feathers for the fashion industry. From the beginning, the ostrich farms were popular photographic subjects, appearing in postcards and many amateur albums from the period.

As the Territory grew, images showing the impact of man's taming of the environment joined those of the developing communities. Fields of hay and grain were being augmented by neat rows of citrus and experimental fields of cotton. Interest in large scale irrigation projects around 1900 resulted in the design and construction of the first hydroelectric dam in the nation, Roosevelt Dam on the Salt River north of Phoenix. Smaller projects, such as the Laguna Dam near Yuma and Granite Reef Dam near Mesa, fulfilled the promise of harnessing Arizona rivers for irrigation and development.

Construction of the Roosevelt Dam was a major

event, and became the focus of local photographers and itinerants, as well as amateurs including engineers, project administrators and local shutterbugs. The albums, photographs, postcards and snapshots from this period provide detailed records of the construction projects, the lives of the workmen, social events, celebrations, picnics and sightseeing trips. The images document the impact on the communities and the subsequent development of towns and agriculture.

In addition to the impromptu record of the Roosevelt Dam and the town that arose at the site, each step of the complex construction project was captured by official contract photographers. From 1906 to 1911, contract photographer Walter Lubkin painstakingly documented the construction, producing an official set of albums as well as photographs and postcards for the popular marketplace.

The construction boom town at Roosevelt was large enough to support its own photographic studio.

The Arizona Souvenir Picture Company produced photographic postcards of the dam construction, town life, and the fauna and flora of the region for local and national markets. The dedication of the dam on March 18, 1911, was attended by dignitaries including President Theodore Roosevelt, and drew hundreds of photographers to record the event.

The relative difficulty of travel across the state fostered efforts to develop powered transportation to supplement the railroad. Lucius Copeland of Phoenix created one of the world's first motorcycles by attaching a steam engine to his high wheeled bicycle in 1883. The motorcycle was memorialized in the studio in a stereograph by Rothrock. Portraits of the proud inventor and his machine appeared in photos and prints. Before long, a three-wheeled version of the steam cycle was produced, and Copeland demonstrated his steam powered vehicles locally and as far away as San Francisco. Copeland apparently maintained his

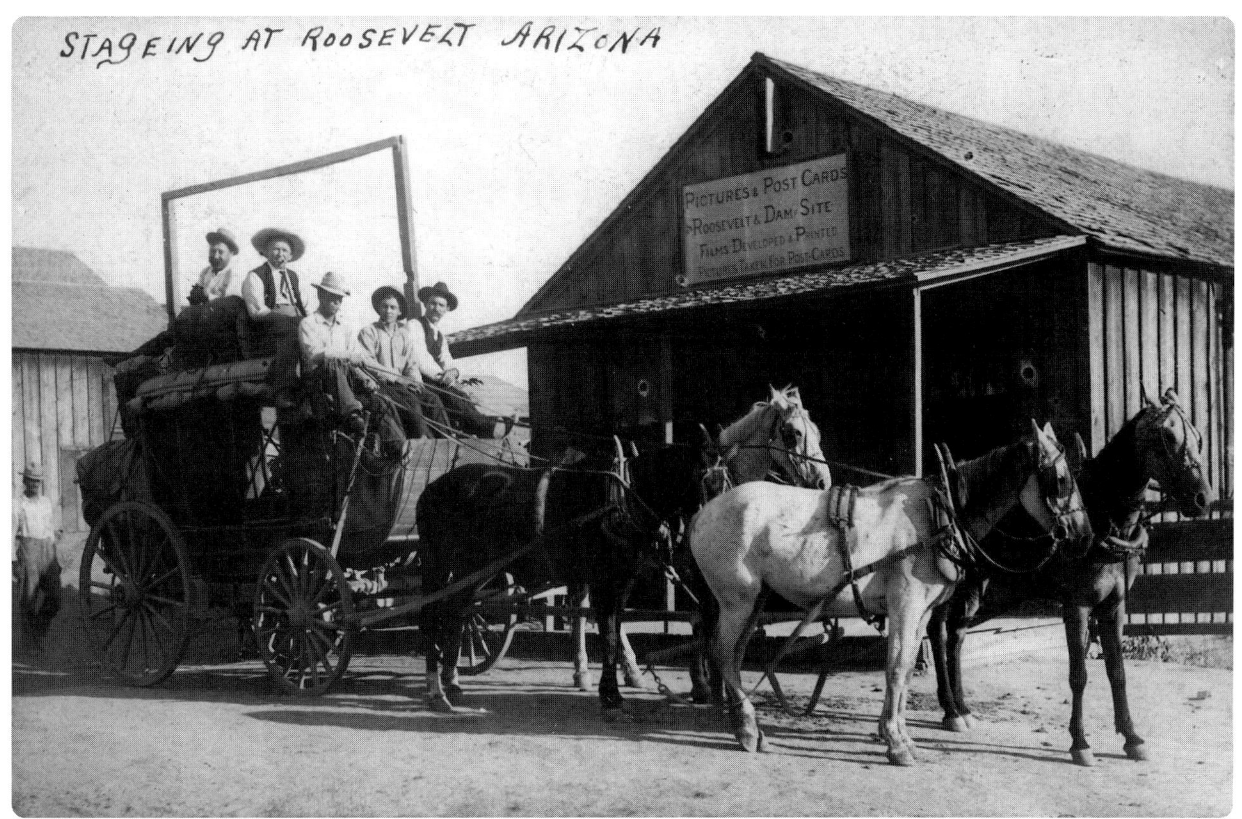

FIGURE 14. *Roosevelt to Mesa stage coach in front of Arizona Souvenir Picture Company Studio, Roosevelt, Arizona Territory. Real photo postcard, photographer unknown, c. 1910. Collection of the author.*

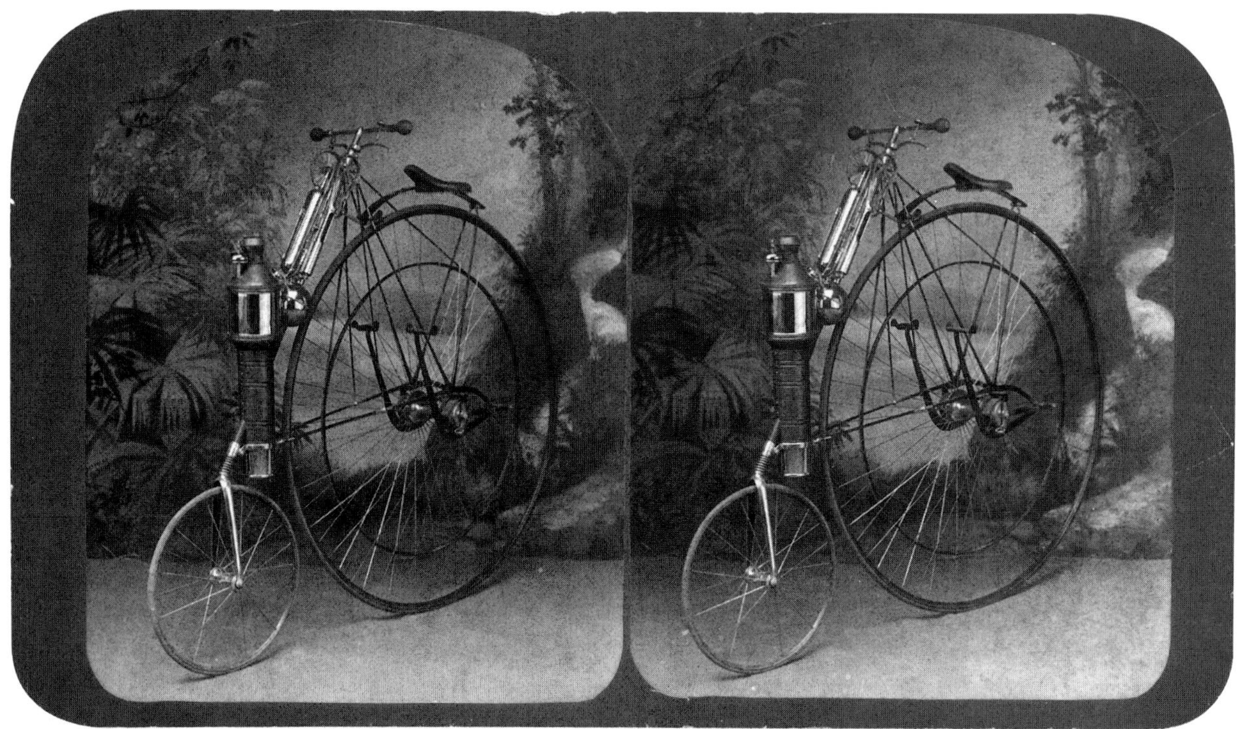

FIGURE 15. *Steam powered Star velocipede developed by Lucius Copeland of Phoenix, Arizona Territory. A machinist at a Phoenix flour mill, Copeland developed one of the earliest motorized cycles, demonstrating it two years before Daimler patented his gasoline cycle in Europe. Copeland's cycle exhibited in Phoenix and Tempe in 1884, and at a circus in San Francisco in 1885. Stereograph by George H. Rothrock, c. 1883. Collection of the author.*

interest in vehicles, and was noted as being the second person to own a four-wheeled automobile in Phoenix.

The wagon roads and trails that crossed the state did little to encourage auto travel, and development of modern roads was slow. Despite the lack of good roads, automobiles were status symbols, owned by the wealthy in towns across Arizona. Images of cars traveling, camping, or delivering mail to the general store or post office were popular and sold widely.

Aviation became a national passion as the Wright brothers and Glenn Curtiss attempted to set new records in biplanes, and European aviators and manufacturers of aircraft competed for dominance of the air. The general public was aware of airplanes through photos and print, but had not seen airplanes fly until the Hudson-Fulton celebration in October, 1909, when over a million people watched Wilbur Wright fly around the Statue of Liberty.

The 1909 Territorial Fair featured a flurry of aerial activity. Mr. O'Dell offered the wealthy and adventurous balloon trips above the fairgrounds, and provided a new forum for local advertising by permitting local businesses to advertise on plaques mounted to the basket. Amateur and professional postcard photographers found the balloon a popular subject. In addition, a locally built glider was displayed in the crafts section of the fair. On the last day, the craft was towed by a car and flew to a height of four feet above the racetrack. Surprisingly few people were present, and the event, the first aeroplane flight in Arizona, received only a brief note in the paper the following day. Arizona's flat land and mild climate made it a natural location for aviation.

As aviators gained confidence and public interest in flight continued to grow, Arizona tried to capitalize on the phenomenon. In 1910, local businesses invited major aviators from around the world to the Phoenix Aero Meet, scheduled for early February. The desire to capitalize on aviation was not unique to Arizona, and Los Angeles beat Phoenix to the punch, staging its own aero meet in January, 1910. The number of aviators represented at the Phoenix meet was limited by crashes and litigation between the Wrights and Curtiss, but interest in the meet was

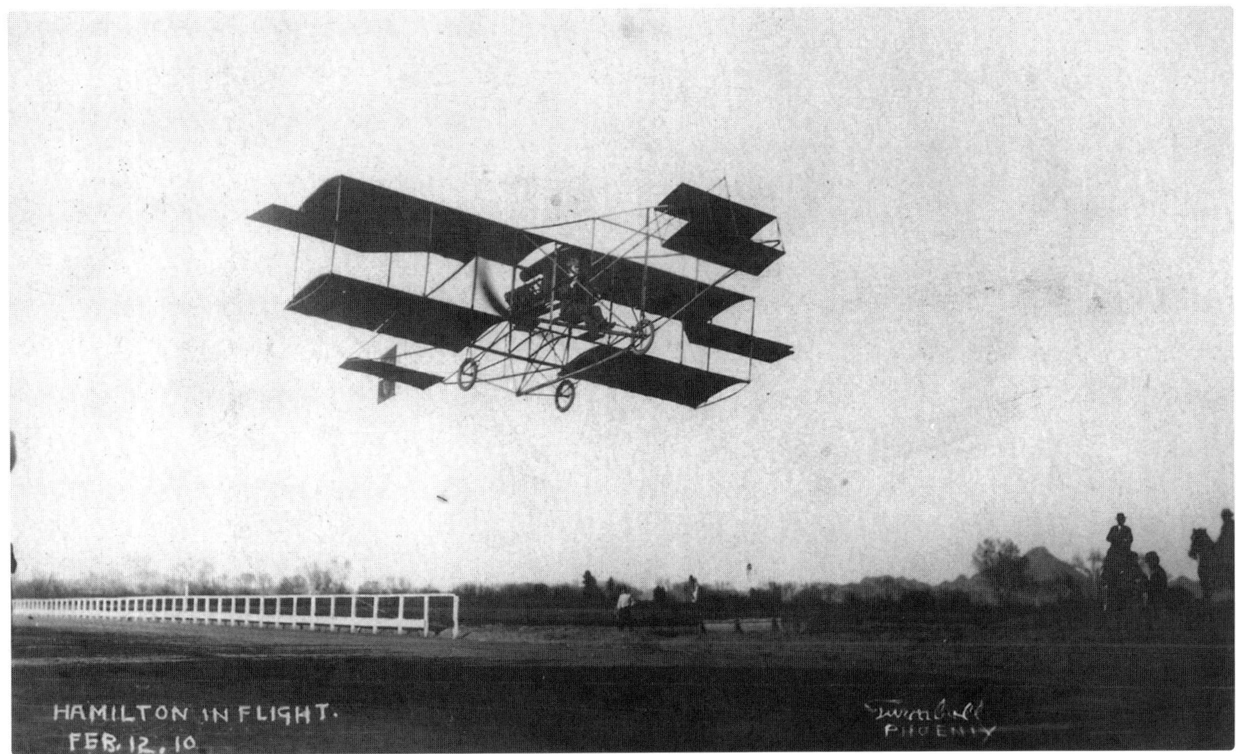

FIGURE 16. *Charles Hamilton at the wheel of the Curtiss biplane at the Phoenix Aviation Meet, flying around the trotting track at the Territorial Fairgrounds. Real photo postcard by Robert Turnbull, February, 1910. Collection of the author.*

keen throughout the Territory. Schools were closed, and the newspapers and local photographers followed every move of the two aviators and Curtiss biplanes that arrived for the meet.

Images of the planes and their competitions with each other, against a local Buick race car named the White Streak, and against a Curtiss motorcycle, were reproduced in papers, sent on the wire services, and sold to the public. In addition to George Sadler, the self-proclaimed official photographer for the event, photographs and postcards were produced and sold by Bob Trumbull, Harrigan and Christie, and probably most other amateur and professional photographers attending the Aero Meet.

While the ease of air travel in Arizona received international recognition, the poor roads and general difficulty in traveling in Arizona was creatively used as a promotional tool. In 1910, the American Automobile Association sponsored A. L. Westgard in a cross-country trip to promote the need for a cross-country highway. Westgard followed the old northern wagon route across Arizona, which became Route 66. The Los Angeles-to-Phoenix auto race, held in conjunction with the 1911 Territorial Fair, drew national attention. Coincidentally, the race followed the same route as a proposed southern route for a cross-country national highway. In 1913, Fisk Tires used Arizona as a backdrop for photographs of their St. Paul-to-Los Angeles tour to demonstrate the dependability of their pneumatic tires. An unknown photographer documented the trip, producing photographic postcards of the car and an advertising banner in numerous difficult travel situations. Soon after the Fisk trip, construction began on Route 66, crossing the northern part of the state. Campgrounds and auto courts, along with the natural scenery, became subjects of postcards, photographs and brochures.

By the time Arizona became a state in 1912, postcard publishers had clearly replaced the individual photography studios as a primary source of visual imagery. The large printers and publishers had been players in the market for years and the high quality printed cards they produced began to replace the photographic cards. Many photographers augmented their own stock by purchasing and selling printed cards from their studios, but the publishers also sold to the stationery, drug, and curio stores which competed in the postcard marketplace.

Though many tribes objected to photography from their first exposure to the media, limitations on photography did not appear until well into the 20th century. In 1899, photographer Ben Wittick commented about the number of photographers at the Walpi Snake Dance. There were people from San Francisco, Chicago, New York, New Orleans and Los Angeles—anybody with a Kodak! Many photographs of the ceremonies from this time depict the legions of photographers throughout the crowd, some with tripods, some hand-holding their cameras, edging into the events themselves.

One of the first and firmest prohibitions began as an attempt to control attendance at the Snake Dance Ceremony at Walpi. An initial plan to limit and control general attendance was ordered in 1913 by the Superintendent of Indian Affairs, after tales reached Washington of still and motion picture photography causing disruption.

In a classic example of poor timing, Victor Miller, a cinematographer for *Pathe's Weekly*, was arrested shortly after the the initial limits were put in place, following an all-night chase across the reservation. Miller had failed in his attempt to smuggle his film off the reservation without signing an agreement promising only non-commercial use.

Unfortunately for Miller and others who supplimented their incomes with images of the ceremonies, a party of politicians including Governor Hunt, President Roosevelt, and ironically several photographers, had been added at the last minute to the limited list of attendees. The disruption to the ceremony caused by the politicians, and portrayal of Miller's dramatic chase, significantly increased the importance of the issue of intrusion to Native American ceremonies. The result of the fiasco of 1913 was an order that "no photographs, still, animated, or out-of-focus," should be permitted thereafter. Few images appear after 1917, and the ban was virtually total by 1920.

With few exceptions, such as the Buehman studio

in Tucson, most of the great 19th century photographers and their descendants failed to make the transition to the new business of photography. By statehood and the early 'teens, the photographic business was almost entirely composed of names that would have been unknown to Arizonans a decade earlier.

The entrepreneurs who succeeded in adapting to the new demands of the marketplace focused less on the entire state, as had their predecessors, and focused on their local area. Cities were established and the local markets supplanted the "export" market for photographs, with the possible exception of photographic postcards. During this era, successful photographic businesses were built on portrait, business and commercial work. Examples of successful local photographic studios during this period include the Kolb gallery at the Grand Canyon, Kelley Studios in Globe/Miami, Tom Bate of Prescott, and the McCulloch brothers in Phoenix.

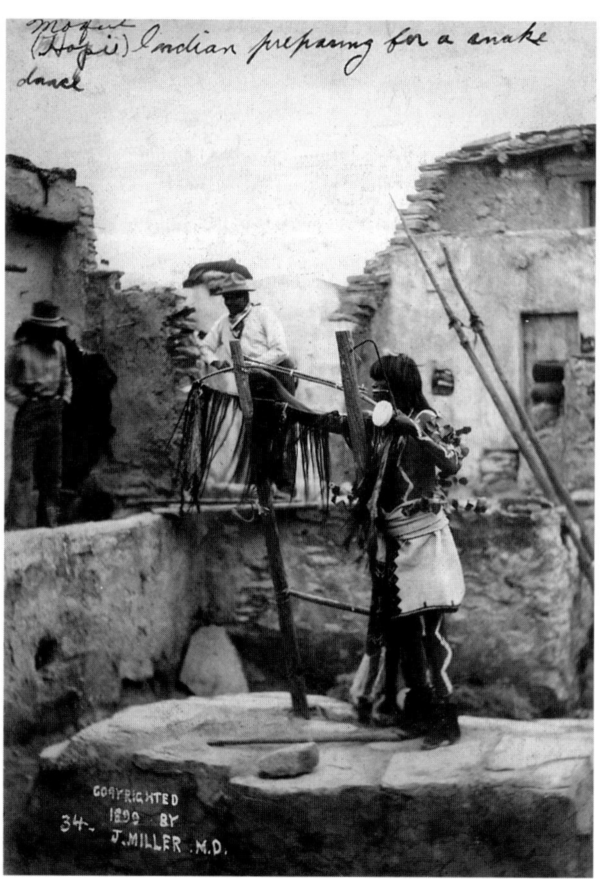

FIGURE 17. *Hopi preparing for the Snake Dance ceremony at Oraibi. Hand-tinted silver print by J. Miller, M. D., c. 1898. Collection of the author.*

26

Many photographers in smaller markets produced exceptional work that is more obscure. A classic example is N. E. Johnson, who captured the explosive growth of Oatman and the Tom Reed, United Eastern and Gold Road mines in northwestern Arizona. To date, little information has surfaced about Johnson, who at one point in his career operated a small studio in the lower level of the St. Francis Hotel. In addition to his ability to document the architecture of the town and growing mines, Johnson had a knack for getting the miners and characters of Oatman to gather (often by the score), and to pose, frequently incorporating hand-written captions within the images, and exhibiting a sense of humor in arrangement of his subjects. Johnson left a small but significant body of postcards and panoramic images of the initial growth and development of the last gold rush in Arizona.

The fascination of war and violence fueled the popularity of photographs of the Civil War during the 1860s. Portraits of Indian war leaders included the fearsome Apache in the 1870s, and disasters, lynchings and executions in every era. The Mexican Revolution coincided with a peak in the popularity of photographic postcards. Millions of "real photo" postcards were produced and collected during the conflict between 1910 to 1916.

Photographers like Calvin Osbon and Walter Horne rose to fame and fortune making and selling postcards of the Revolution, beginning in 1914 when American troops invaded and occupied Vera Cruz. Local photographers along the border competed with enterprising professional and amateur photographers to capture images of life along the border for the growing market.

The border between Arizona and Mexico was a volatile boundary during the Mexican Revolution. Agua Prieta, Naco, and Douglas saw considerable action after Pancho Villa raided Columbus, New Mexico in 1916. Initially 5,000 troops from Arizona, New Mexico and Texas were called to armed service. By September, nearly 200,000 army and National Guardsmen were on active duty along the U. S. border. Soldiers sent millions of cards to their friends and families back home, creating a huge market for portraits and images

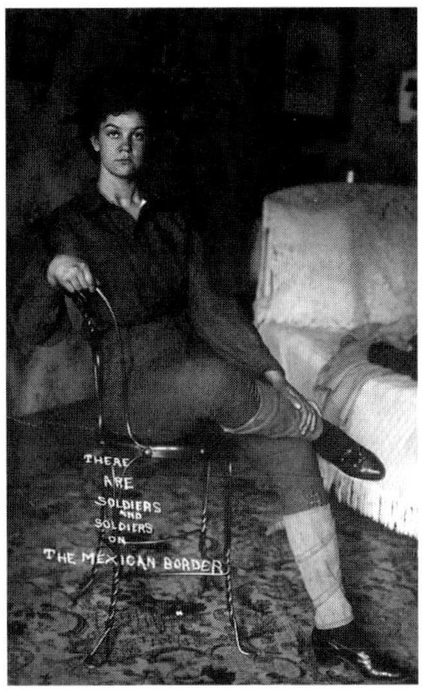

FIGURE 18. *Prostitute wearing soldier's uniform in the red light district of Douglas, Arizona during the Mexican Border action. Real photo postcard, photographer unknown, c. 1915. Collection of the author.*

of the sites and scenes of the conflict. During its peak in 1916, one photographer indicated that he was producing almost 5,000 cards a day.

Typical subjects included images of the Mexican Bandits, action scenes of the conflict, executions, burned and bloated bodies, reminiscent of the images of Civil War battlefields, and scenes of the military camps. This was a time of transition for the military, and the postcard images capture both cavalry and horse-powered armaments and supply wagons, as well as gasoline powered trucks, armored vehicles and motorcycles.

The border insurgency was the first war where airplanes played a part. Beginning with seaplanes used in Vera Cruz, airplanes captured the interest of photographers following the troops. Aerial images of the camps and troops, the carnage caused by the first aerial bombing, and portraits of the first military aviators were among the postcard images made.

Fire is perhaps second only to war as a popular draw to the public's attention, and there were many in old Arizona to lure photographers eager to capture the images of conflagration. The reliance on wooden buildings, densely arranged in most towns, the use of open flames for light and heat, and the relative scarcity of water led to frequent and serious fires.

Jerome saw fire decimate almost its entire business district in 1894. Another blaze destroyed the center of town in 1898. As soon as the damaged area had been rebuilt, it was lost again to an arson fire in 1899.

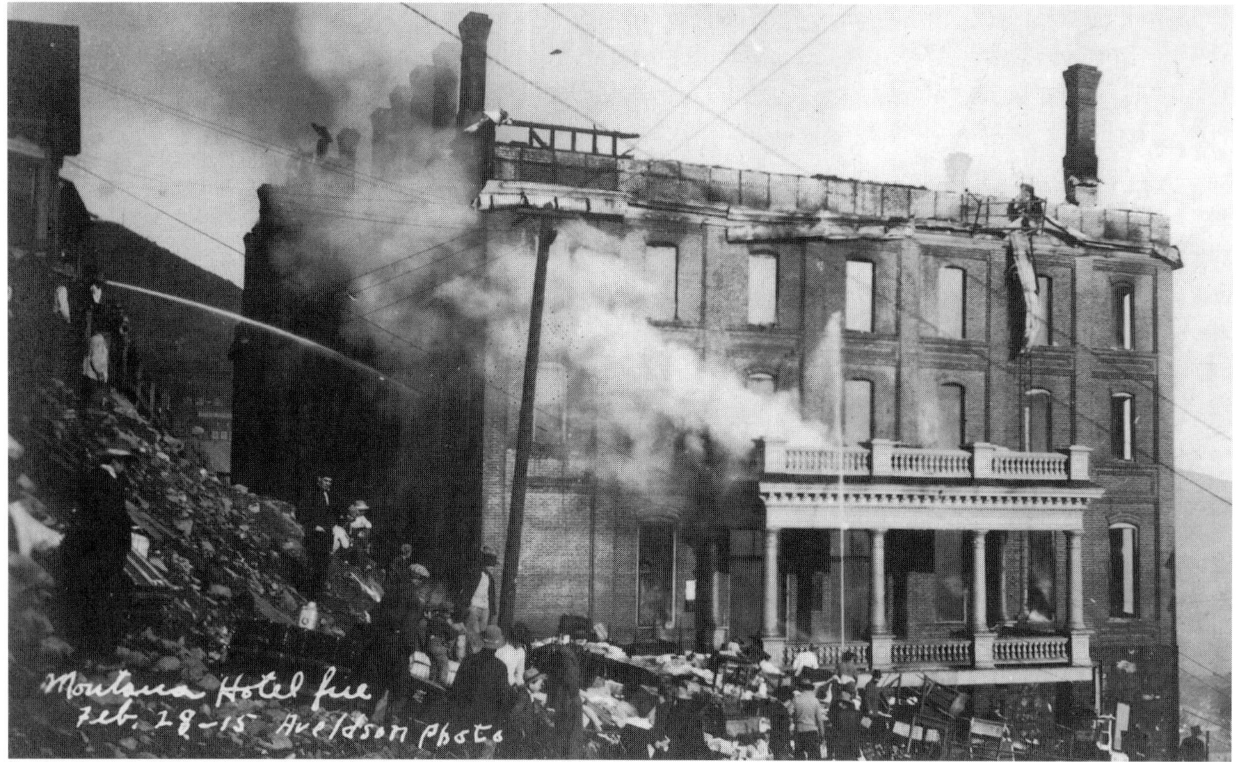

FIGURE 19. *The Montana Hotel immediately after the fire and before demolition a few days later, Jerome, Arizona. Real photo postcard, photographer unknown, February, 1915. Collection of the author.*

The photographer Aveldson of Jerome created a series of images of the burning of the Montana Hotel in 1915. The guests' trunks are shown lying in the street where they landed after being thrown out of the windows, with locals viewing the fire seated at tables and chairs from the dining room, which had been carried outside, tablecloths and all, just ahead of the fire.

The booming downtown section of Ray, Arizona, burned completely to the ground, the tallest remnants in the rubble were shorter than a wagon wheel. Clifton, Miami, and virtually all of the mining camps paid the consequence for flimsy construction, crowded living quarters, and carelessness as flames destroyed buildings and took lives.

Even more established communities felt the impact of fire, despite local brigades, water systems and equipment. An overturned lantern started the blaze that leveled Whiskey Row and all but two of Prescott's 35 saloons and most of the businesses around the courthouse square in 1900. In Bisbee, both the businesses downtown, and the growing housing developments that were filling the canyons surround-ing it, were decimated by fire repeatedly during the first decades of the 20th century. Even Phoenix saw a major landmark, its high-class Adams hotel, burn twice between 1900 and 1910.

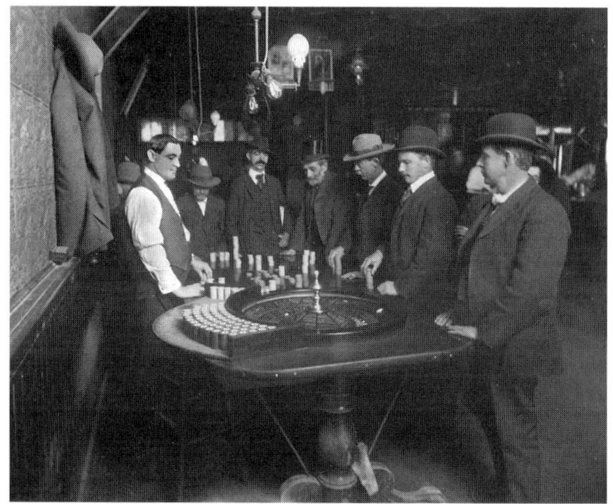

FIGURE 20. *Game of roulette at the Orient Saloon on Main Street, Bisbee. Dayton "Date" Graham, first Bisbee City Marshall and first lieutenant in the Arizona Rangers, and Tony Downs are first and second from right, respectively. Mounted silver print by William Irwin, 1906. Collection of the author.*

Gambling had been officially banned throughout the Territory in 1907, and the bars and clubs on the U.S. side of the border were relatively calm compared to those available a few miles south in Mexico. As a result, the gambling clubs and bars just over the border were popular sites for troops and locals alike. Images of the casinos, hostesses, and other forbidden pleasures reflected life among the young troops along the border, which others apparently found vicariously stimulating.

Labor-management disputes had been a part of the Arizona scene for decades. Mining unions, dominated by the International Workers of the World (IWW, or Wobblies) attempted periodic negotiations for higher wages and improved working conditions, which led to strikes. Postcards caught images of labor unrest, from the copper strikes of U. S. miners in Cananea, Mexico, in 1906, to the IWW strikes in Globe and Jerome, and the Bisbee deportations in 1916. George Dix documented the deportation at Bisbee beginning with Sheriff Wheeler's posse of non-union sympathizers identified by arm bands. Dix's images document the round-up of over 1,250 union members at gunpoint and their forced march to the baseball stadium, then to cattle cars, as they were run out of town by rail to Columbus, New Mexico.

In Globe, the National Guard was called out to protect the mine from striking workers. An unidentified photographer created a compelling series of images of the strikers' march through town, the conflict with the troops, and the removal of the wounded by truck. Jerome and other mining communities also saw strikes and labor unrest during this period. Though photographs of the deportation and union conflicts were produced, they apparently were not generally distributed and are relatively uncommon today.

After the World War I, the country was ready for change. The "War to End All Wars" had just been won. Development of industries that had flourished

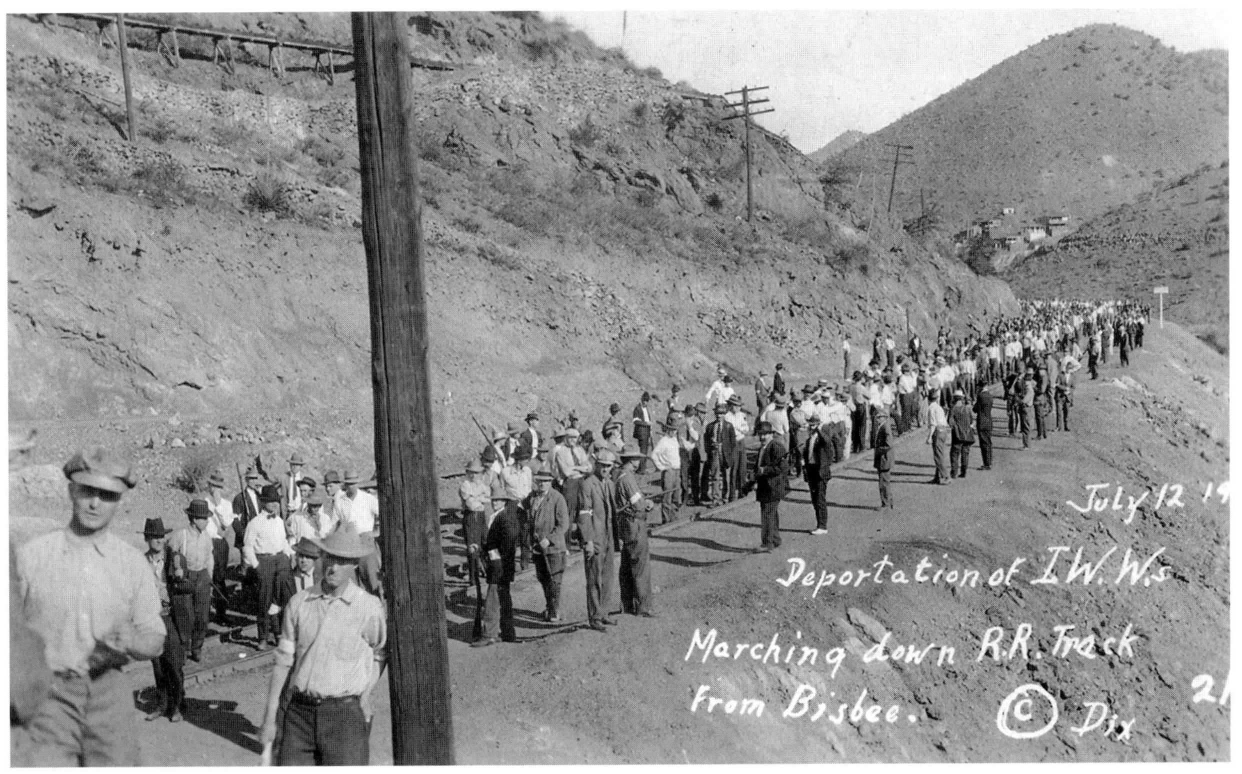

FIGURE 21. *Sheriff Wheeler's Deputies marching IWW strikers from downtown to the baseball stadium where they were held before being forced out of town during the Bisbee Deportation. Real photo postcard by George Dix, July, 1916. Collection of the author.*

during the war became a focus of attention. Communication technologies and mass media continued to develop and photography's role in business and social documention changed.

As the second decade of the century ended, the Wild West became anachronistic, with romantic portrayals in pulp and movies replacing the real images of bygone days. Dude ranches became popular, and travel and tourism become major economic forces in the state. Captions on stereographs of cowboys that had been marketed since the 1890s by publishers like Keystone, changed from descriptions of the brave tamers of the west, to descriptions of the busy, alert, mounted herdsmen whose duty it was to keep cattle together. The old time cowboy was portrayed as a thing of the past, replaced by efficient feedlots. Captions asked viewers, "Have you ever played cowboy?" The West was growing up.

The market for postcards and stereoviews continued to shrink as motion picture shows and higher quality photomechanical reproduction reached new mass markets. Movie theaters brought images of national and world events, and photomechanical reproductions in magazines and newspapers provided tangible records for people to share with family and friends. Even small local papers began to add photographic illustrations, and scrap books began to edge out postcards and photographs as records of community events.

The telephone become increasingly commonplace, and the immediacy of a phone call supplanted the old picture postcard for everyday communication. Businesses in outlying areas, like the Kolb gallery at the Grand Canyon, no longer had to rely on postcards to order groceries and supplies from stores in town. A simple phone call would do. Postcards became less important as communication tools and social documents, although they remained popular as tourist mementos.

The photographic studio finally pushed the itinerant photographer almost out of existence as portraiture became a mainstay. The newspaper "stringer" became one of the last incarnations of the survey and itinerant photographers who had visually documented the development of the state. Roads were built,

initially around the towns, and eventually between them, and the automobile became available to the middle class.

Arizona is indebted to the intrepid photographers who captured images of the environment, personalities, and events that shaped the development of the Territory. Their legacy was crucial to the investment, promotion, and growth of the state. Though the number of photographers and volume of images produced is small compared with many other western states, they form a compelling portrait of Arizona's evolution, from barren home of Navajo and Apache who threatened travel routes to the gold fields of California, to a bonanza of gold, silver and copper mining, to the Arizona of today, an international economic force.

The fascination with the history of photography that began in the 1970s continues to mature. Photographs are studied and analyzed for the information they contain, not simply as illustrations for the printed word. Slowly, a body of knowledge is forming about the men and women who produced these historic documents. Private and public collections are beginning to consolidate and organize photographic images of Arizona's past so they can be studied and interpreted. Study of this valuable resource by time period, format, and process adds depth to the analysis of images, and of the events and subjects they depict. Analysis of mount information, such as studio name and location, has begun to refine dating of photographs and to provide at least some assistance in verifying (and questioning) the pencil notations and attributions that have been added to the mounts of many images over time. Hopefully, this body of knowledge will continue to grow.

This book is an attempt to add to the visual resource of images of Arizona, rather than to repeat images readily available from other sources. The images that follow have been reproduced here in original form, such as full stereographs with mounts, rather than cropped as has been common in the past. Many of these images have rarely been seen in print before, and many more are yet to be discovered or revealed.

Portfolio of Arizona Images

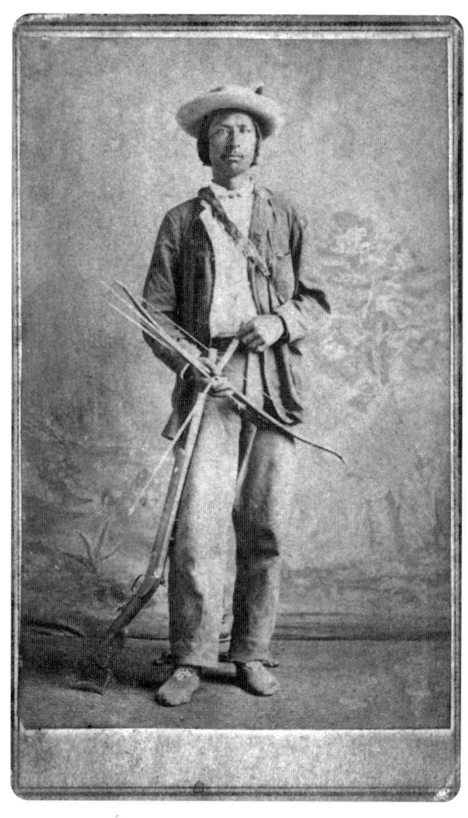

Studio portrait of Apache scout identified as Mr. Daniel McCorey, Chief of Arizona Scouts. Carte-de-visite, photographer unknown, c. 1867. Collection of the author.

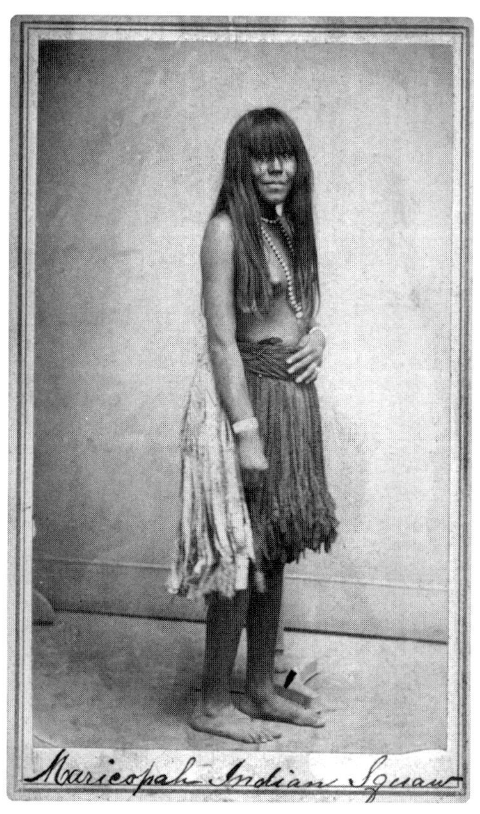

Studio Portrait of Maricopa woman. Carte-de-visite, photographer unknown, c. 1867. Collection of the author.

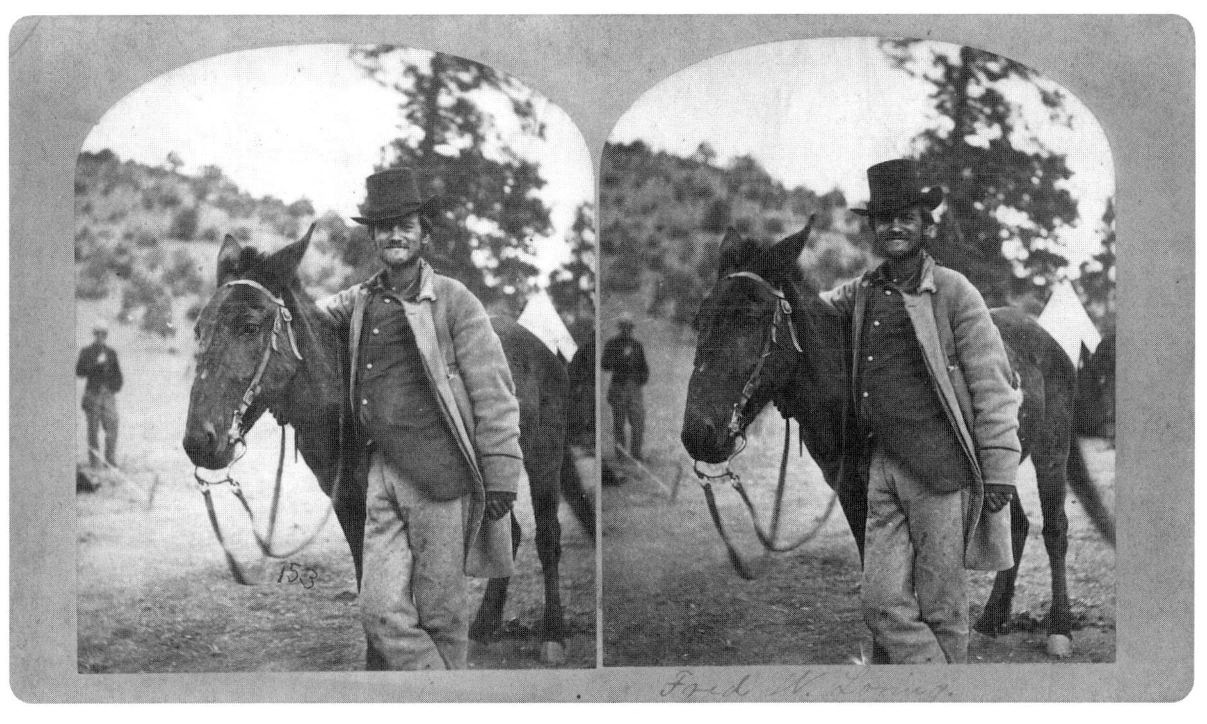

Fred W. Loring, general assistant and correspondent for Appleton's Journal, *and his mule "Evil Merodach," at Wheeler expedition camp taken before departing for Wickenberg en route to San Bernadino, California. Loring was killed by Apache-Mohave less than two days later, on November 5, 1871. Stereograph by Timothy O'Sullivan, November, 1871. Collection of the author.*

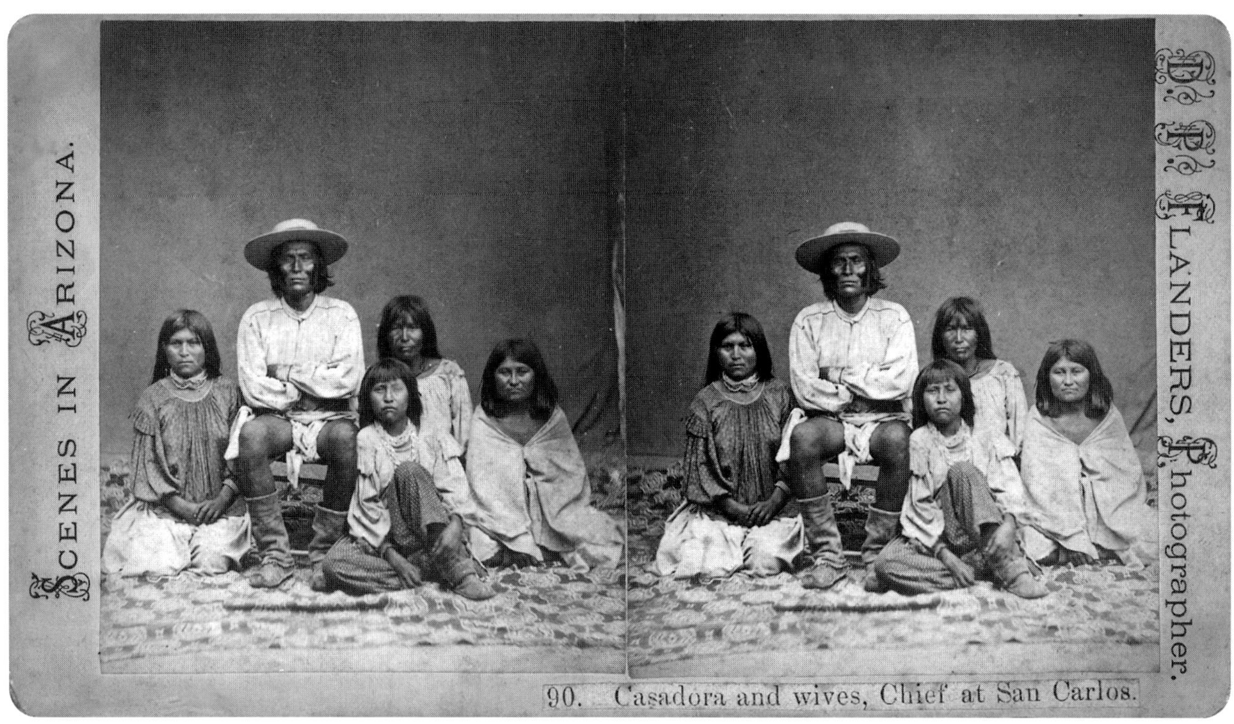

Casadora, Arivaipa Apache Sub-Chief, and wives at the San Carlos Reservation. A few months earlier, Casadora surrendered to Captain Hamilton, and returned to the reservation, diffusing the tension after Pedro and renegade Apache attacked a wagon train which sparked the departure of Apache from the San Carlos Reservation and the "Outbreak" of 1874. Stereograph by Dudley Flanders, Summer, 1874. Collection of the author.

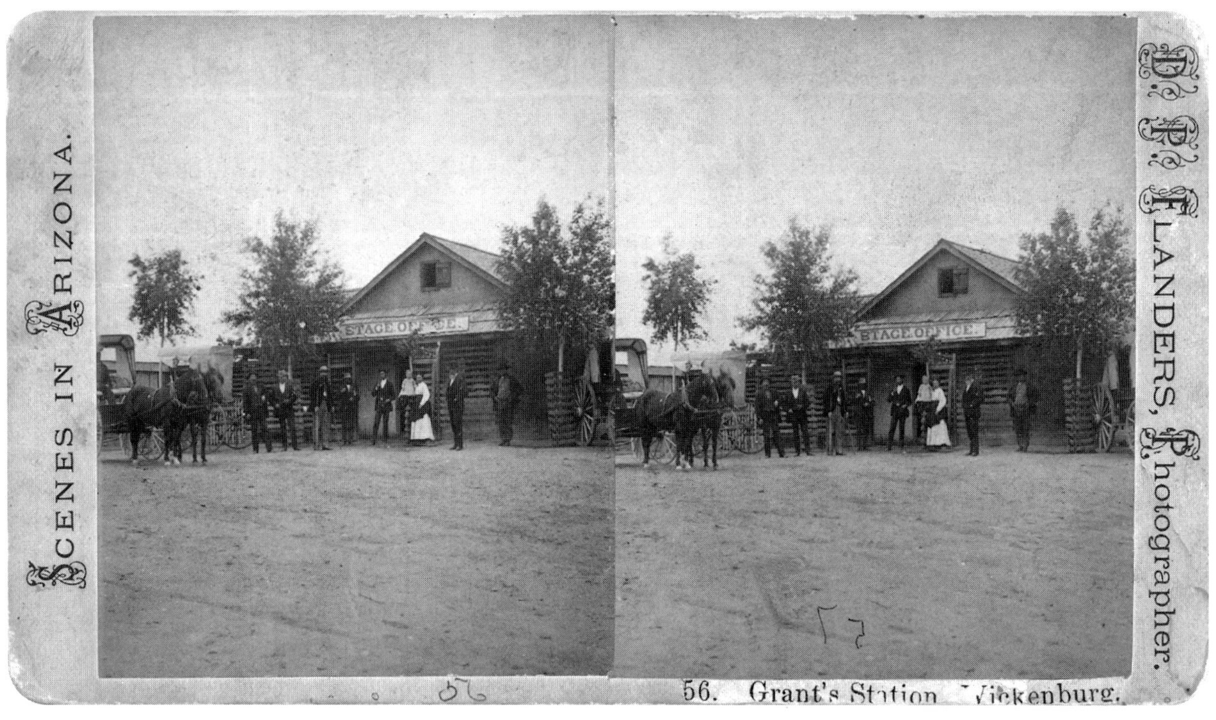

Grant's Station, a Butterfield Stage stop in Wickenberg, Arizona Territory. Stereograph by Dudley Flanders, Spring, 1874. Collection of the author.

34

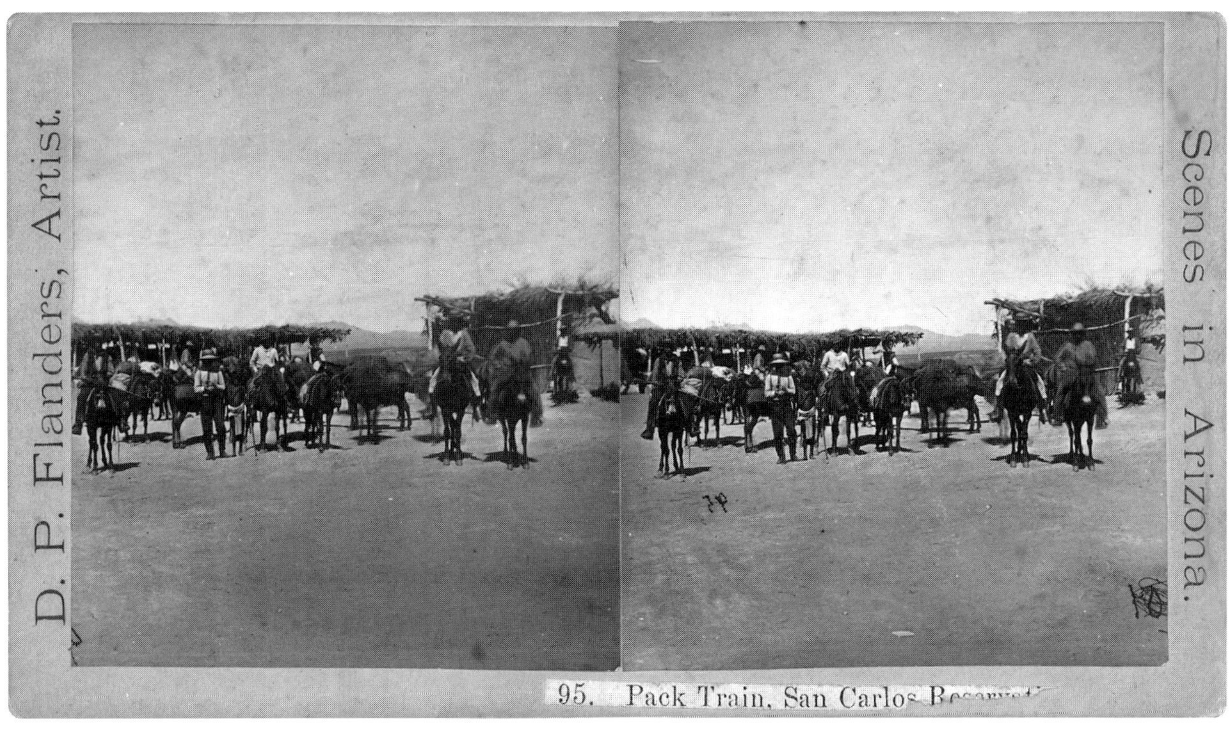

Pack train of the Flanders photographic excursion from Tucson to San Carlos, Summer. Stereograph by Dudley P. Flanders, 1874. Collection of the author.

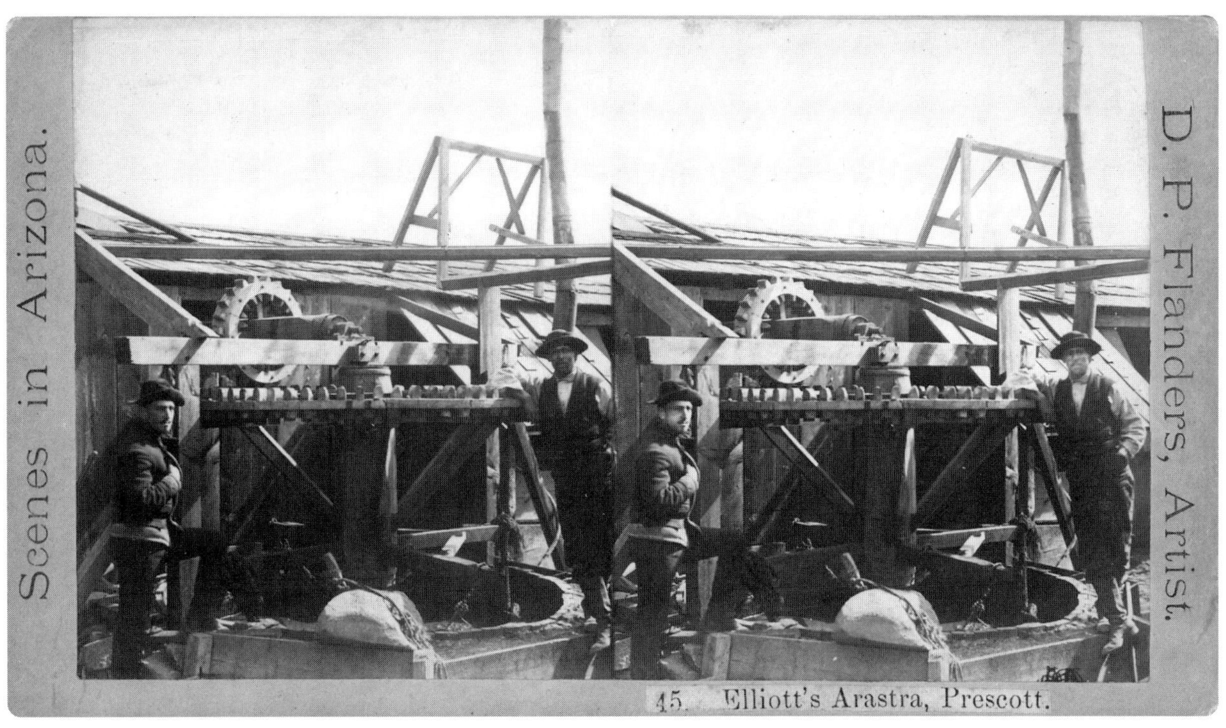

Elliott's arastra, a powered ore crushing apparatus in Prescott. Stereograph by Dudley P. Flanders. Collection of the author.

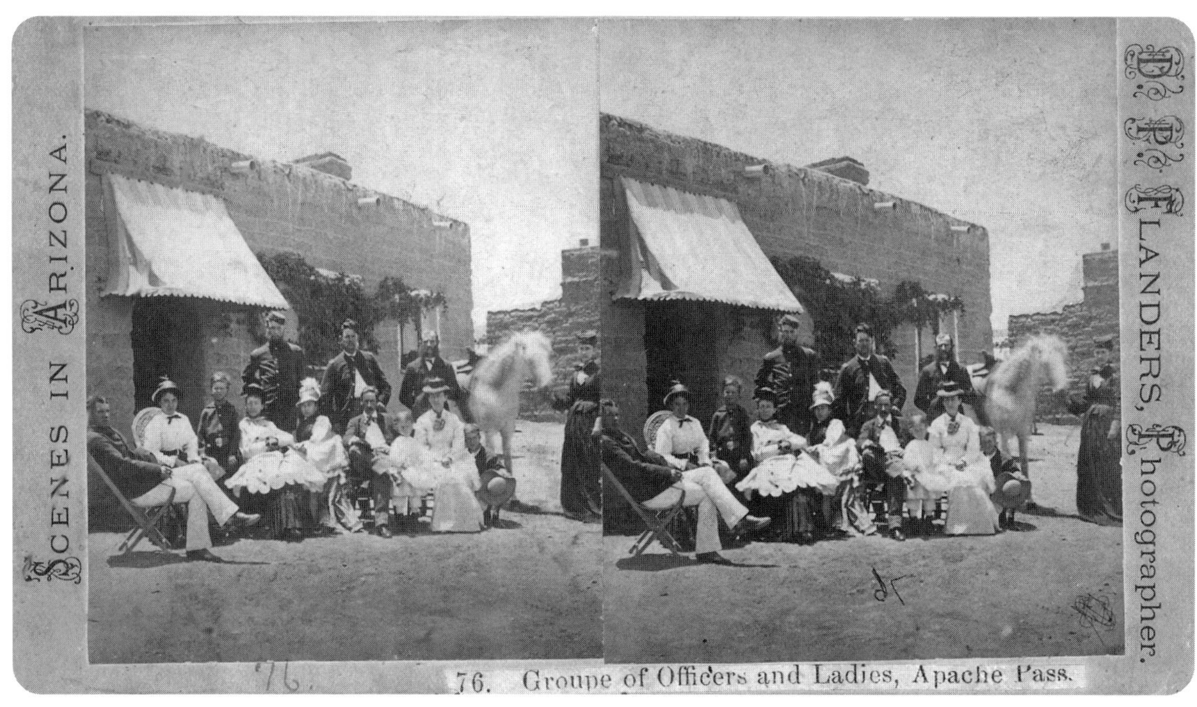

Officers and Ladies at Fort Bowie, Apache Pass, Cochise County, in typical summer attire—wool uniforms, long sleeves, and full petticoats. Stereograph by Dudley Flanders, July or August, 1874. Collection of the author.

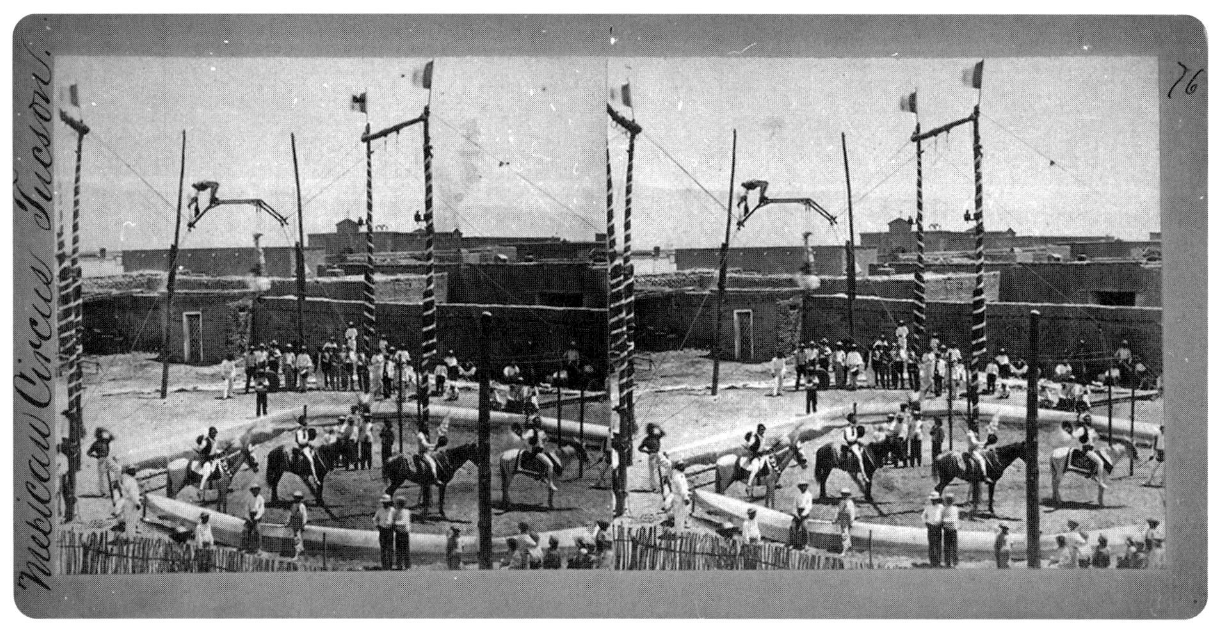

Mexican Circus performing in the square in Tucson, Arizona Territory. Stereograph by Dudley P. Flanders, Summer, 1874. Collection of C. Wesley Cowan, Historic Americana.

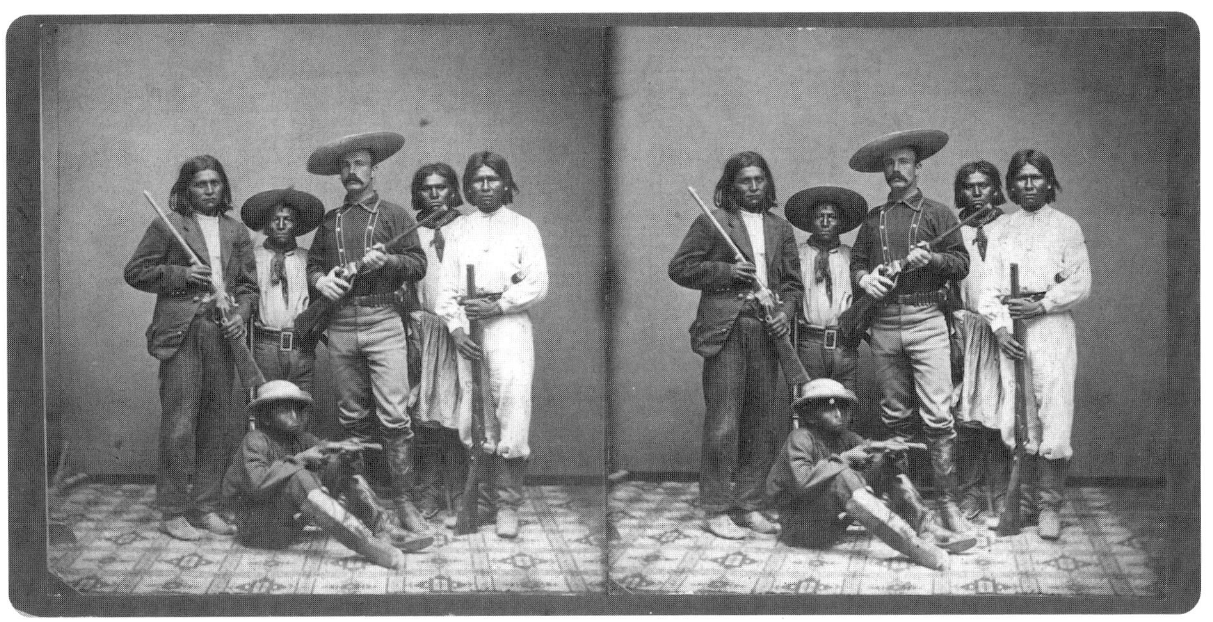

John Clum, Apache Agent and his Apache Scouts at San Carlos Reservation soon after his arrival on August 8, 1874. Clum was one of the most successful agents working with the Apache. After leaving his position at the reservation, Clum became publisher of the Tombstone Epitaph, *and later, postmaster of Alaska. Stereograph by Dudley P. Flanders. Collection of the author.*

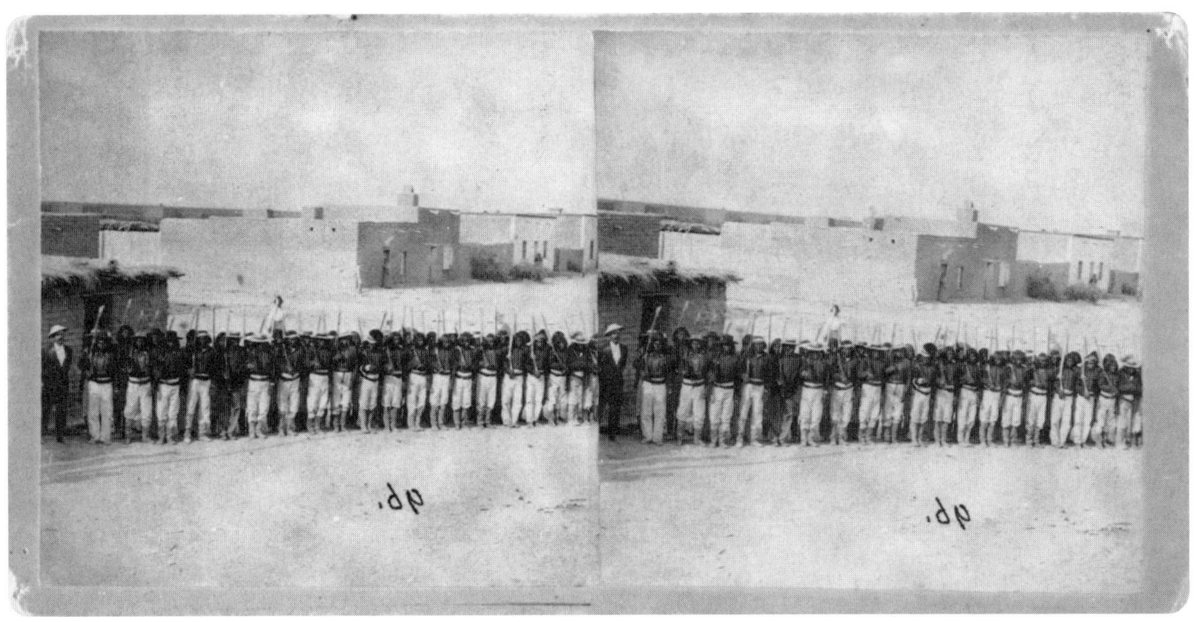

San Carlos Indian Agent John Clum with his Apache Police in formation during a visit to Tucson, Arizona Territory. Probably taken during a visit to diffuse anti-Indian sentiment. Stereograph by Henry Buehman, c. 1876. Collection of the author.

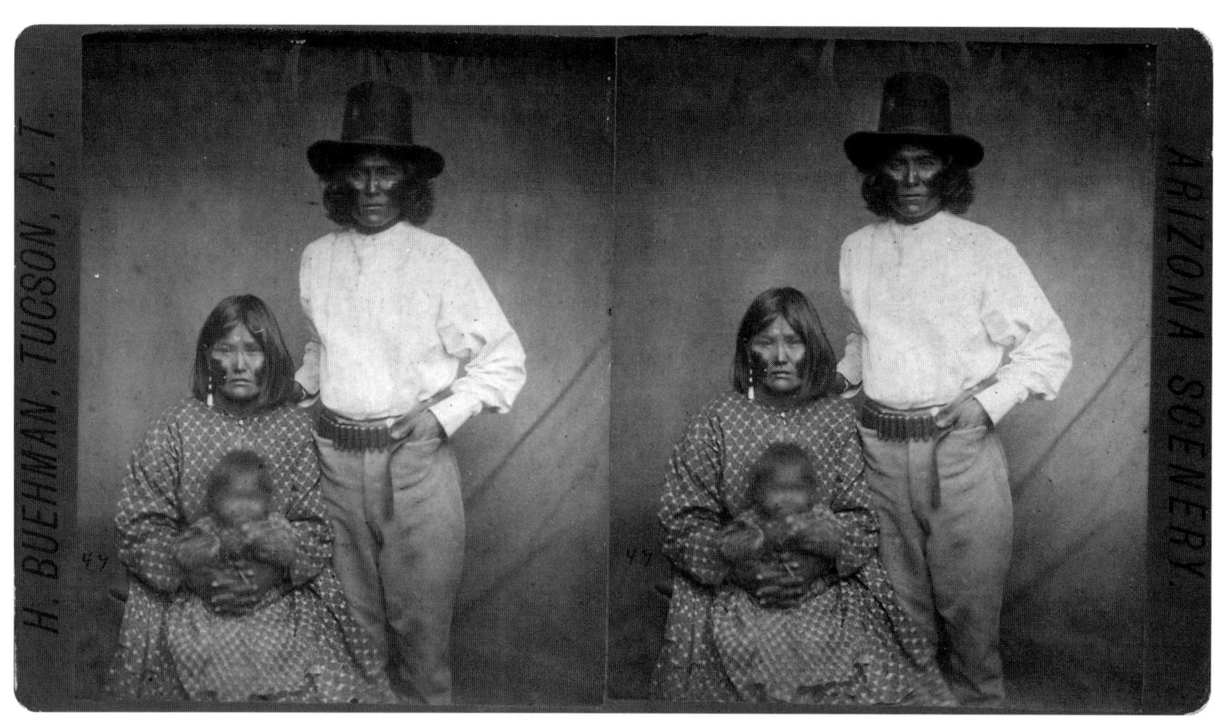

"Handsome Charlie" with wife and child, probably taken at San Carlos Reservation. Stereograph by Henry Buehman, c. 1878. Collection of the author.

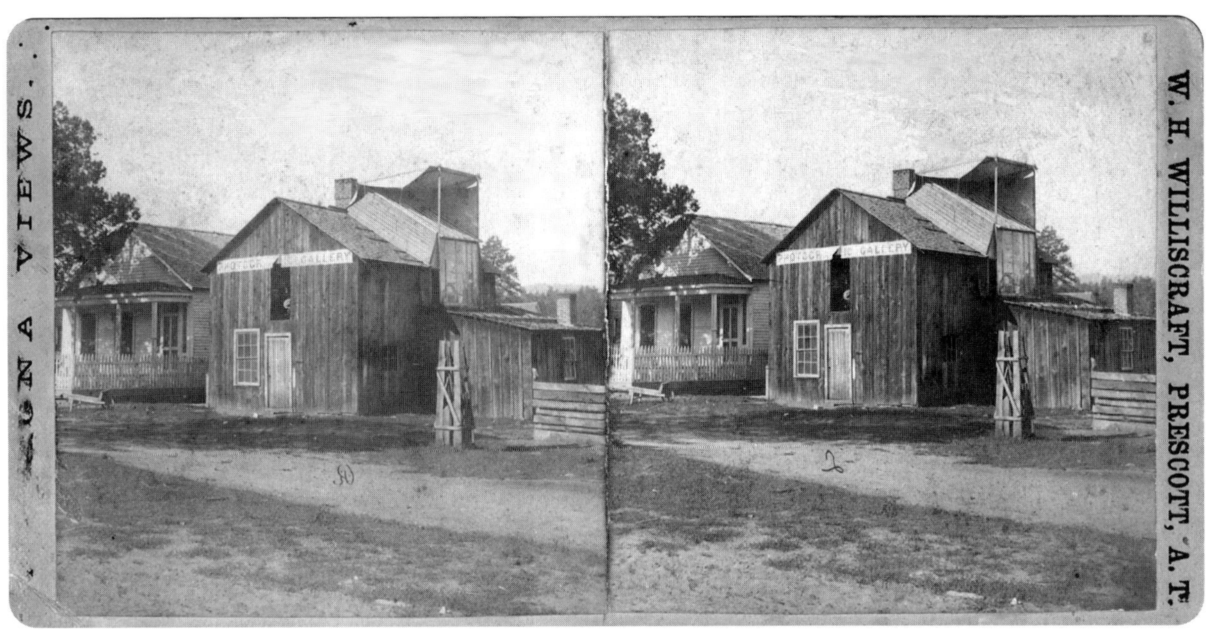

First photographic gallery in Prescott, Arizona Territory, established by F. A. Cook and N. P. Pierce, and subsequently used by E. M. Jennings, William McKenna, D. F. Mitchell, William Williscraft, Dudley P. Flanders and their operators. Stereograph by William Williscraft or operator, c. 1875. Collection of the author.

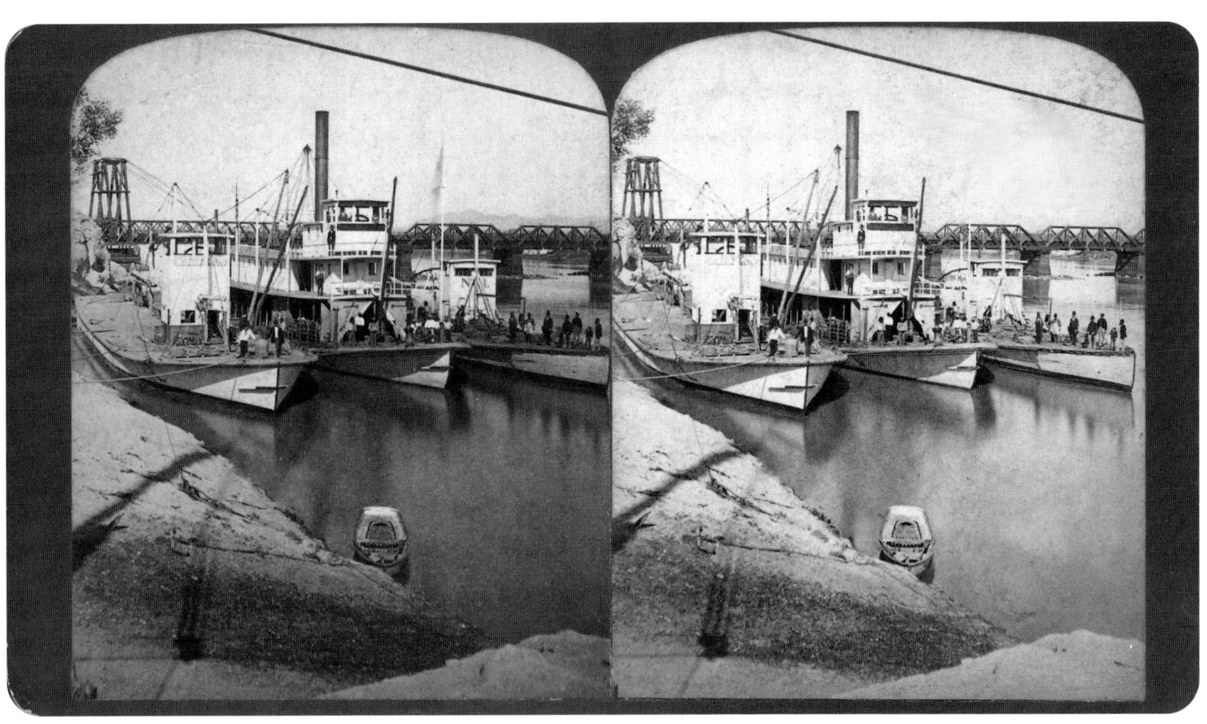

Paddle wheel steamers and barges on the Colorado at Yuma, Arizona. Stereograph by C. R. Savage, 1878. Collection of the author.

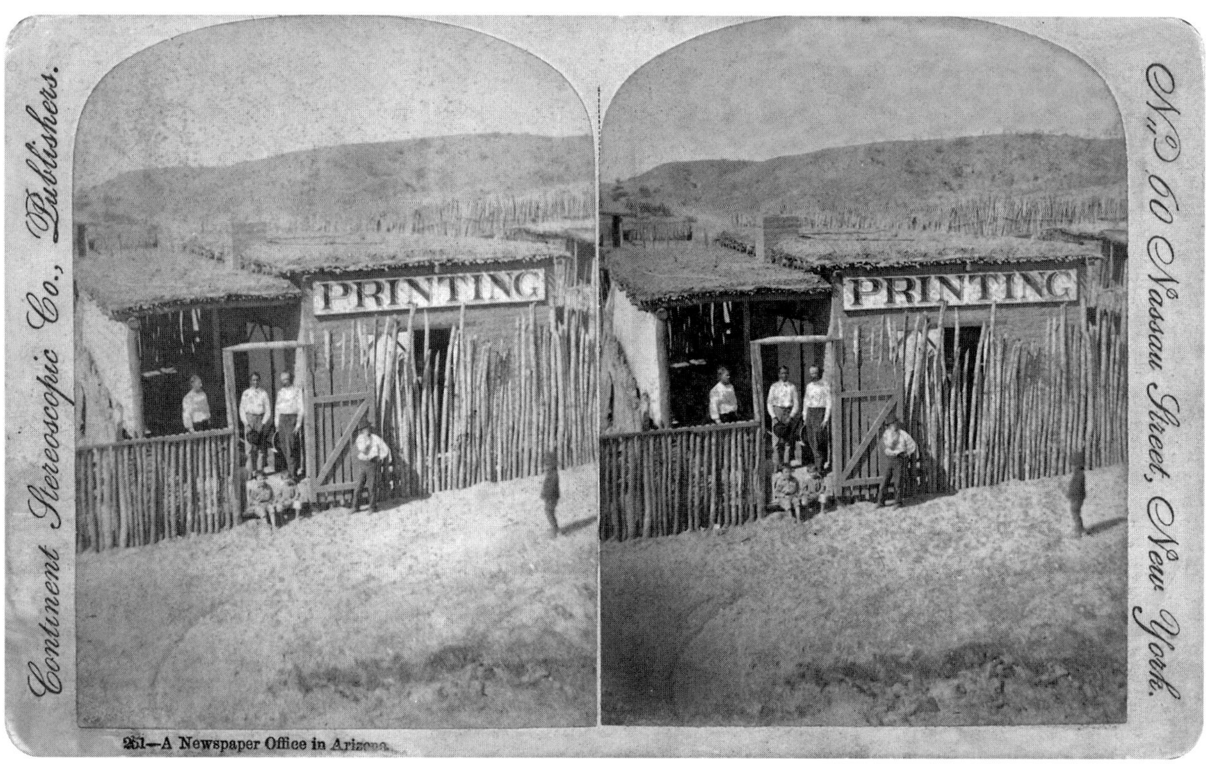

Facade of newspaper office and printer, Ehrenberg, Arizona Territory. Stereograph published by Continent Stereoscopic Company, photographer unknown (probably Enoch Conklin), c. 1878. Collection of the author.

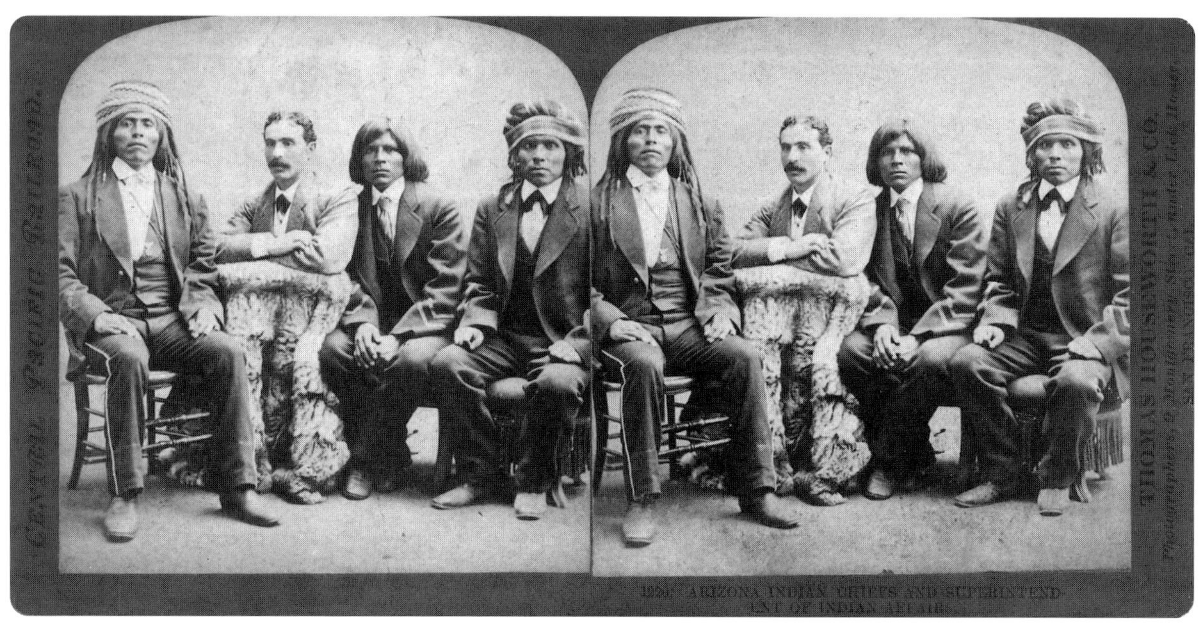

Arizona Indian Chiefs and Superintendent of Indian Affairs, Carlos Aratu, Apache Mohave chief's son (at left), Louis Morajo, Pima Indian Chief (2nd from right). Stereograph by Thomas Houseworth, c. 1880. Collection of the author.

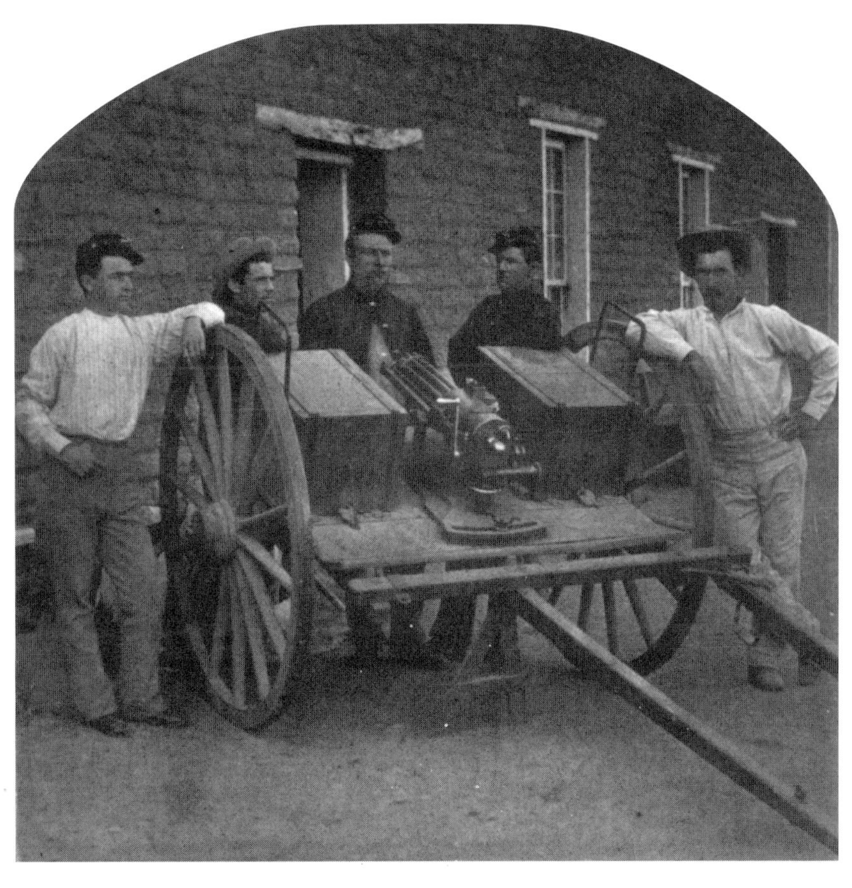

Officers and staff with gattling gun at Ft. McDowell. Photographer unknown, stereograph, c. 1878.
Courtesy of Sharlot Hall Museum.

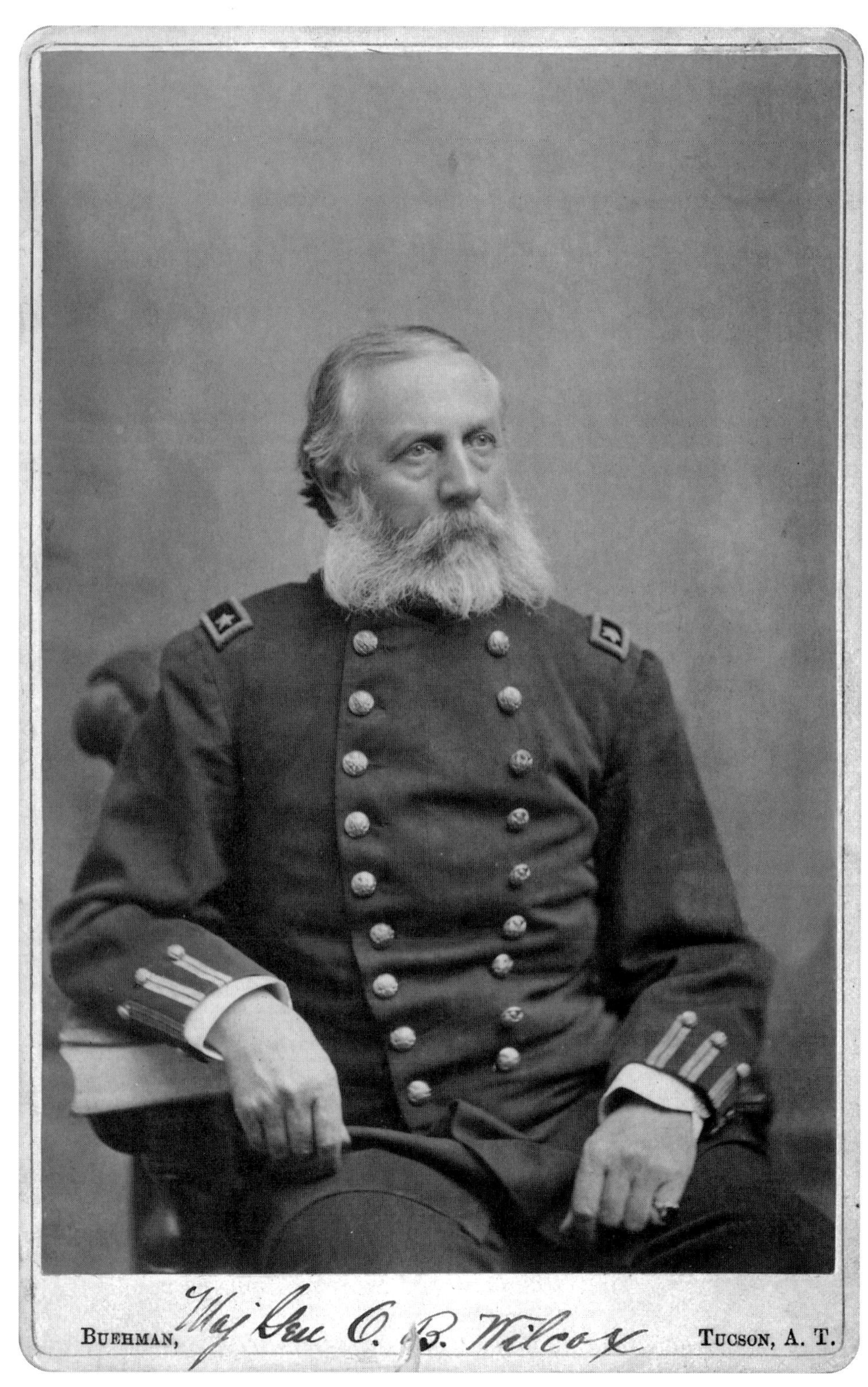

General Orlando Bolivar Wilcox, military commander of the Territory of Arizona from March 8, 1878, to September 4, 1882. Cabinet card by Henry Buehman, c. 1881. Collection of the author.

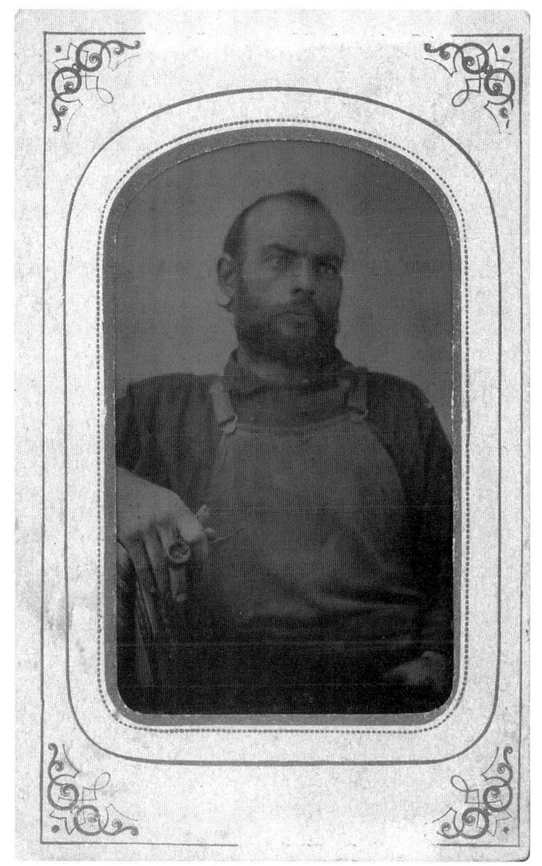

Portrait of Schroeder, a photographer active at Ft. Huachuca, Bisbee and Wilcox, from around 1885 into the 1890s. Carte-de-visite sized tintype, photographer unknown. Collection of the author.

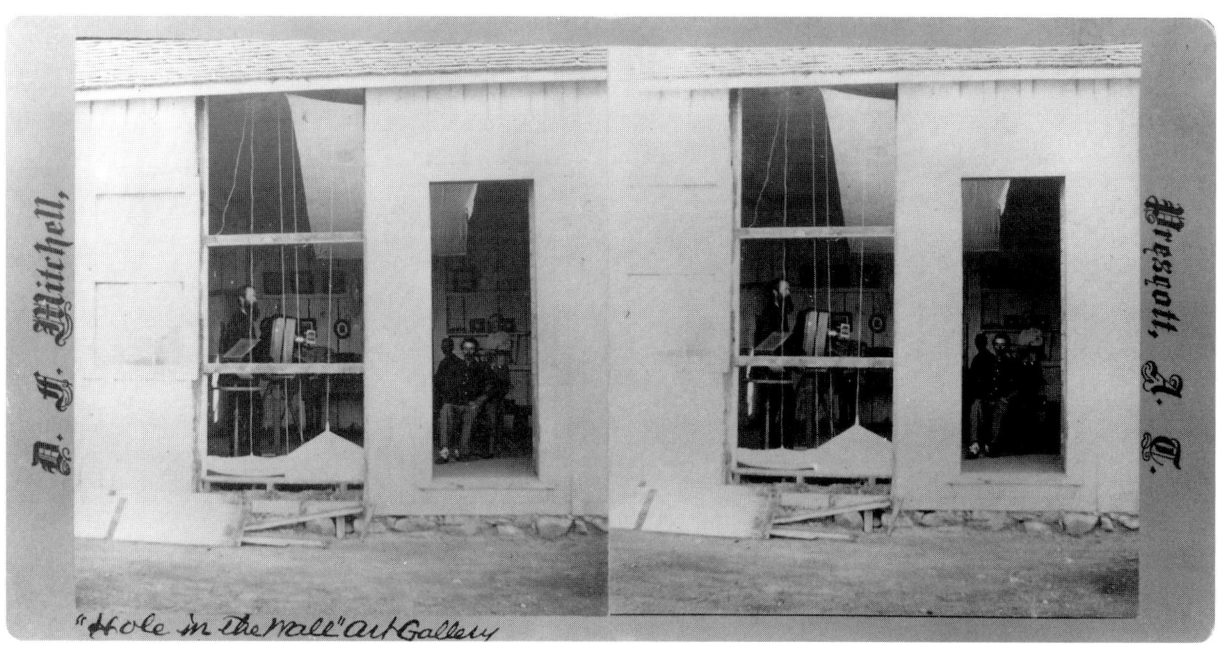

Exterior of the Hole in the Wall Art Gallery, Camp Verde. A photographer at work in his studio. Stereograph by Daniel F. Mitchell. Courtesy of Sharlot Hall Museum.

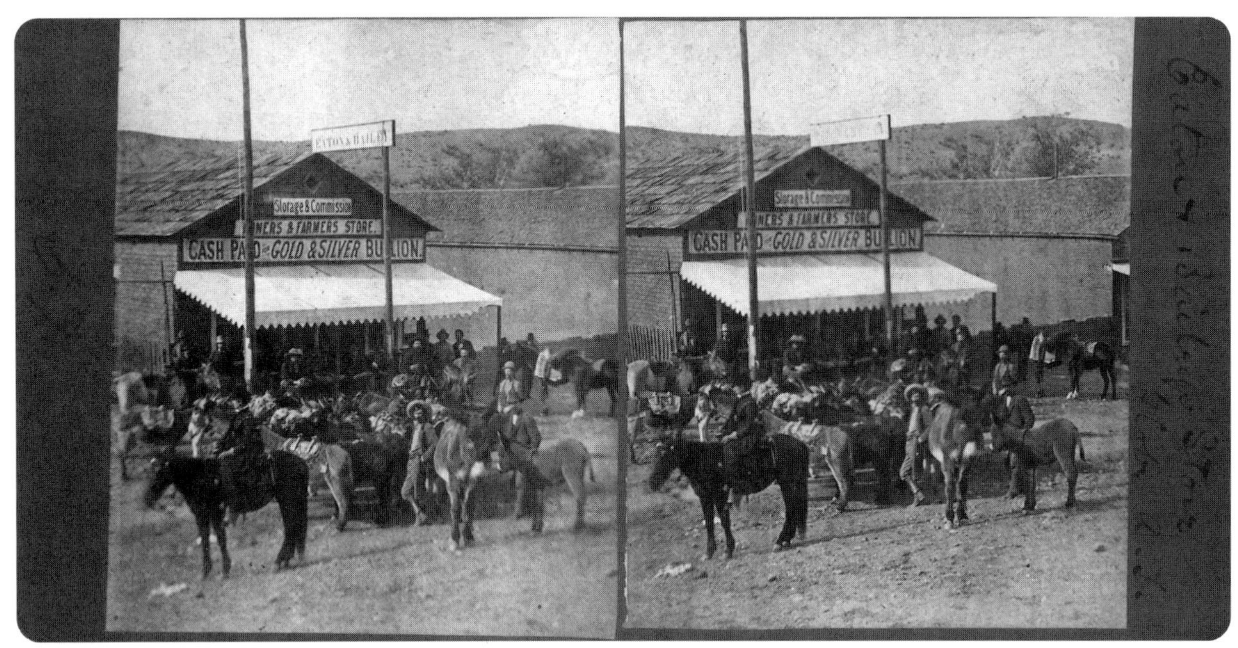

Miner's rig in front of Eaton and Bailey's Mercantile, Globe, Arizona Territory. Stereograph by Charles O. Farciot, c. 1889. Collection of the author.

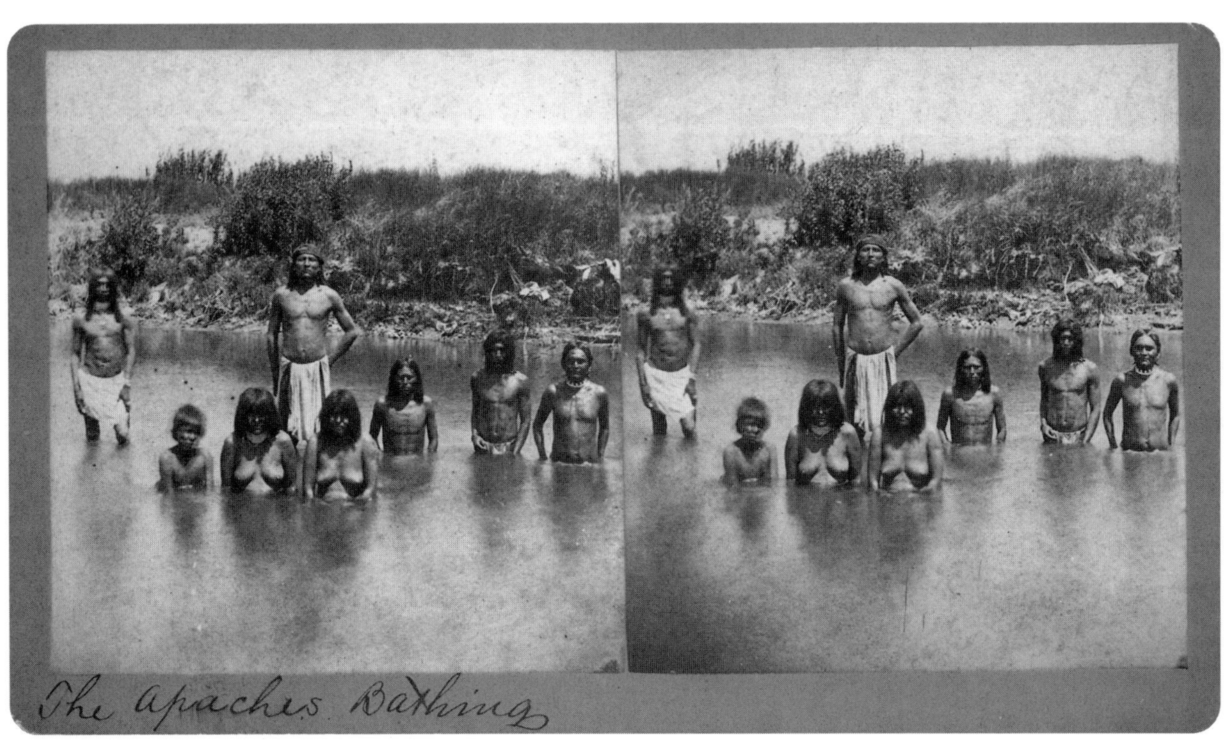

Group of Apache bathing in the Verde River near Fort McDowell. Stereograph by J. C. Burge, c. 1883. Collection of the author.

44

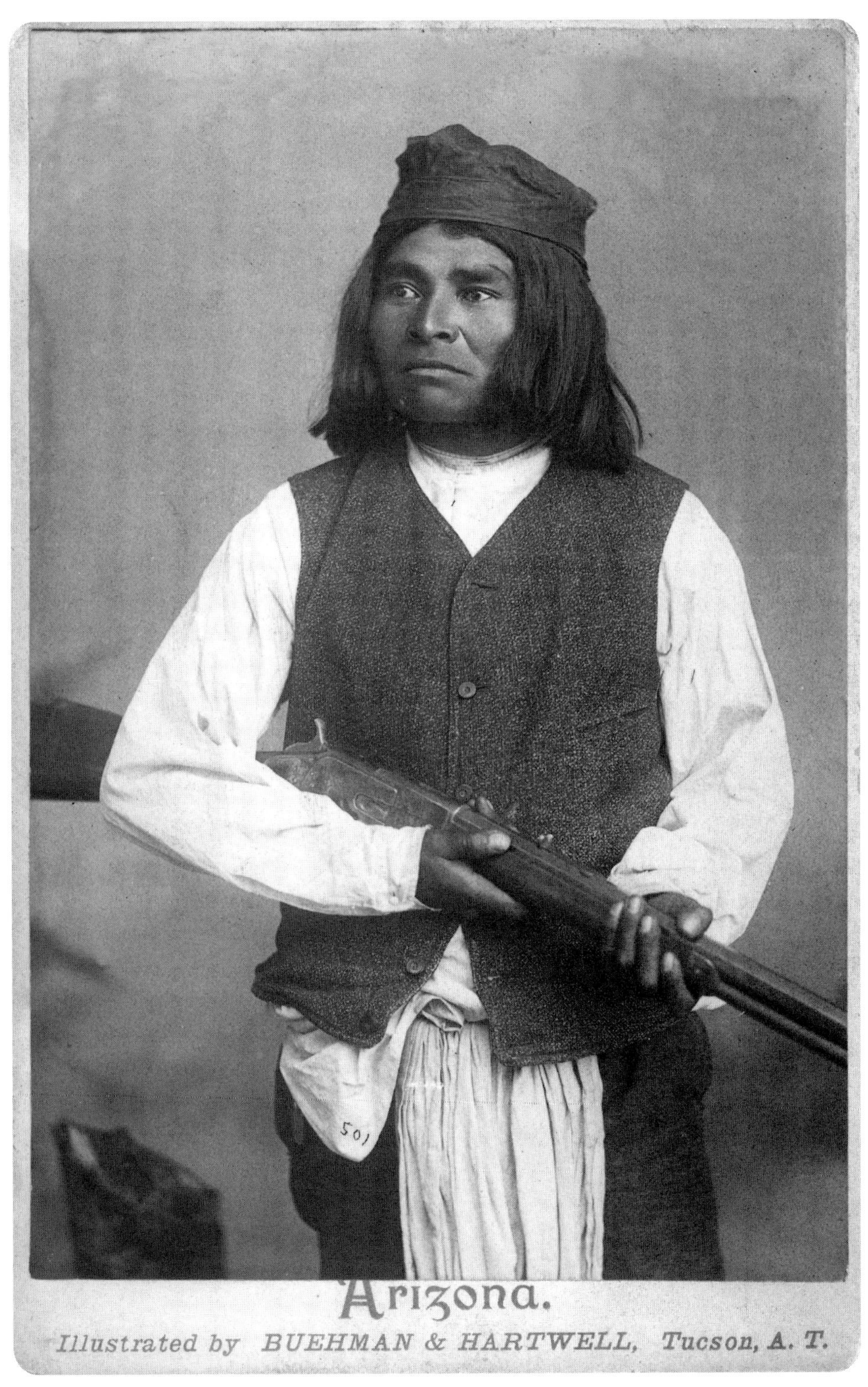

Studio portrait of Chatto, Apache scout, location unknown. A sub-chief of Chihuahua, Chatto and his band surrendered in 1884, and were sent to San Carlos. In 1885, Chatto acted as a scout to General Crook during efforts to recapture Geronimo. Cabinet card by Buehman and Hartwell photographers, c. 1885.

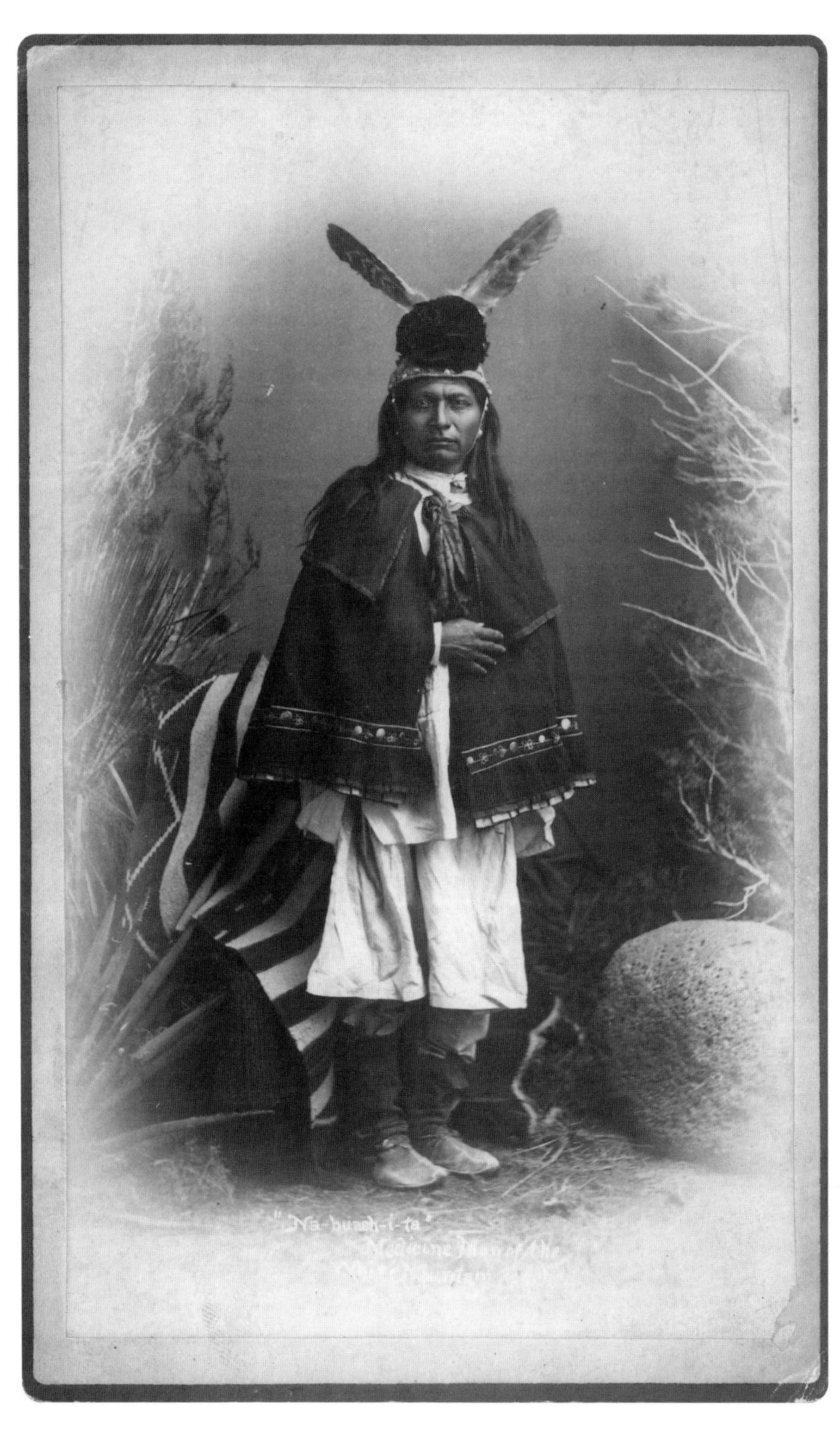

Studio portrait of Na-Buash-I-Ta, medicine man of the White Mountain Apache. Boudoir card by A. F. Randall, c. 1884. Collection of the author.

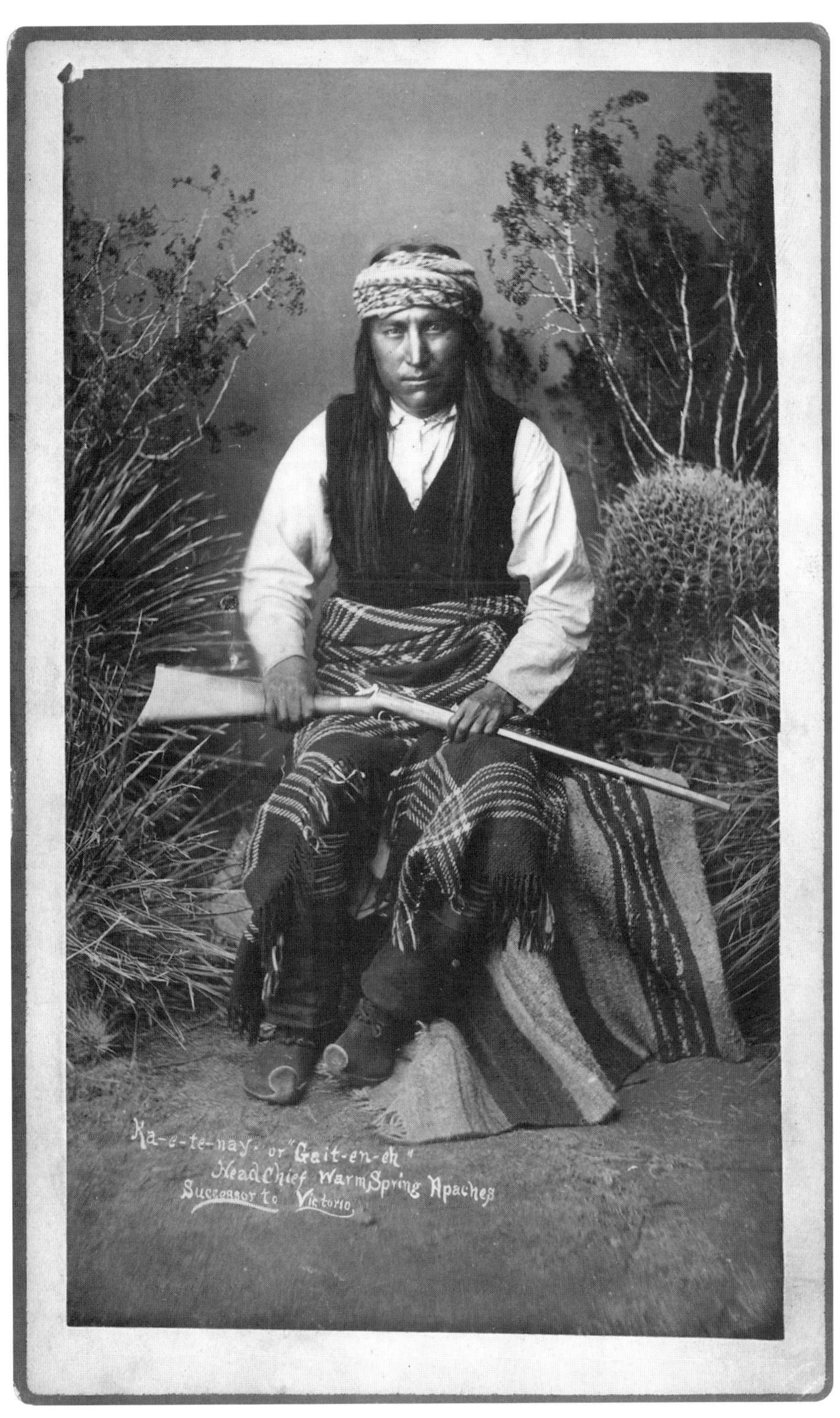

Studio portrait of Ka-e-te-nay, or Gait-en-eh, successor to Victorio, Chief of the Warm Springs Apache.
Ka-e-te-nay was sentenced to three years in Alcatraz for his attempts to cause an uprising in 1884. Boudoir card
by A. F. Randall. Collection of the author.

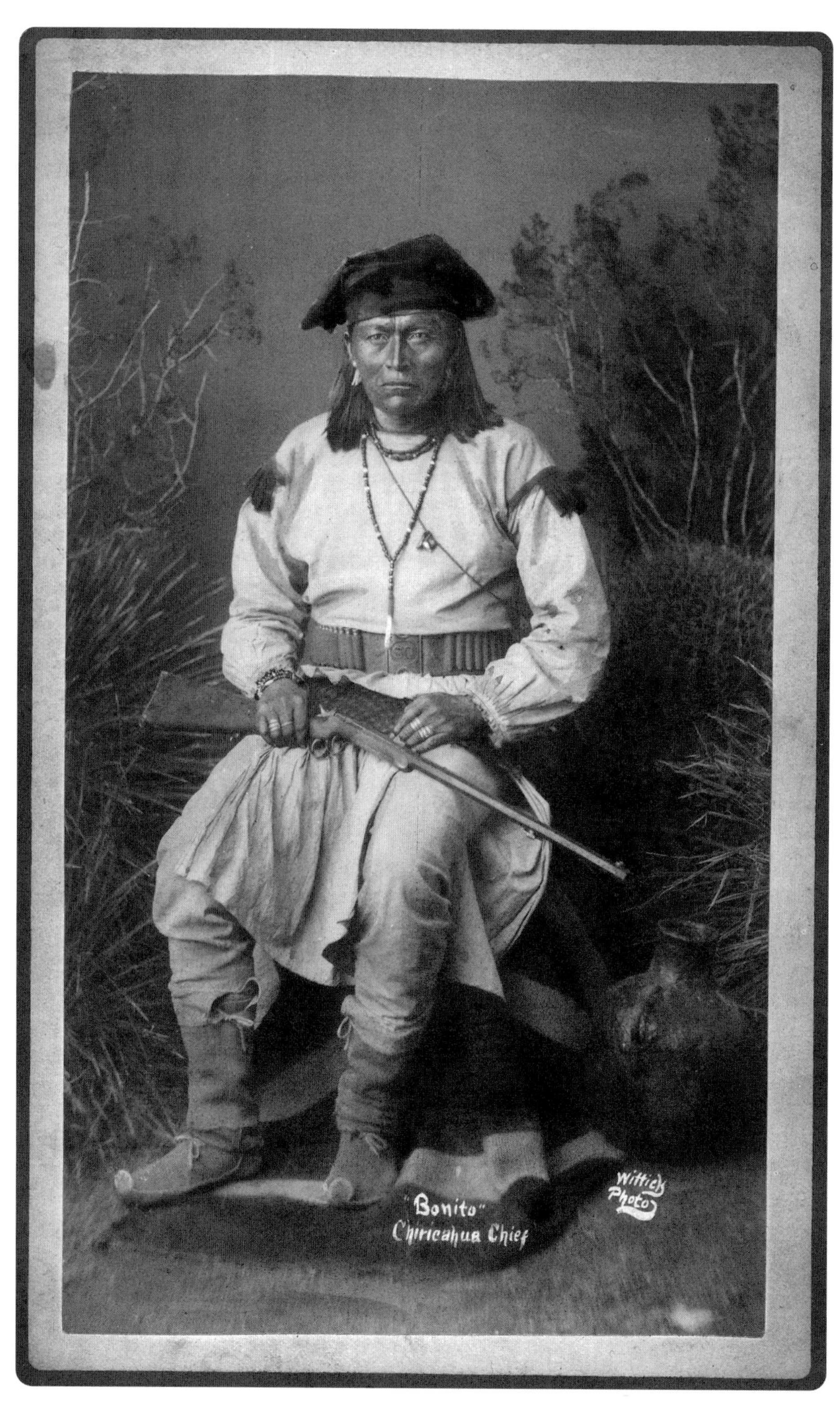

Studio portrait of Bonito, Warm Springs Apache Chief, who with his band, left the San Carlos reservation for Mexico in 1883. Boudoir card by Ben Wittick, c. 1884. Collection of the author.

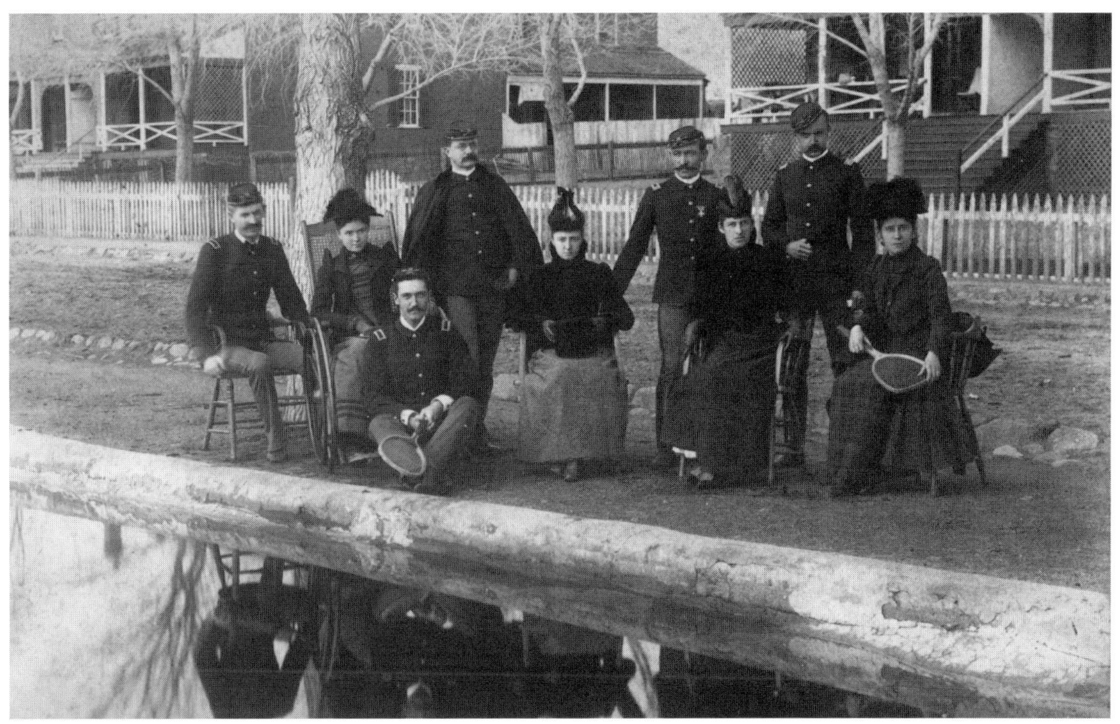

Group of officers and wives at Ft. Grant, Arizona Territory. The second man from right is Lt. Robert Doddridge of the 10th Cavalry, who served at Ft. Thomas from 1885–86 before moving to Ft. Grant, where he served until 1892. Boudoir card by Andrew Miller, c. 1888. Collection of the author.

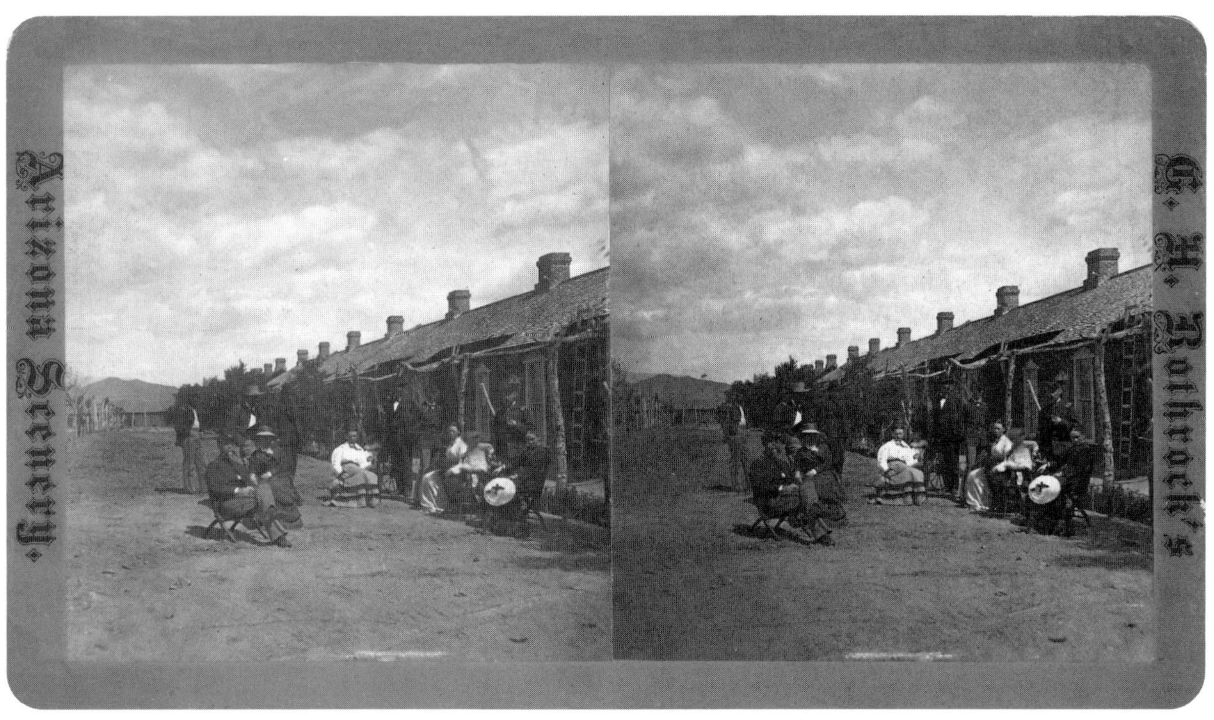

Officers and wives in front of Officer's Quarters, Ft. McDowell, north of Phoenix, Arizona Territory. Stereograph by George. H. Rothrock, c. 1885. Collection of the author.

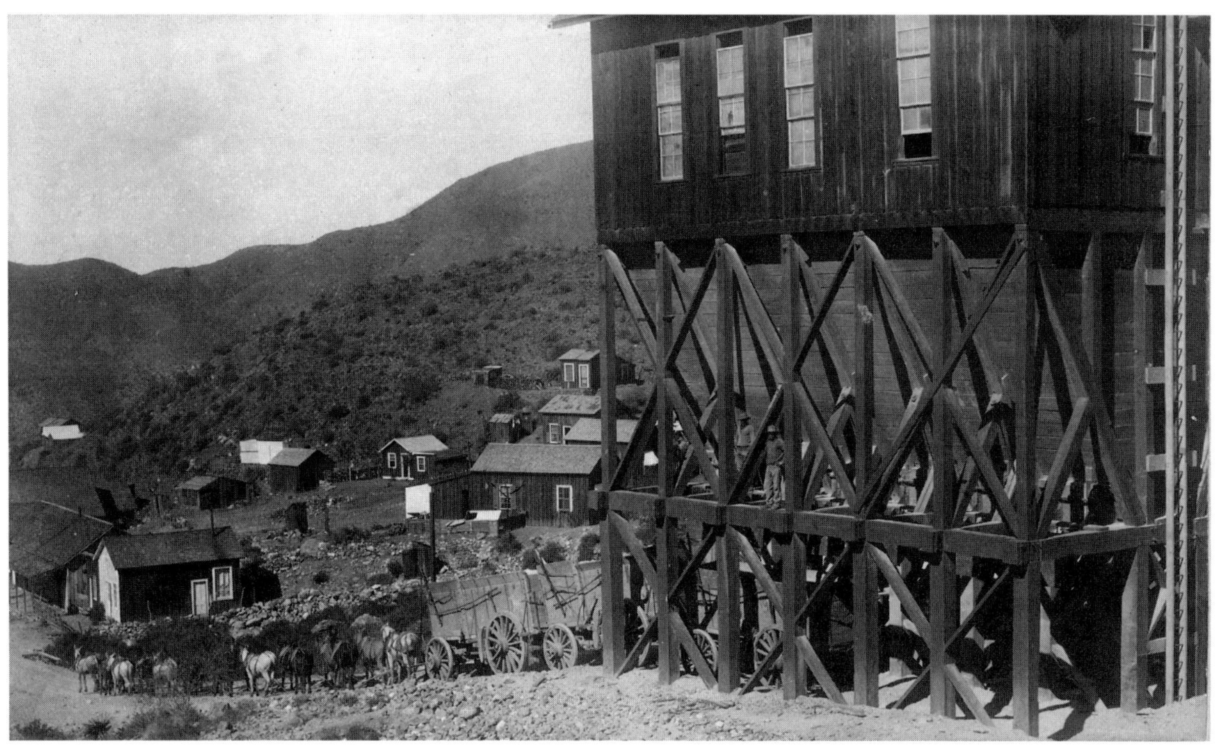

Detail of ore bins and wagons preparing to leave Silver King, Arizona Territory. Mounted albumen photograph, photographer unknown (possibly E. A. Bonine), c. 1882. Collection of the author.

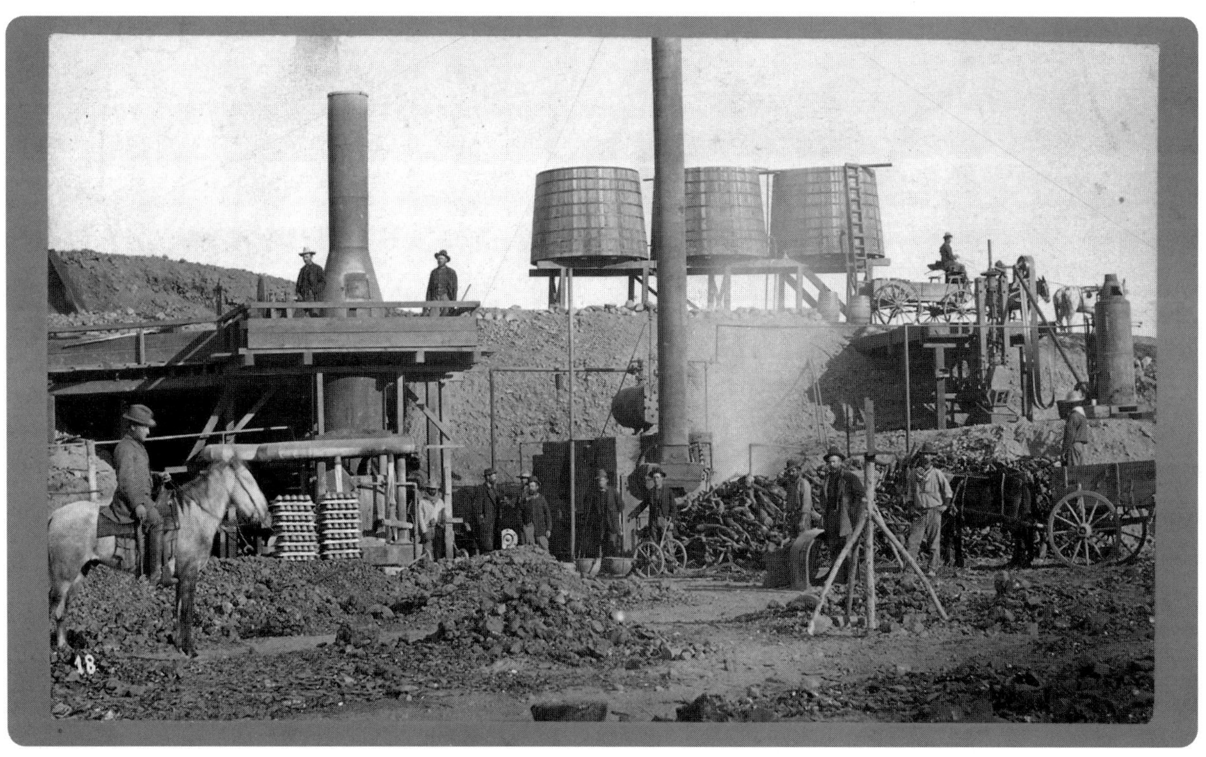

Carefully arranged photograph showing the stages necessary to process metals: from right to left—the ore arrives, the arastra or stamp mill is used to crush the ore, which is then refined, purified, and poured into molds. Finally, the ingots are stacked while the owner looks on. Boudoir card by Elias Bonine, c. 1885. Collection of the author.

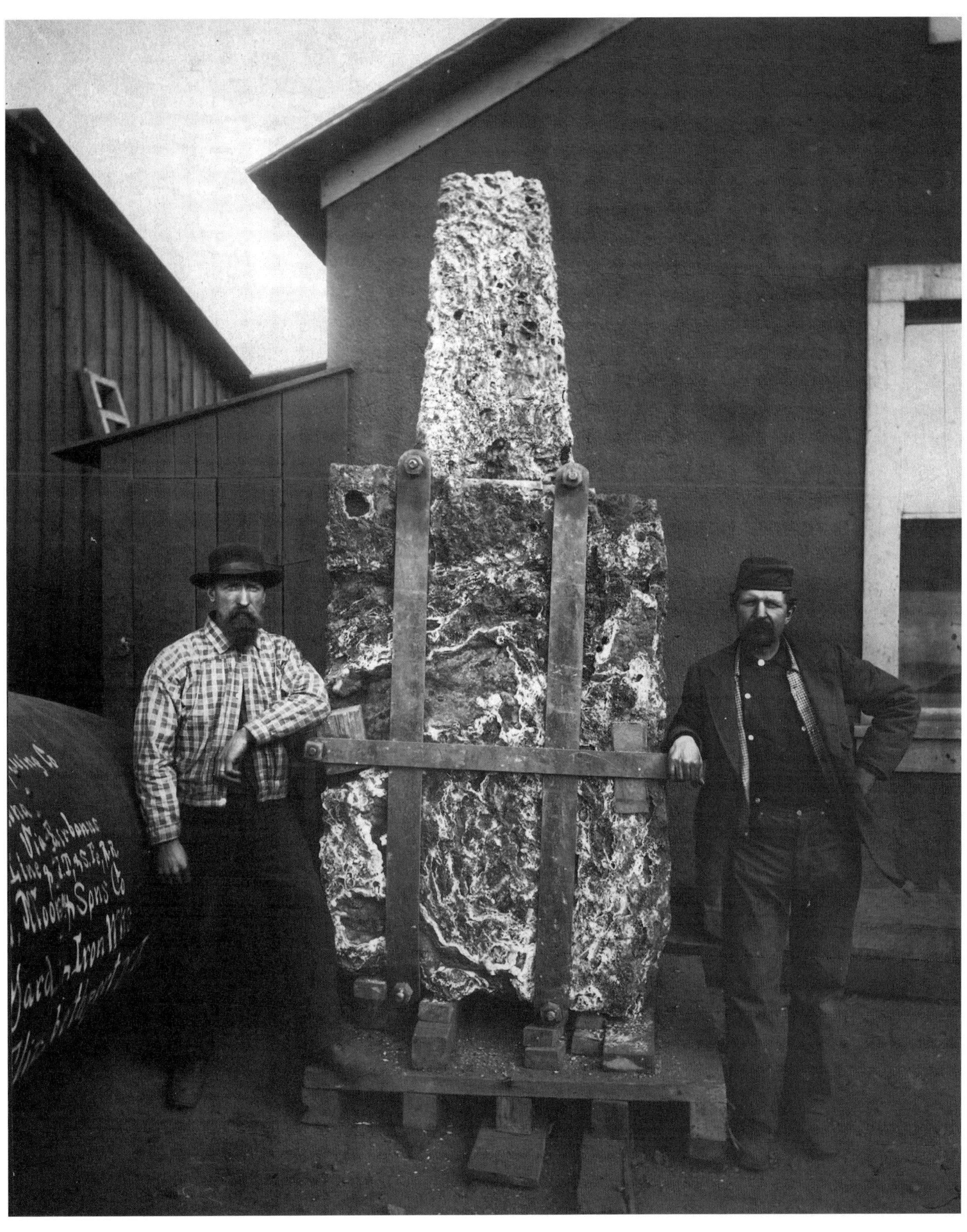

Native copper taken out of the Copper Queen mine by J. S. Williams, being packed for shipment to Chicago for display at the 1893 Columbian Exposition. Mounted albumen print, photographer unknown. Collection of the author.

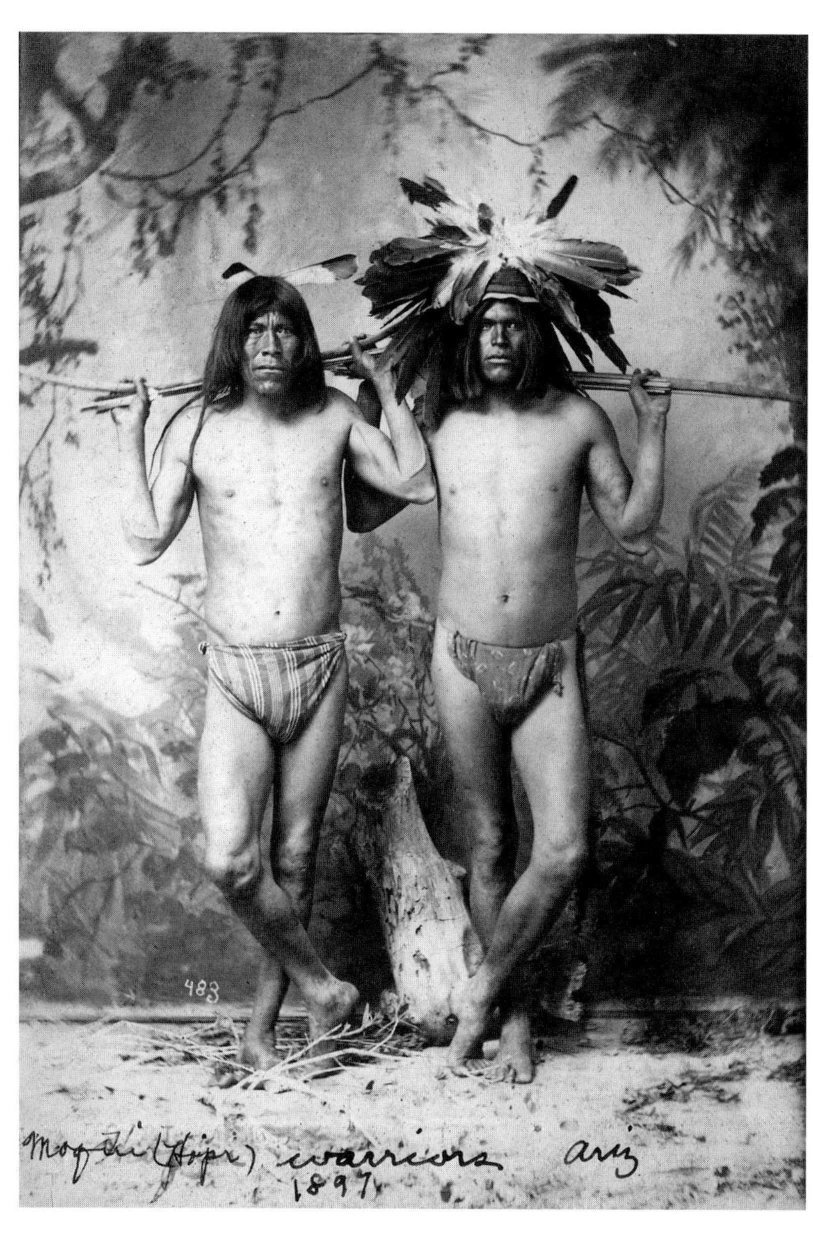

Studio portrait of two unidentified Moqui (Hopi) warriors, Phoenix, Arizona Territory.
Mounted silver print, photographer unknown (probably F. A. Hartwell). Collection of the author.

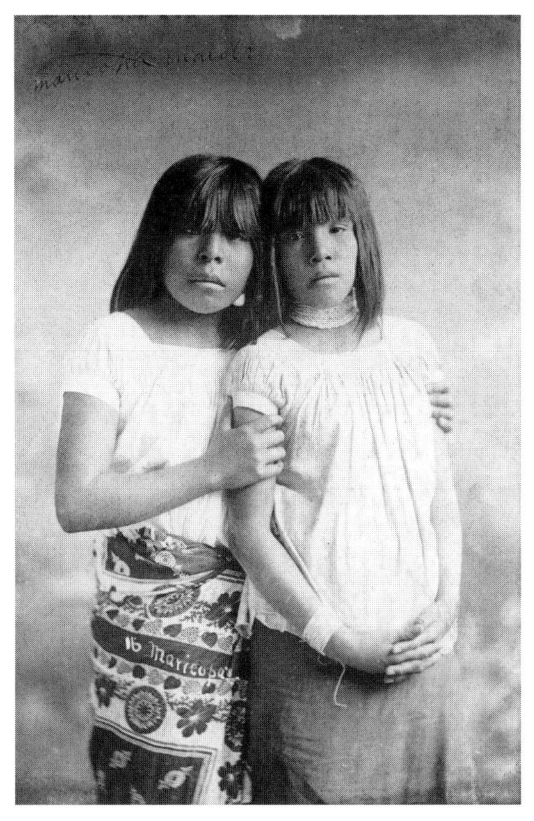

Studio portrait of Maricopa women, Phoenix, Arizona Territory. Mounted silver print, photographer unknown (probably F. A. Hartwell), c. 1898. Collection of the author.

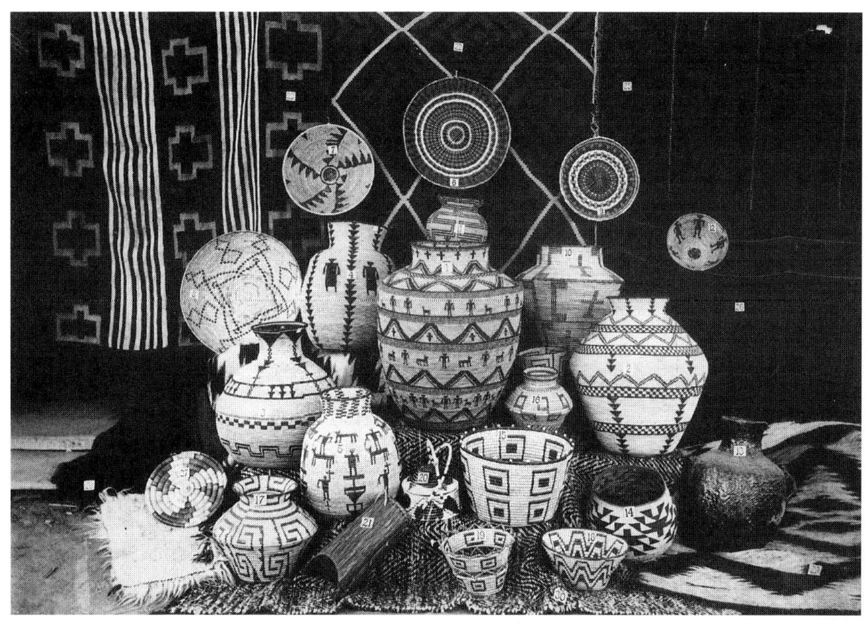

Native American rugs and baskets. Mounted silver print, photographer unknown (probably F. A. Hartwell), c. 1898. Collection of the author

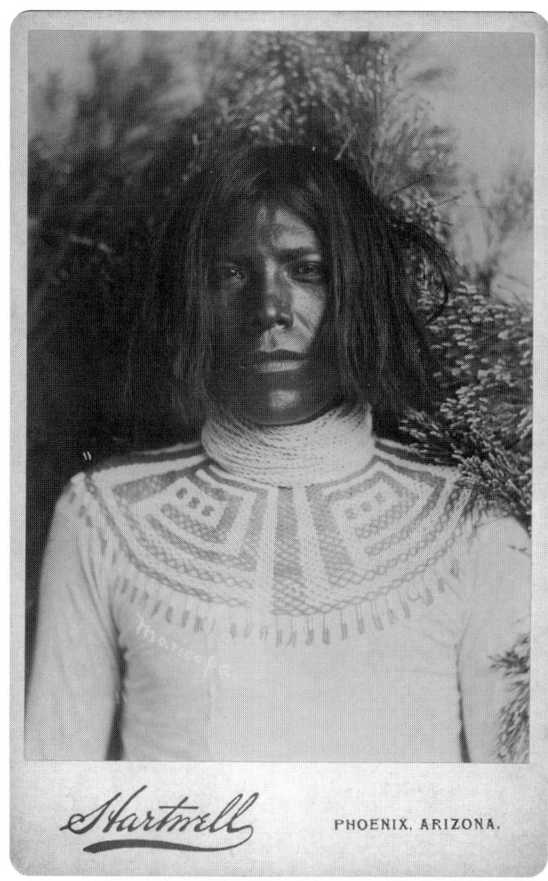

Unidentified studio portrait of Apache, Phoenix, Arizona Territory. Cabinet card by F. A. Hartwell, c. 1898. Collection of the author.

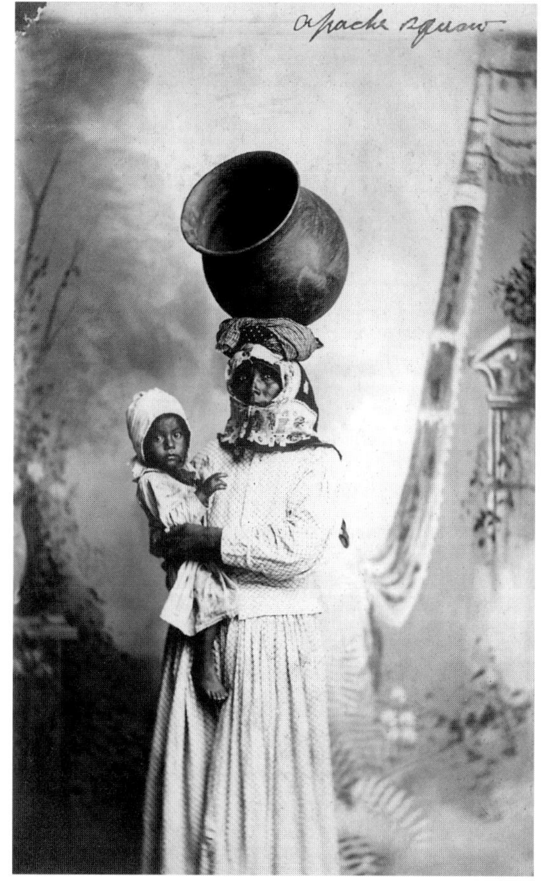

Studio portrait of unidentified Apache woman with child, Phoenix, Arizona Territory. Mounted silver print, photographer unknown (probably F. A. Hartwell), c. 1898. Collection of the author.

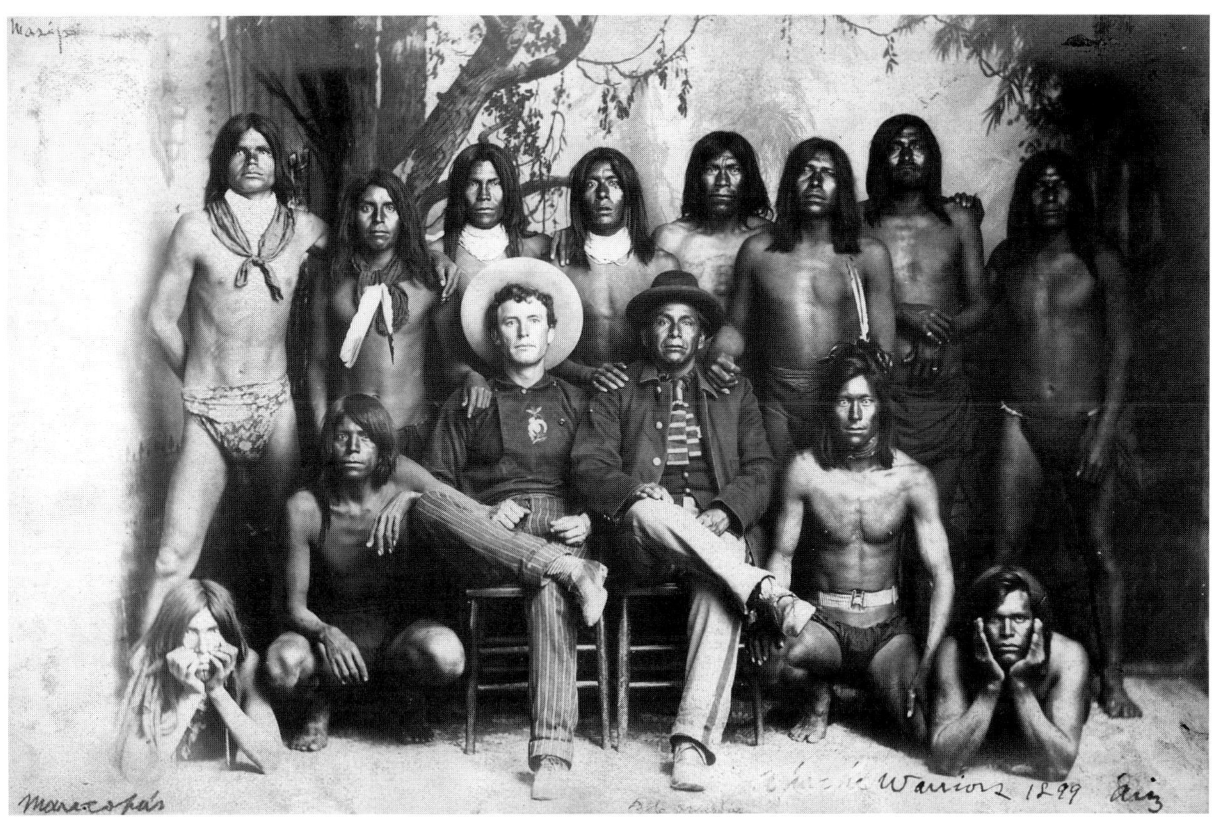

*Unidentified studio portriat of group of Maricopa and Apache with cowboy. Mounted silver print, photographer unknown (probably F. A. Hartwell),
c. 1899. Collection of the author.*

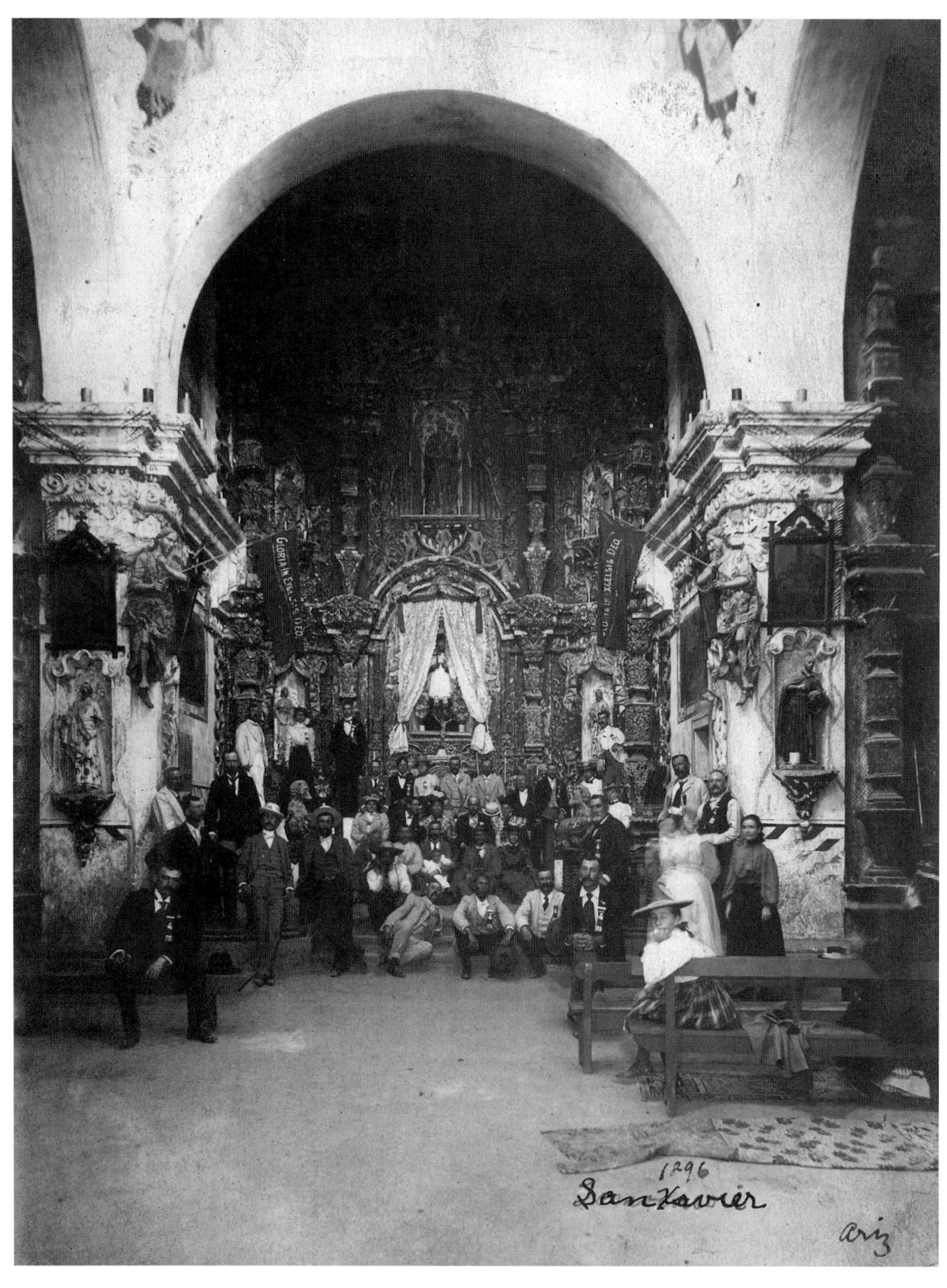

Unidentified group in the interior of San Xavier del Bac Mission, South of Tucson, Arizona Territory. Mounted silver print, photographer unknown (probably F. A. Hartwell), c. 1896. Collection of the author.

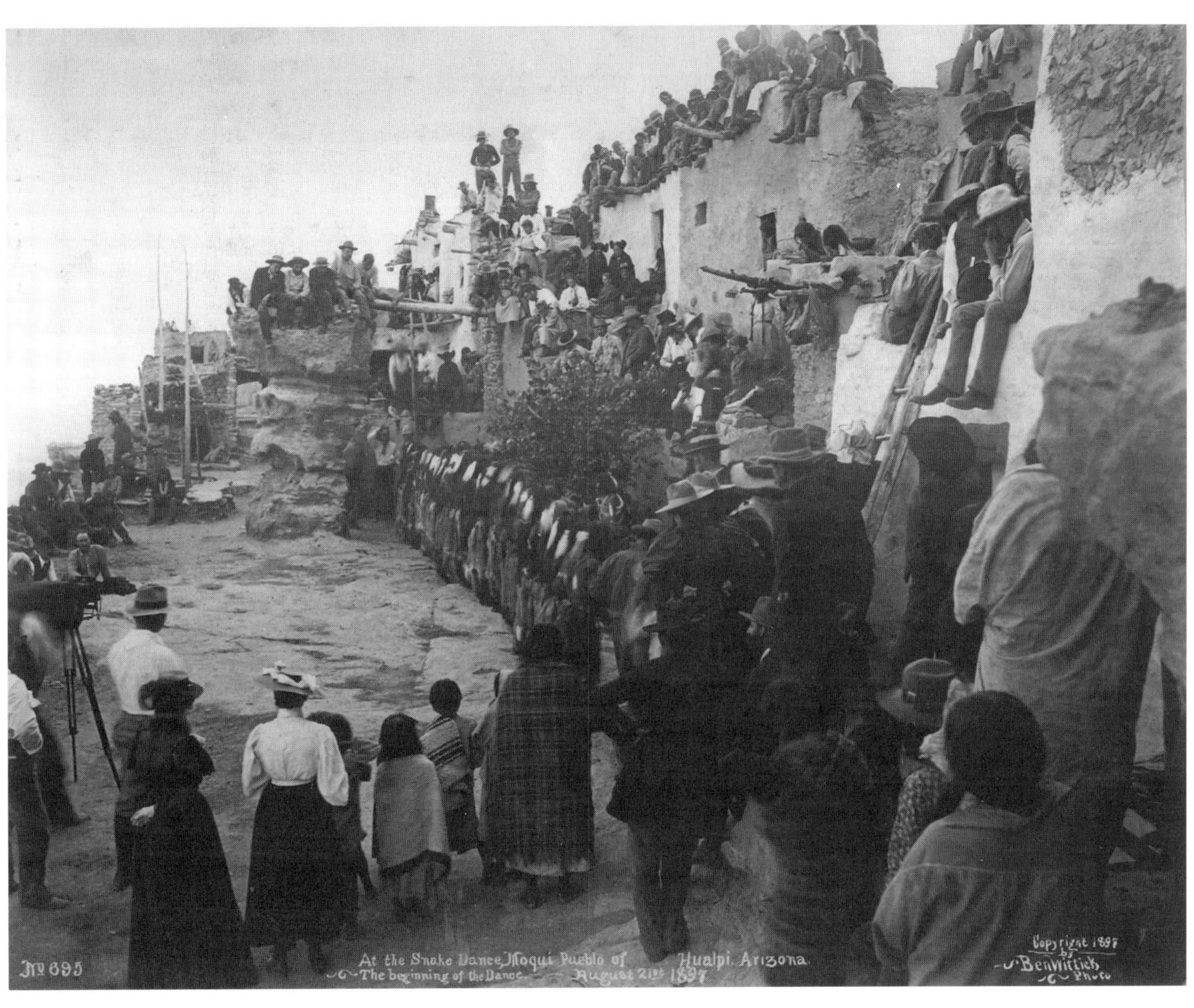

The beginning of the Snake Dance, Moqui Pueblo of Hualpi. Mounted albumen print by Ben Wittick, August 21, 1897. Collection of the author.

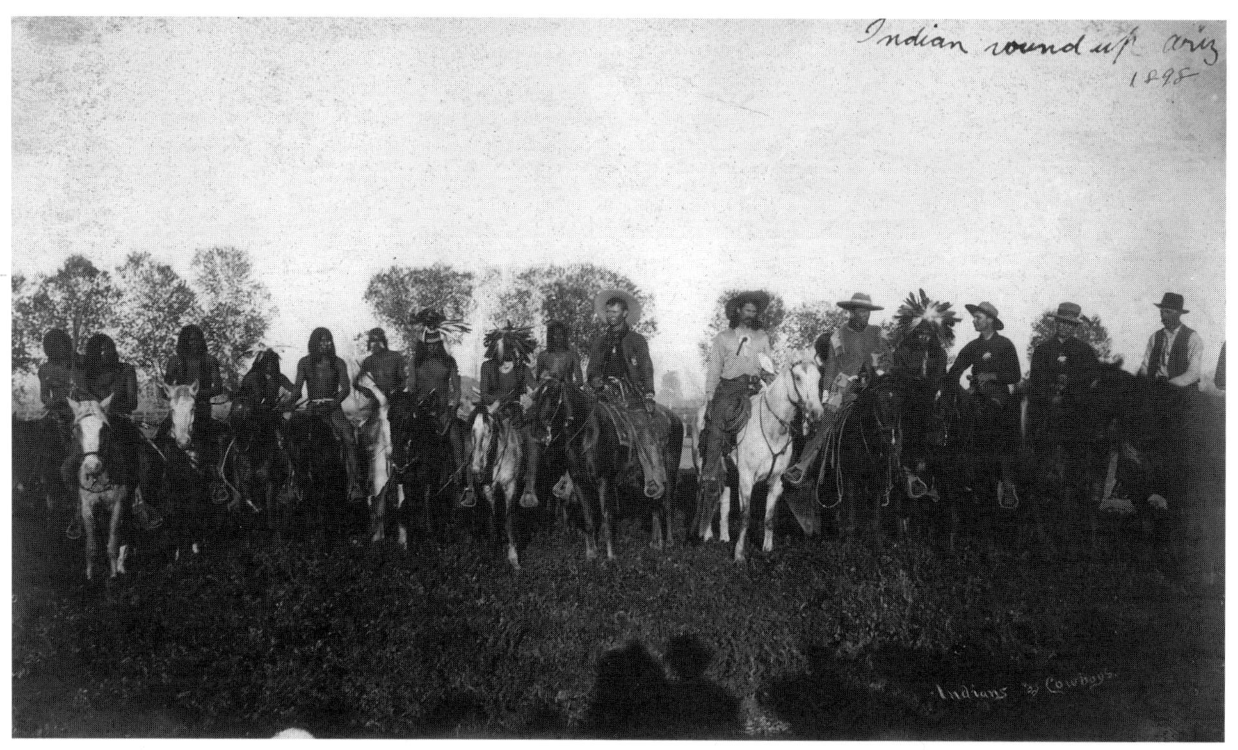

Unidentified group of Maricopa, Apache and cowboys taken near Phoenix, Arizona Territory, at the Indian Roundup. Mounted silver print, photographer unknown (probably F. A. Hartwell), c. 1898. Collection of the author.

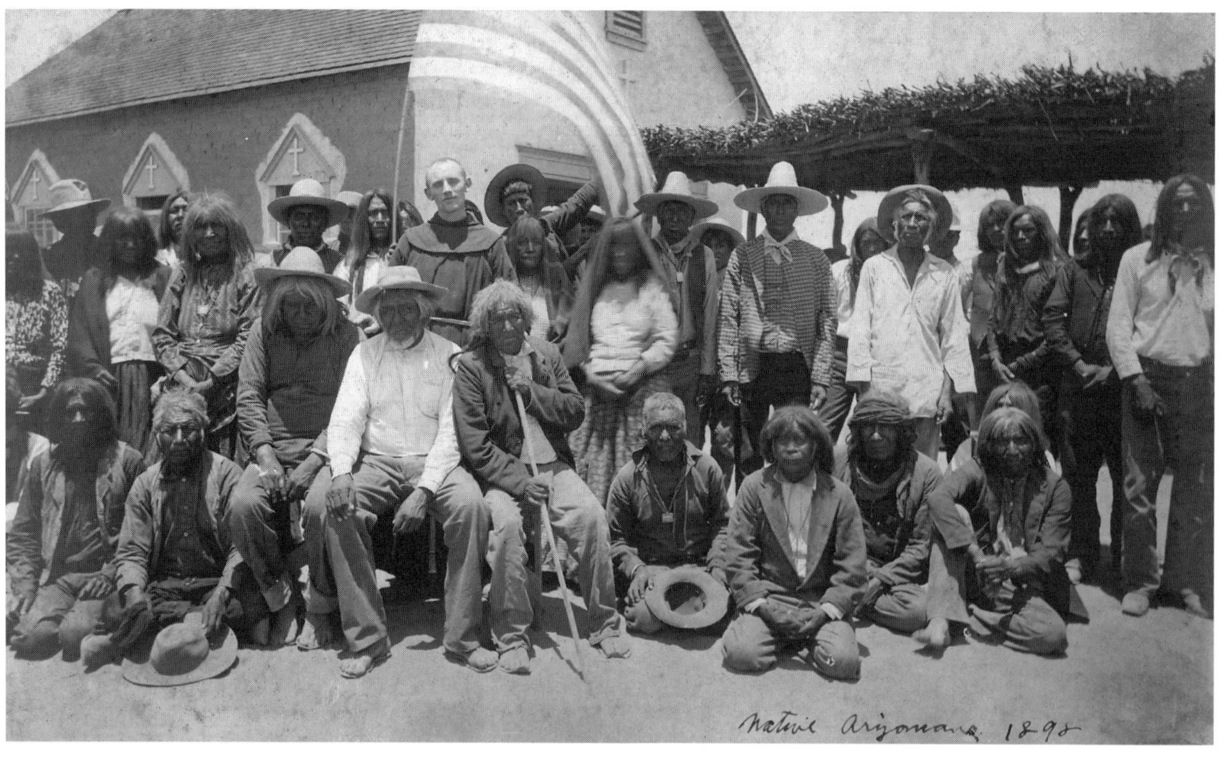

Unidentified group of Pima and Papago with priest at mission near Phoenix. Mounted silver print, photographer unknown (probably F. A. Hartwell), c. 1898. Collection of the author.

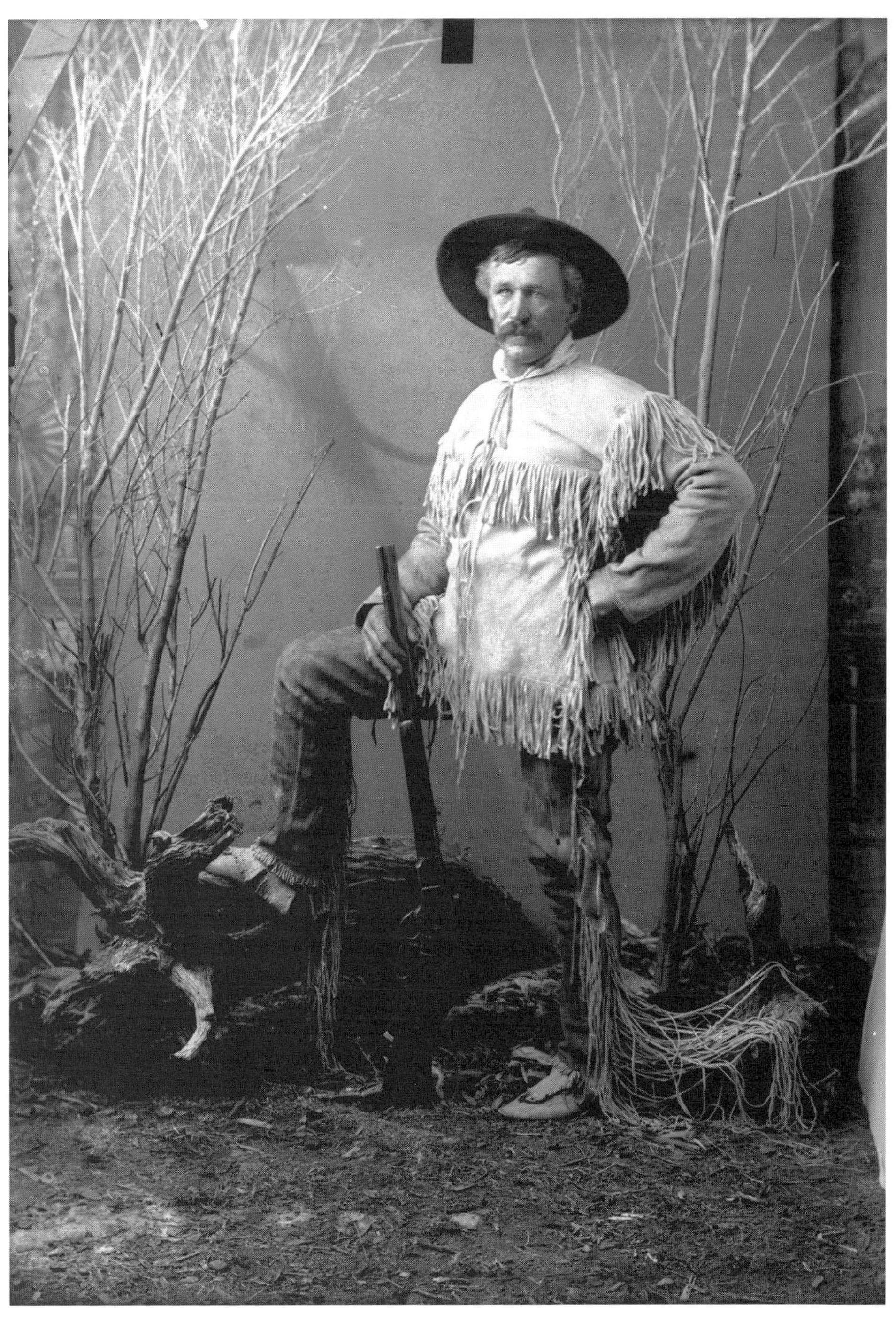

Studio portrait of William J. Flake. Flake purchased the Stinson ranch in northeastern Arizona in 1878. Another settler in the area was Erastus Snow. The new town was named Snow Flake, after the two settlers, and later became the county seat of Apache County. Photographer unknown, print from original dry plate negative, c. 1895. Collection of the author.

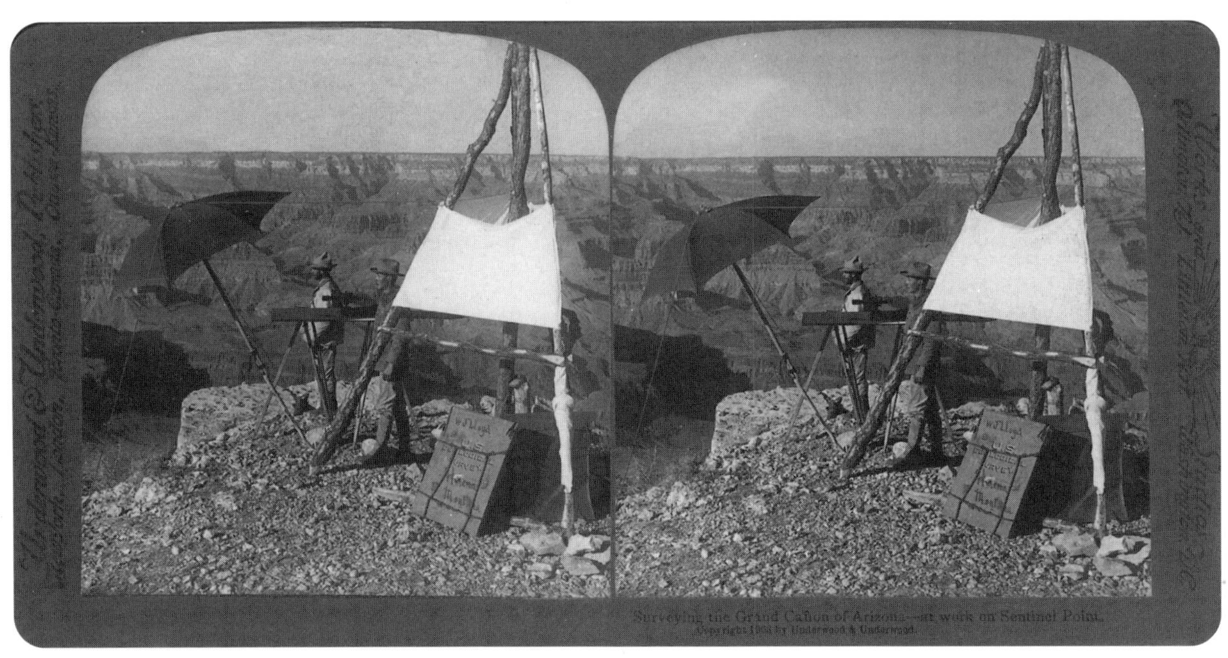

Surveyors of the U. S. Geological Survey at Sentinel Point, Grand Canyon. Stereograph published by Underwood and Underwood, photographer unknown, 1903. Collection of the author.

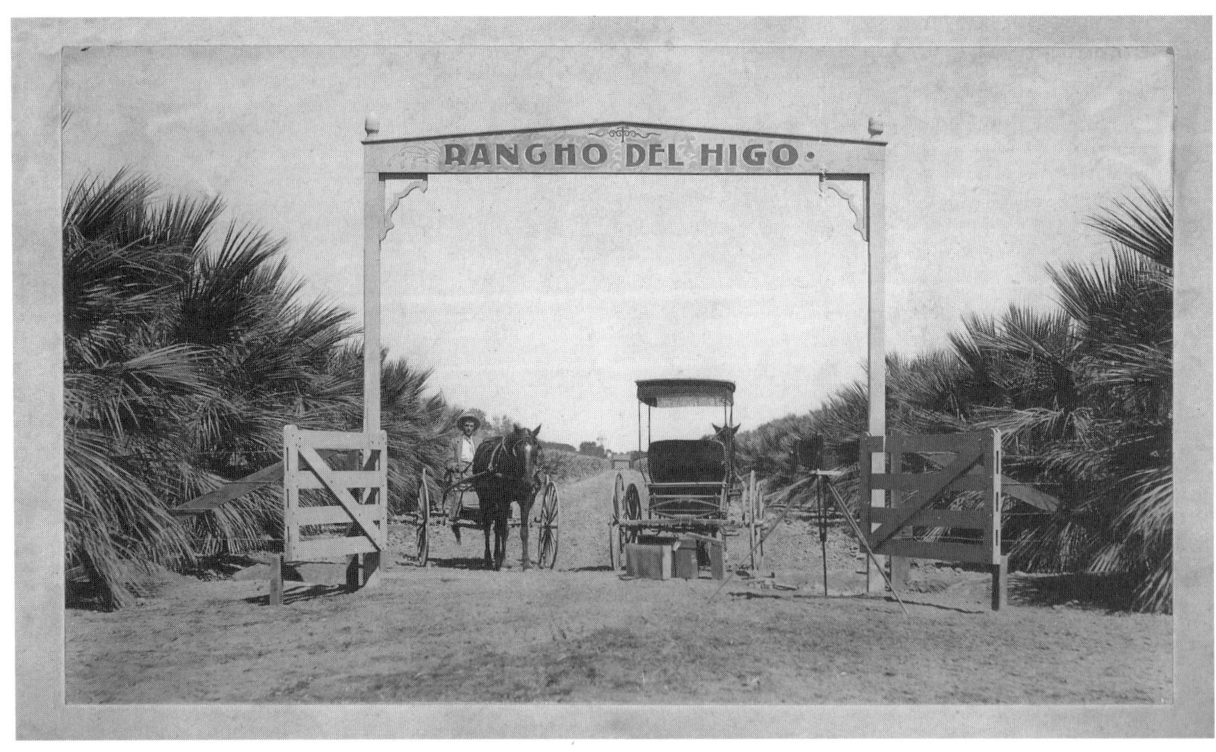

Photographers Messinger and Altenburgh at work at the entrance Rancho del Higo, Glendale, Arizona Territory. Boudoir card by Messinger and Altenburgh, c. 1898. Collection of the author.

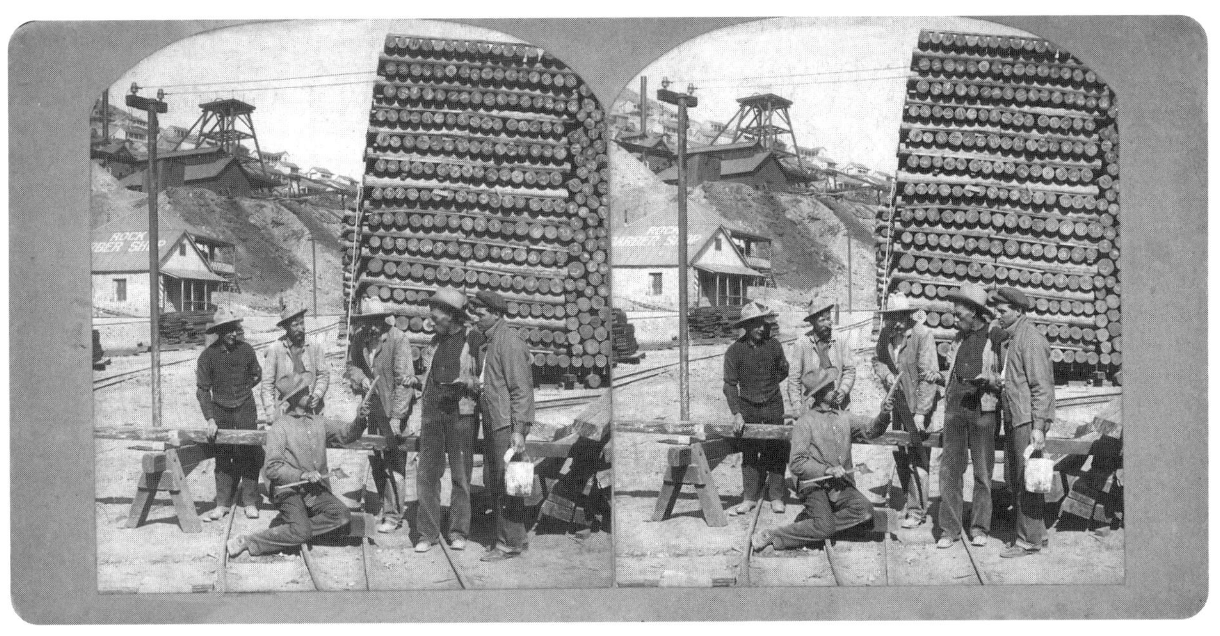

Telephone installation crew at Morenci, Arizona Territory. From left to right (standing): Wallace Doherty, Mr. Phillips, Fred McDougal, Gilbert H. Davidson (foreman), Harry Coody, William Fraser (seated). Stereograph by Arthur H. Davidson, c. 1903. Collection of the author.

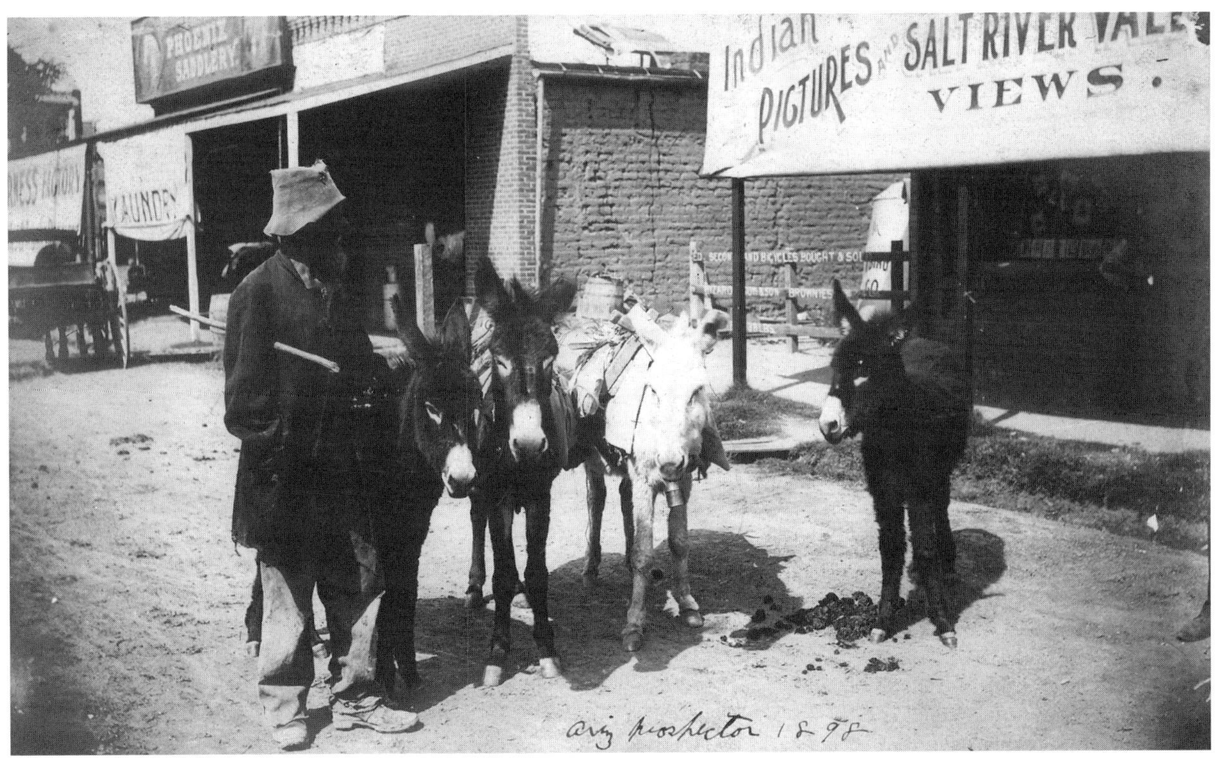

Arizona prospector, Col. Poston, in front of photographic studio in Phoenix, Arizona Territory. Mounted silver print, photographer unknown (possibly F. A. Hartwell), 1898. Collection of the author.

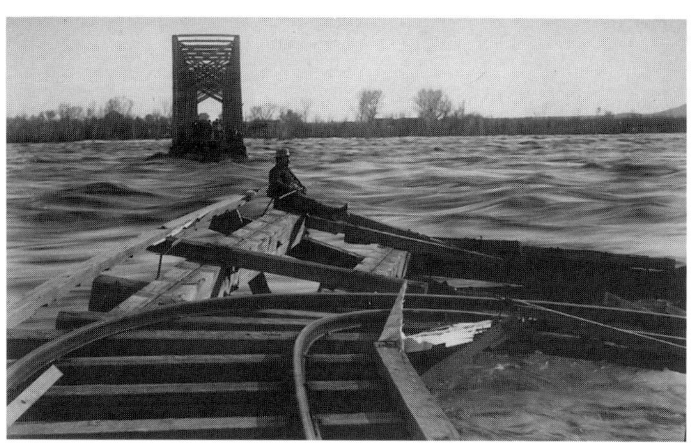

Looking south across the Salt River and the Tempe railway bridge during the flood of 1891. Boudoir card by George Rothrock. Collection of the author.

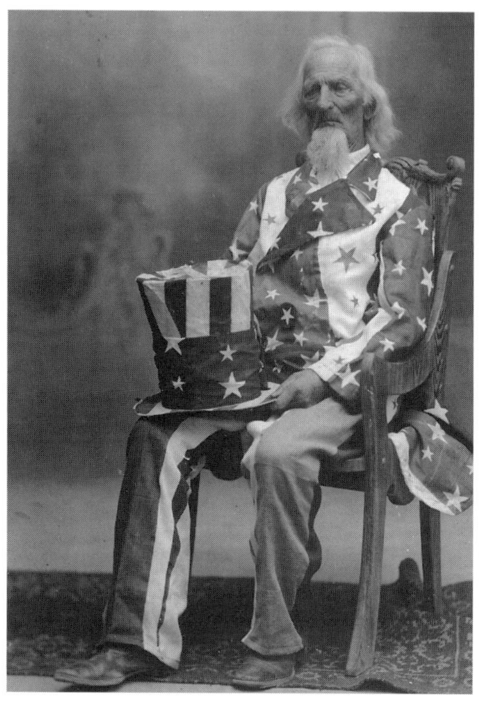

Unidentified man dressed as Uncle Sam, Tucson, Arizona Territory. Mounted silver print by Henry Buehman, c. 1900. Collection of the author.

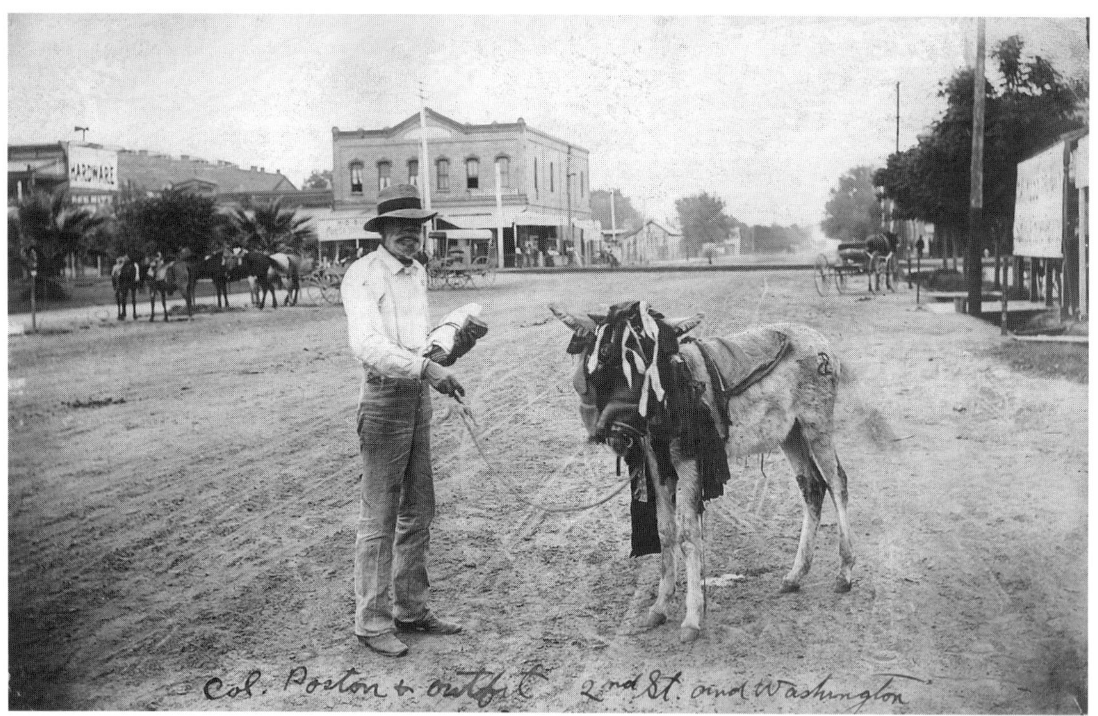

Col. Poston & outfit, 2nd Street and Washington in Phoenix, Arizona Territory. Known as the Father of Arizona, Charles D. Poston arrived in Arizona soon after the Gadsden Purchase and served as its first Congressman, Commissioner of Indian Affairs, and Registrar of the U. S. Land Office. He was active in mining and exploration throughout his life. Mounted silver print, photographer unknown (probably F. A. Hartwell), c. 1898. Collection of the author.

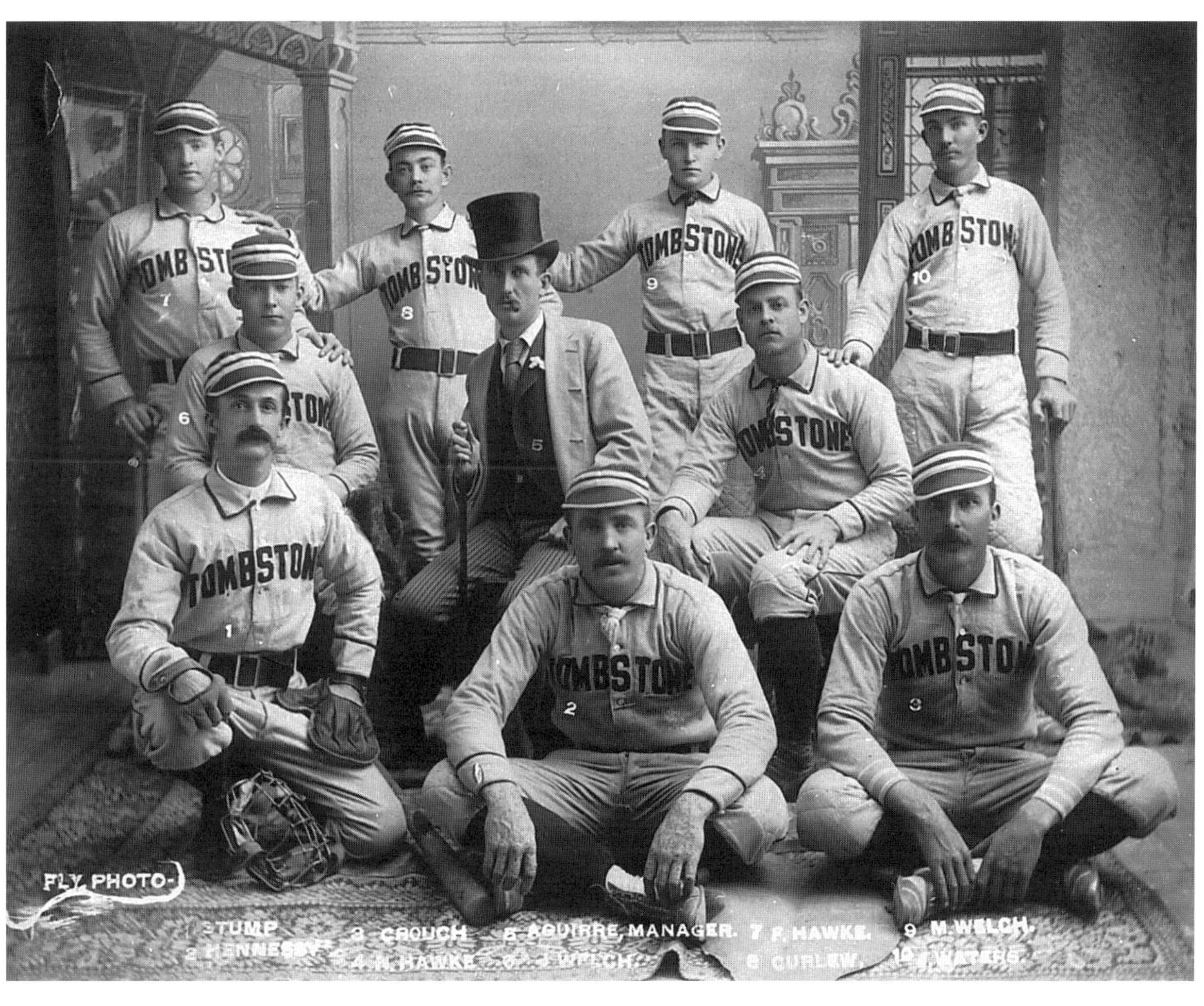

Tombstone baseball team Portrait: Identification by number—1. Stump; 2. Hennessy; 3. Crouch; 4. N. Hawke; 5. Aguirre, Manager; 6. J. Welsch; 7. Hawke; 8. Curlew; 9. M. Welch; 10. J. Waters. Mounted albumen print by Camilius Fly, c. 1883. Collection of Silver Lady Antiques, Tombstone.

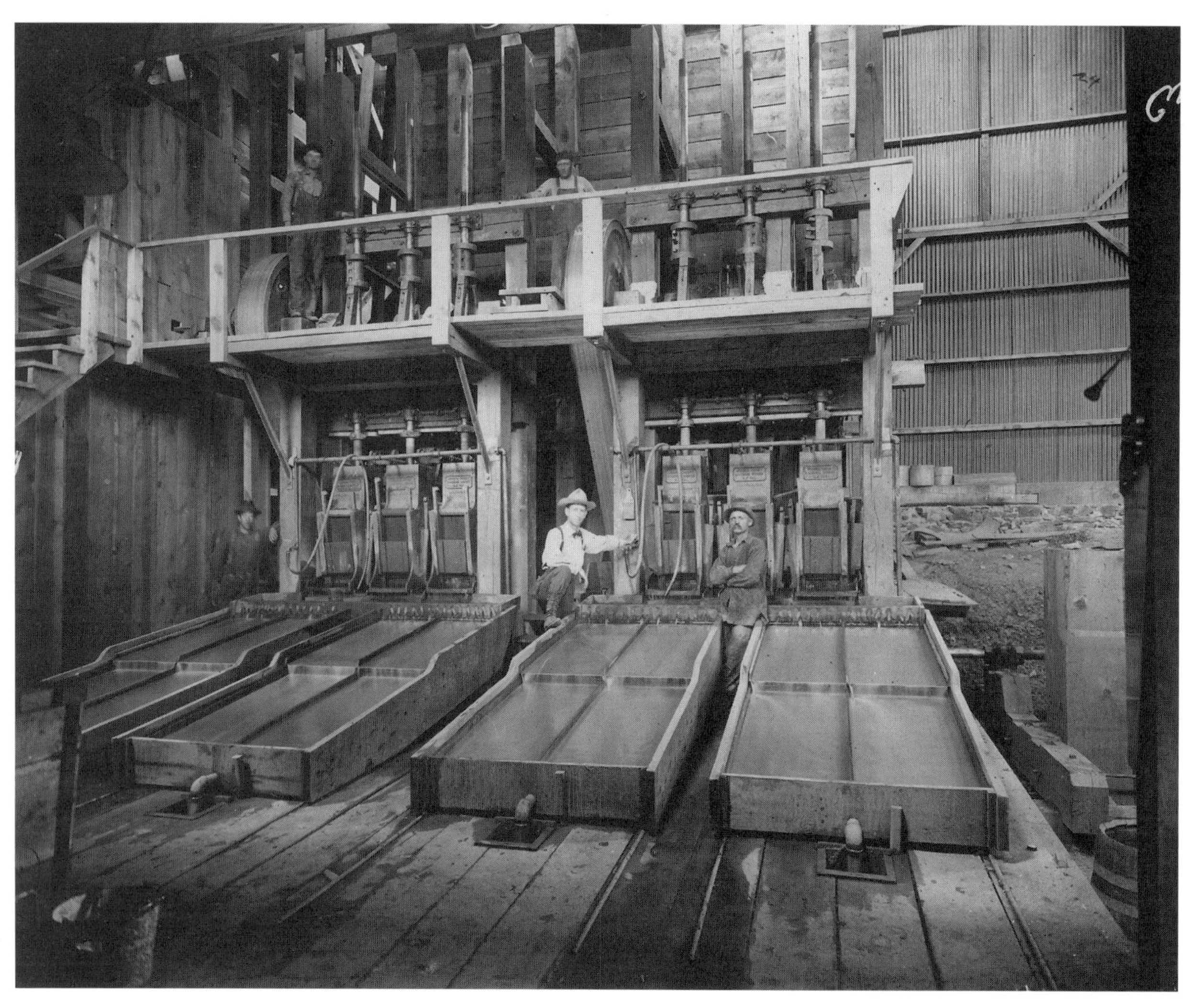

Interior of a six stamp processing plant at the Iron King mine, west of Humboldt, Arizona Territory. In 1907 the mine produced 1,253 ounces of gold, 35,491 ounces of silver and 3,933 pounds of copper. Silver print by A. E. Suppinger, c. 1903. Collection of the author.

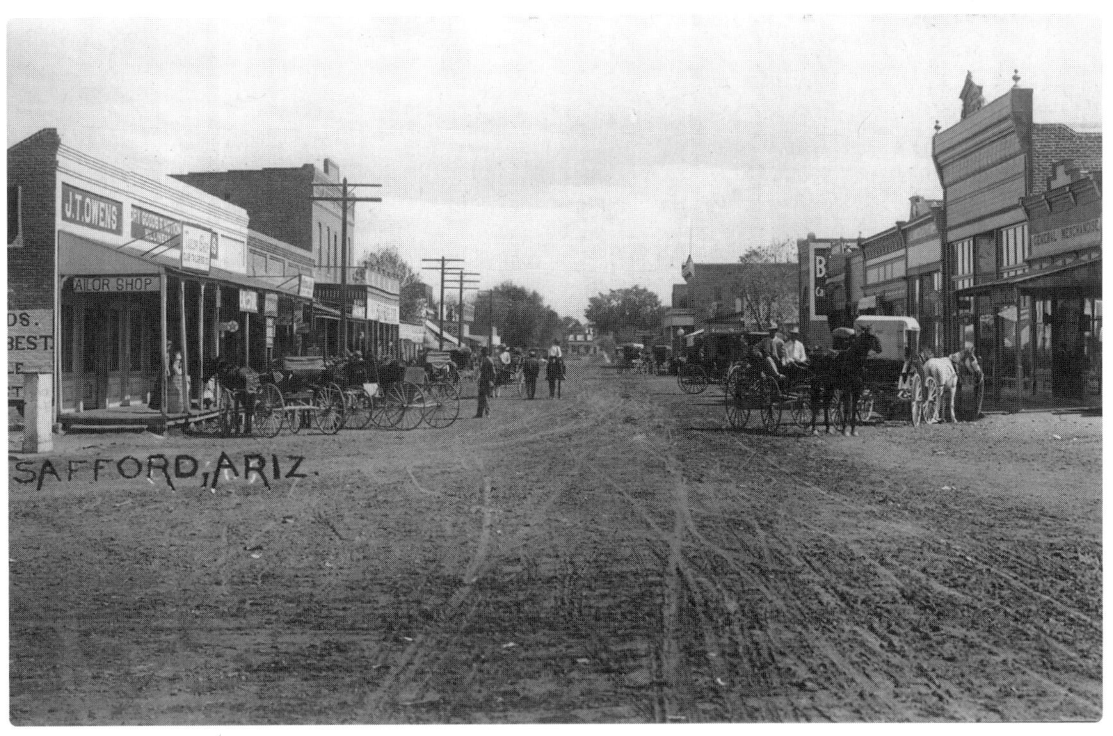

Main Street, Safford, Arizona Territory. Real photo postcard, photographer unknown, c. 1907. Collection of the author.

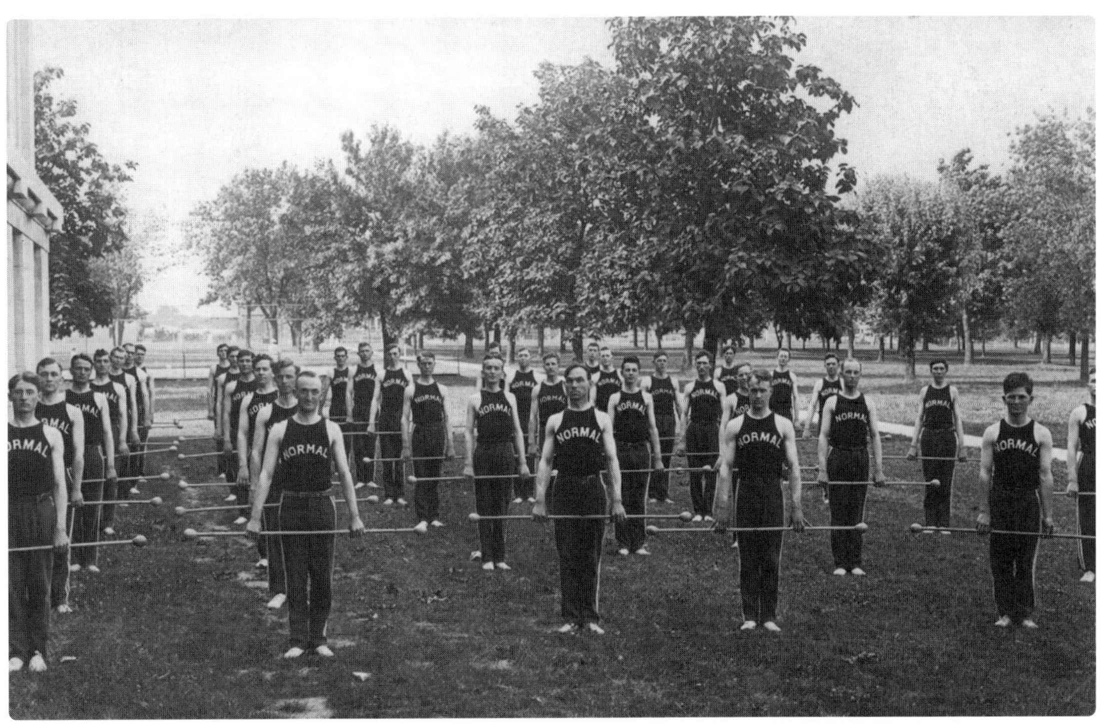

Undergraduate gymnastics class at Tempe Normal School (now Arizona State University). Real photo postcard, photographer unknown, c. 1908. Collection of the author.

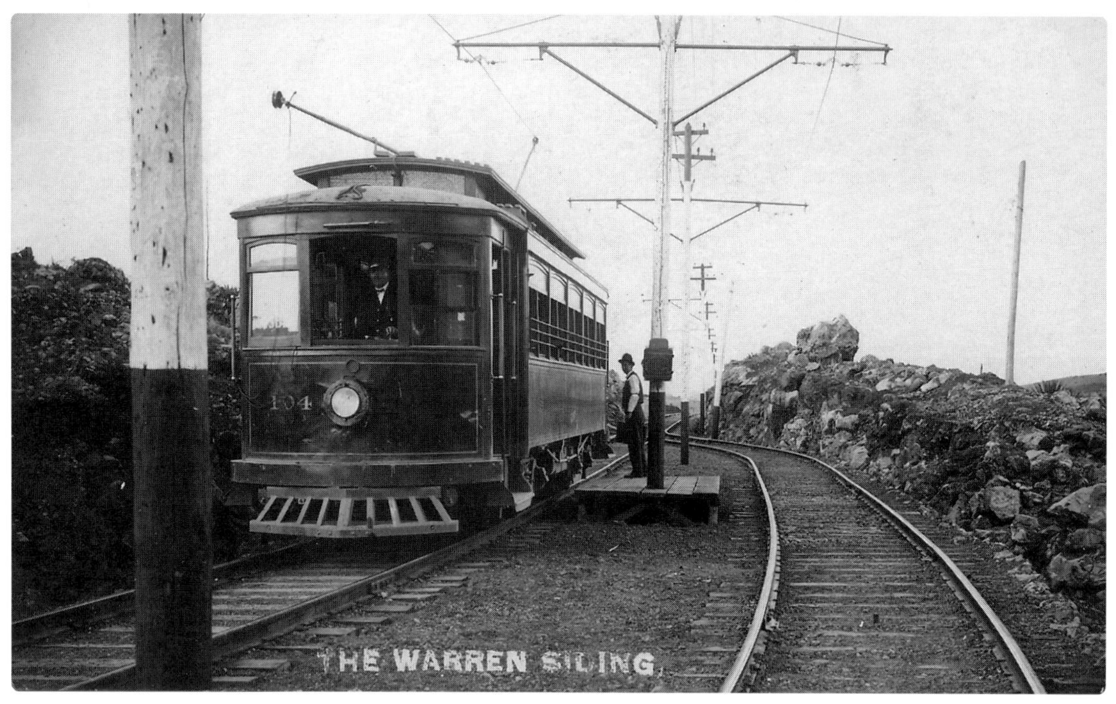

Street car #104, Bisbee to Warren route at the Warren siding. Real photo postcard, photographer unknown, c. 1909. Collection of the author.

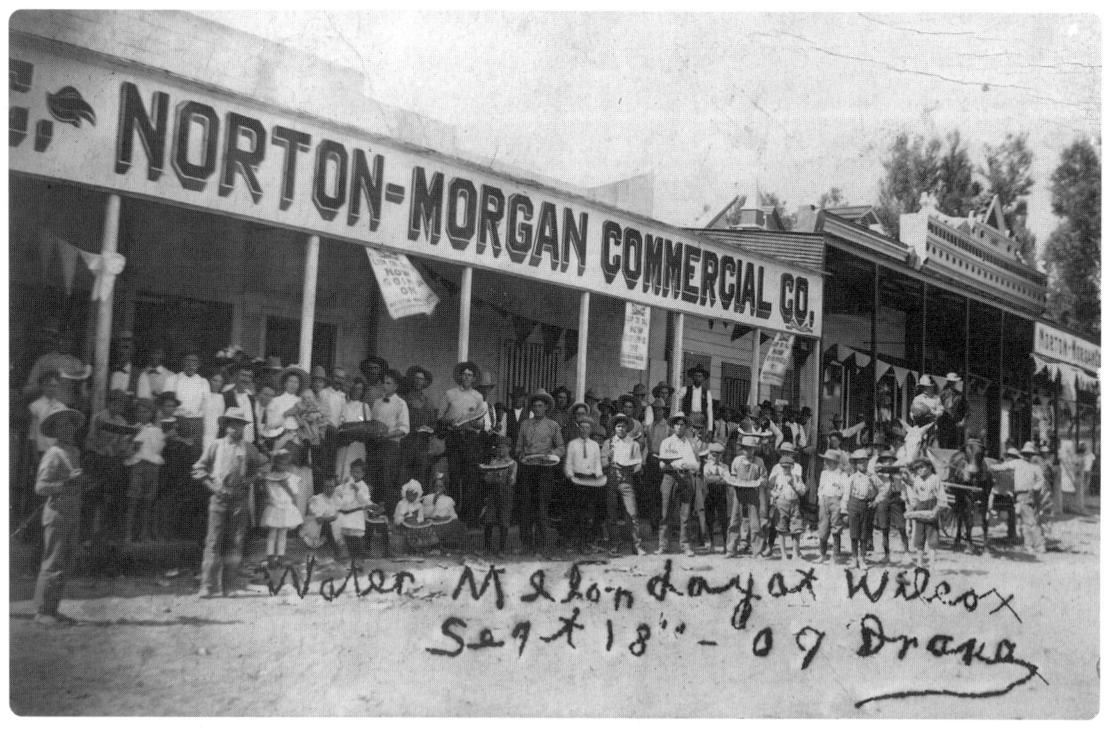

Watermelon Day celebration in front of the Norton-Morgan Commercial Company, Wilcox, Arizona Territory. Real photo postcard, photographer unknown, September 18, 1909. Collection of the author.

66

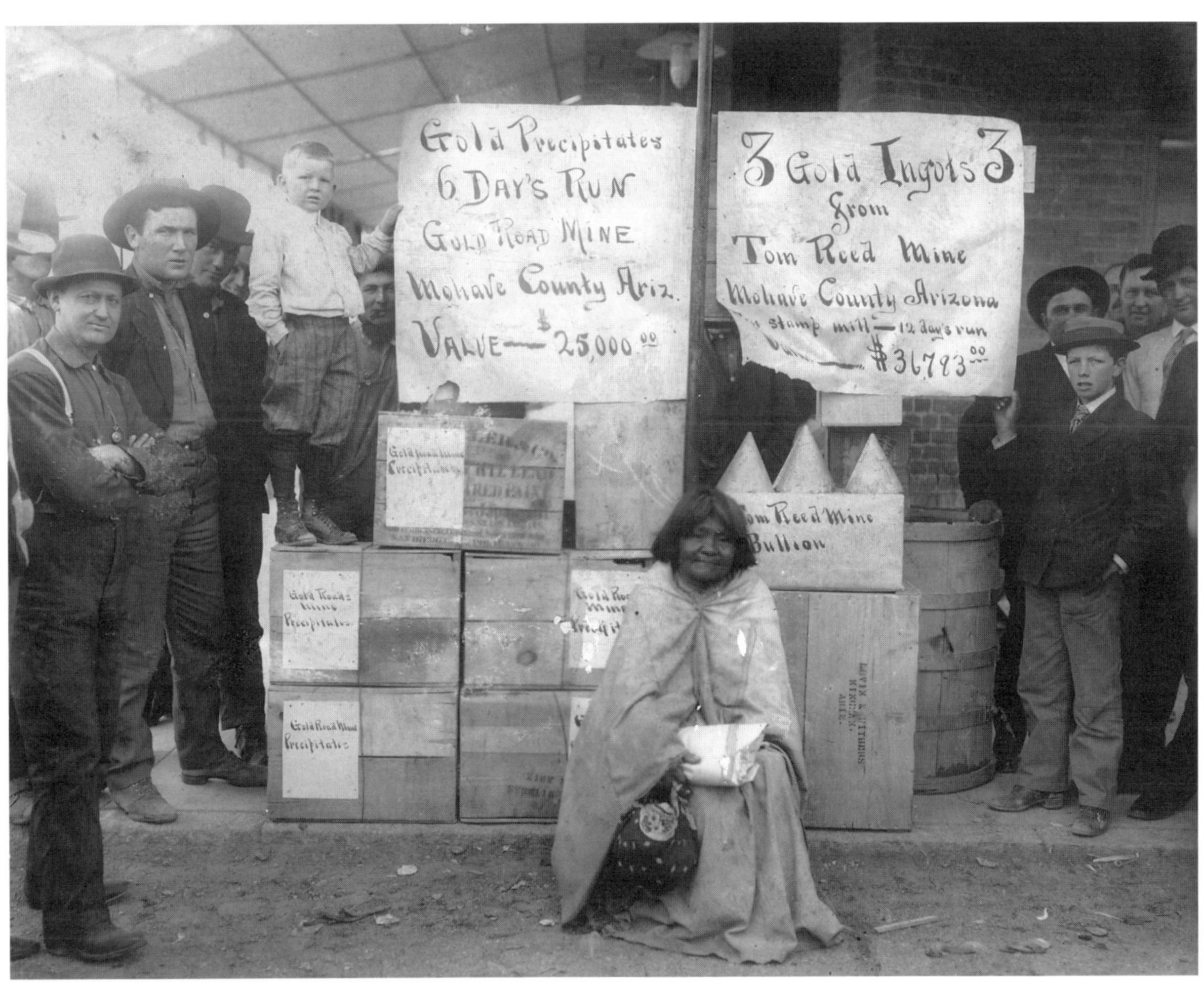

Ingots and precipitate produced during a six day period from the Tom Reed Mine, Oatman, Arizona Territory. Total value estimated at $61,793 with gold at $25 per ounce. Mounted silver print by N. E. Johnson. Collection of the author.

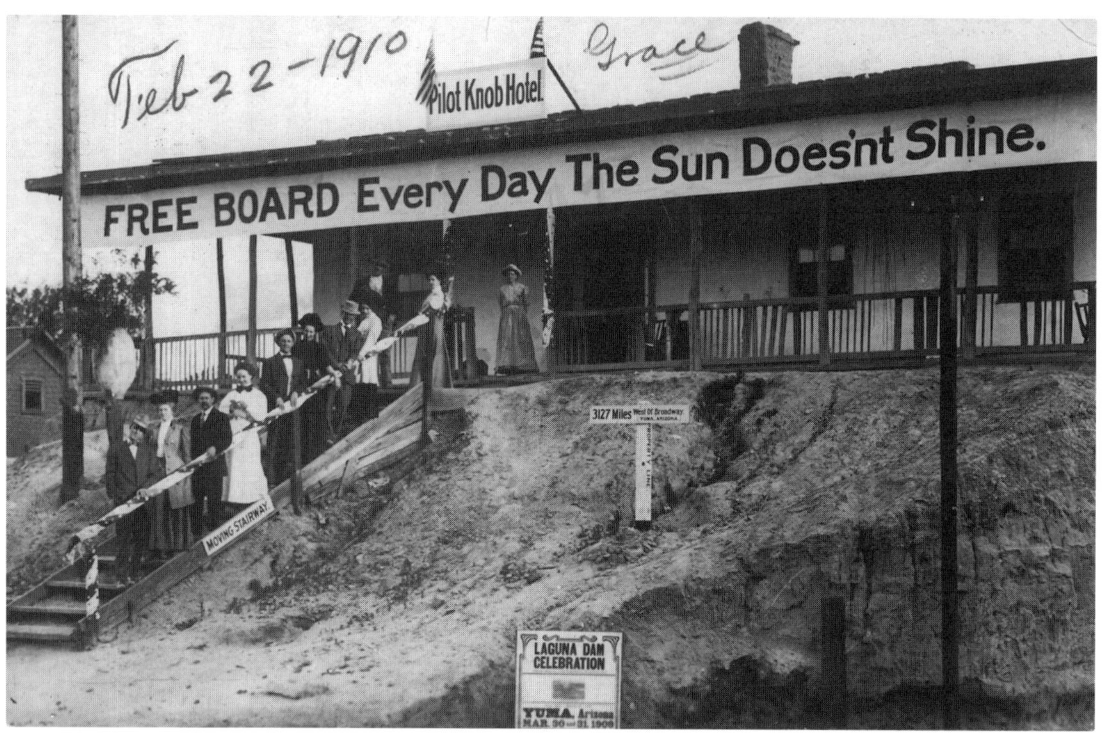

Pilot Knob Hotel with guests posed on the "Moving Staircase" (a parody on escalators in the large cities), Yuma, Arizona Territory. Real photo postcard, photographer unknown, February 22, 1910. Collection of the author.

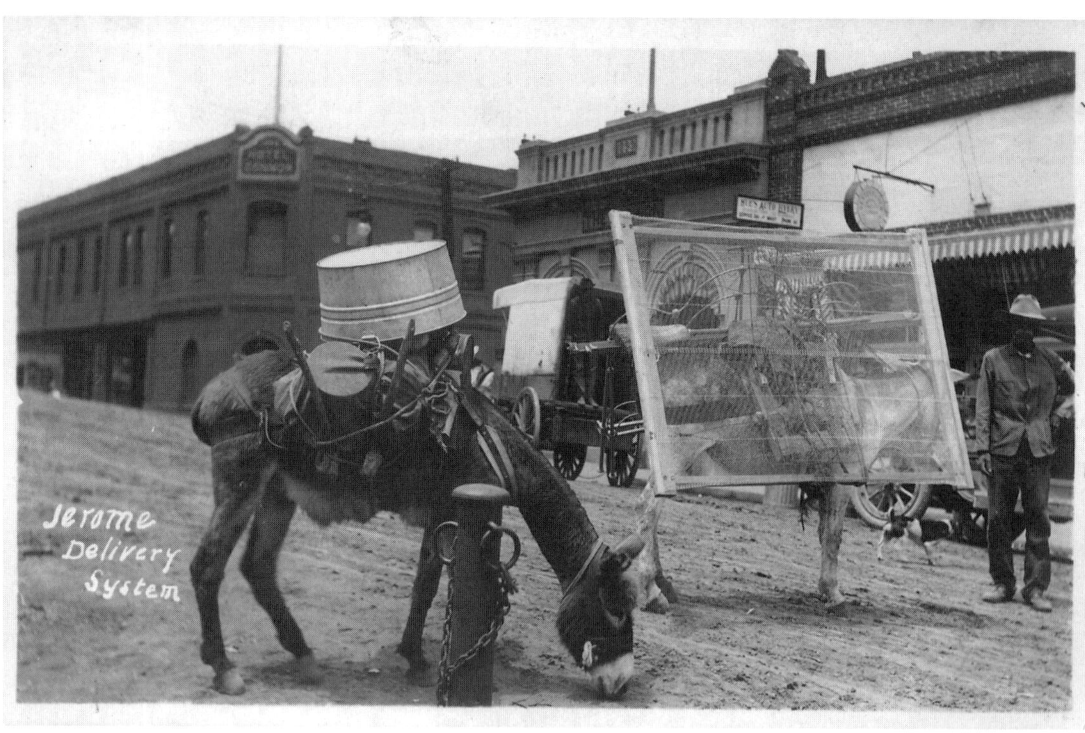

Moving day in Jerome. Due to terrain, mules were regularly used for transporting materials through the steep streets of of Jerome. Real photo postcard, photographer unknown, c. 1916. Collection of the author.

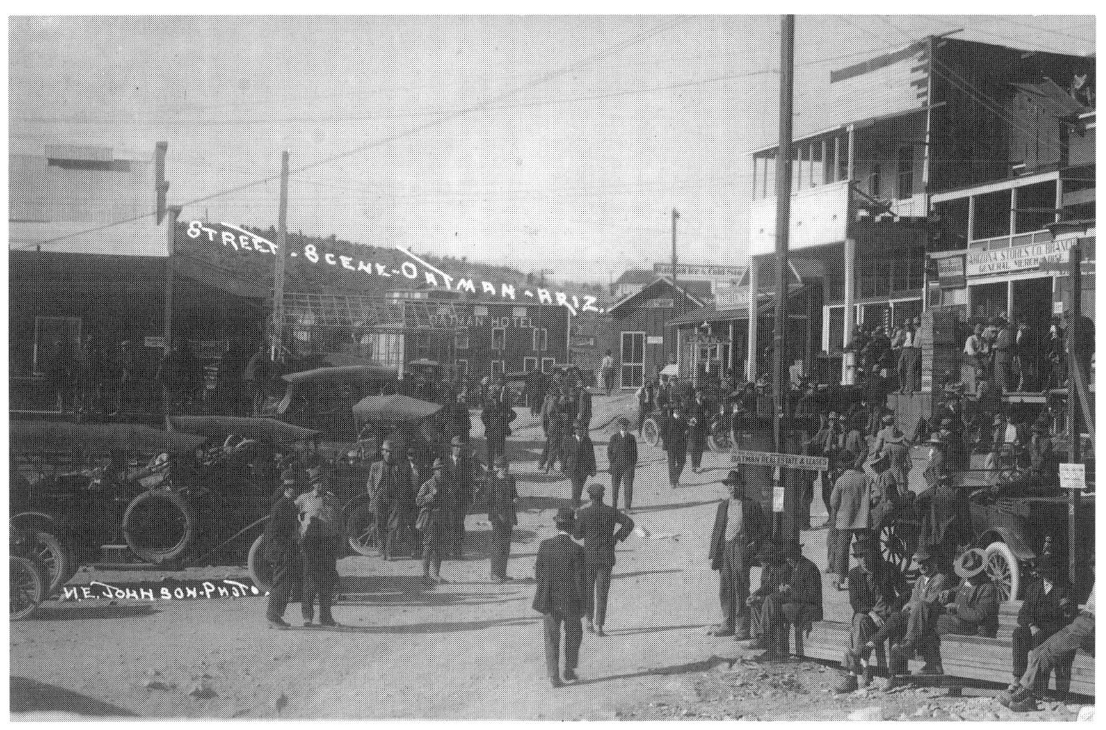

A busy day in downtown Oatman, Arizona. Real photo postcard by N. E. Johnson, c. 1915. Collection of the author.

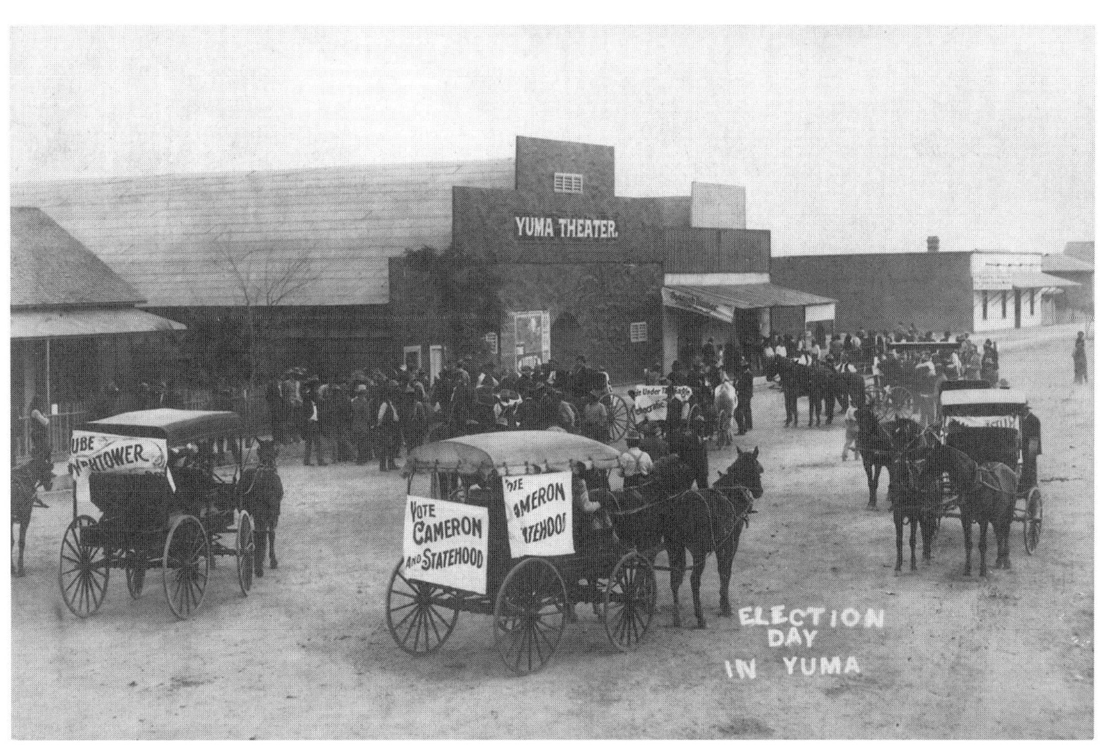

Polling place and campaign wagons for election of delegates to the Constitutional Convention of 1909. Photographer unknown, real photo postcard. Collection of the author.

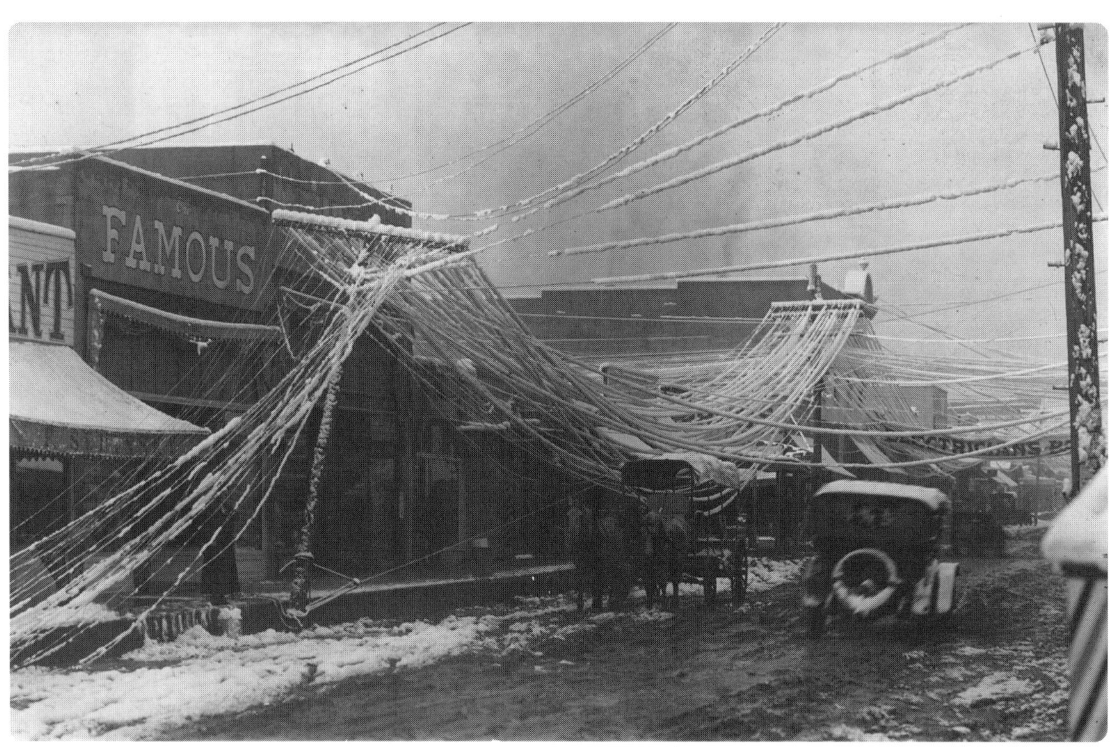

Telephone wires after winter storm in Miami, Arizona. Real photo postcard, photographer unknown, c. 1916. Collection of the author.

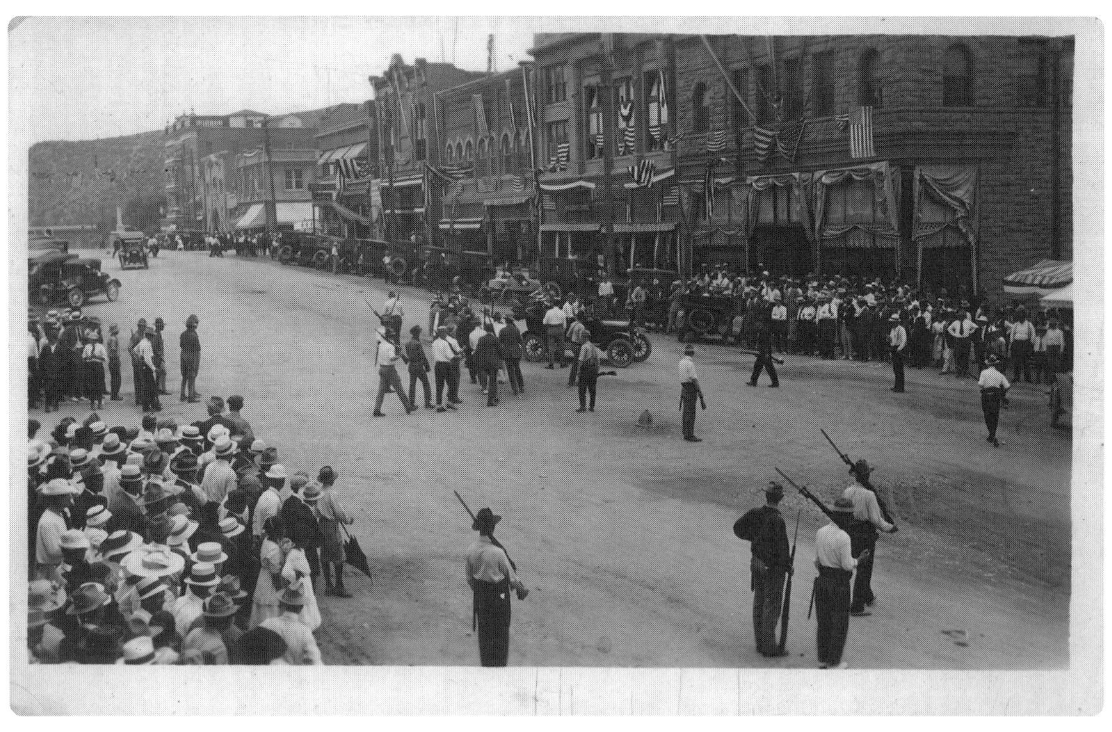

Mining union protesters and National Guard disrupting 4th of July parade in Globe. Real photo postcard, photographer unknown, c. 1916. Collection of the author.

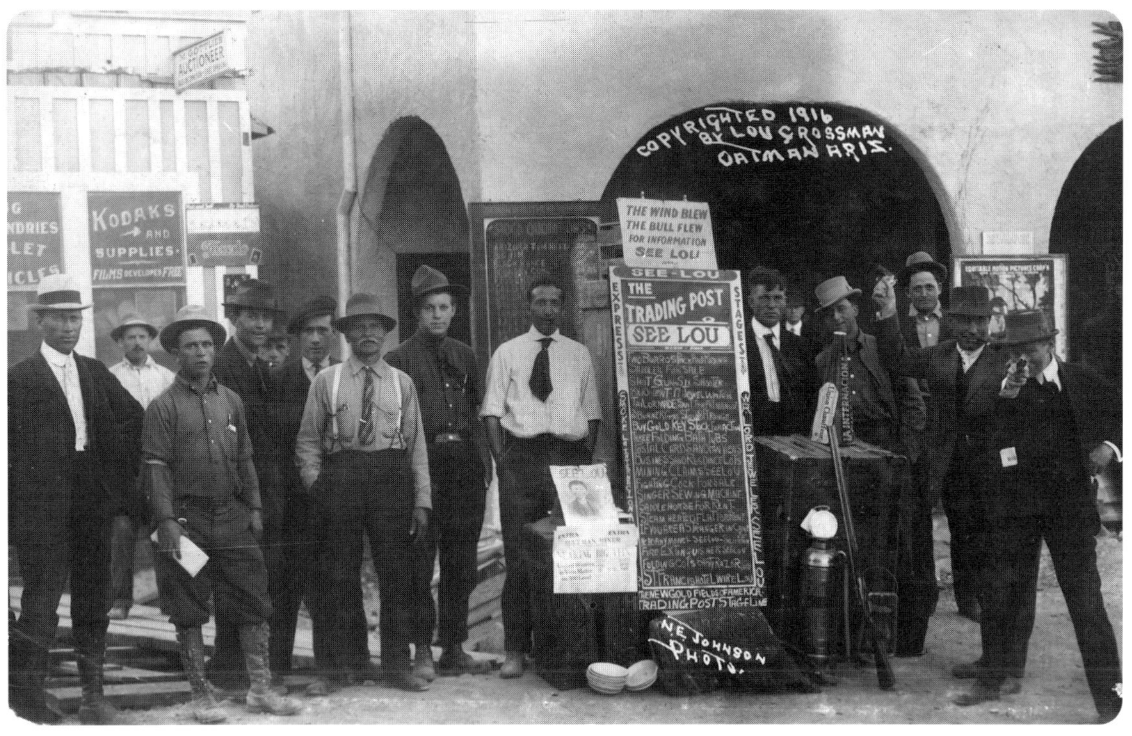

Advertisement for Lou Grossman's trading post in front of motion picture theater, Oatman. Real photo postcard by N. E. Johnson, c. 1916. Collection of the author.

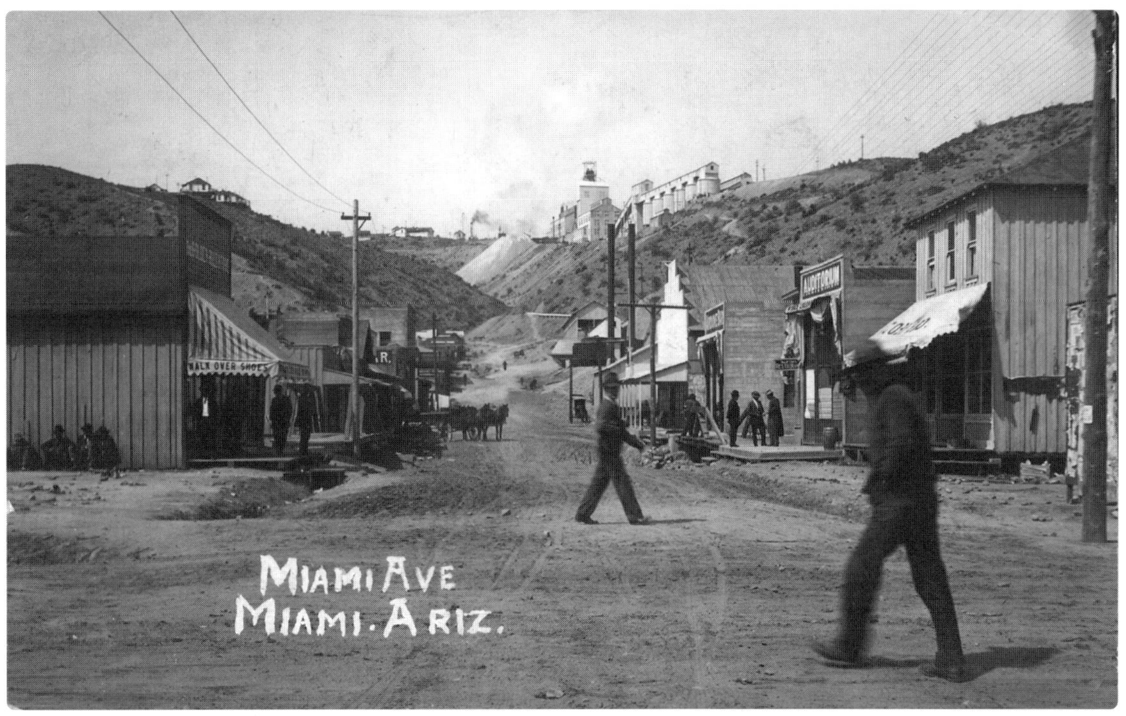

Miami Street, Miami, Arizona, c. 1915. Real photo postcard, phgotographer unknown. Collection of the author.

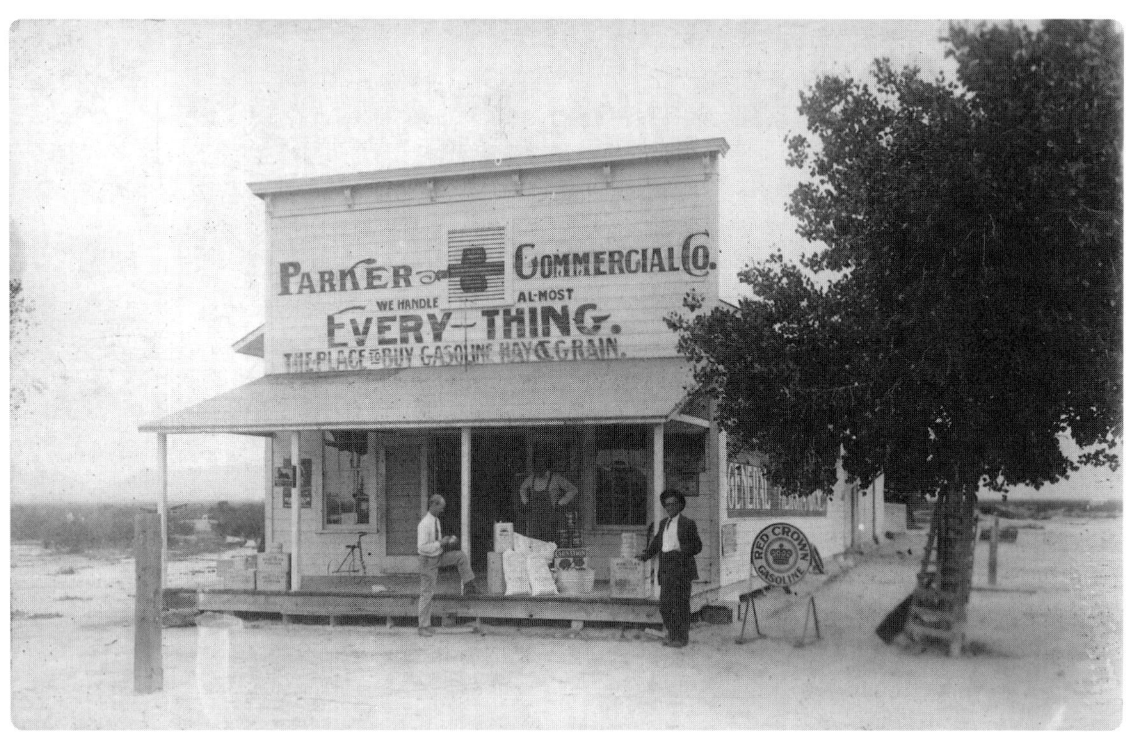

Parker Commercial Company, north side of the tracks near Wenden. Real photo postcard, photographer unknown, c. 1918. Collection of the author.

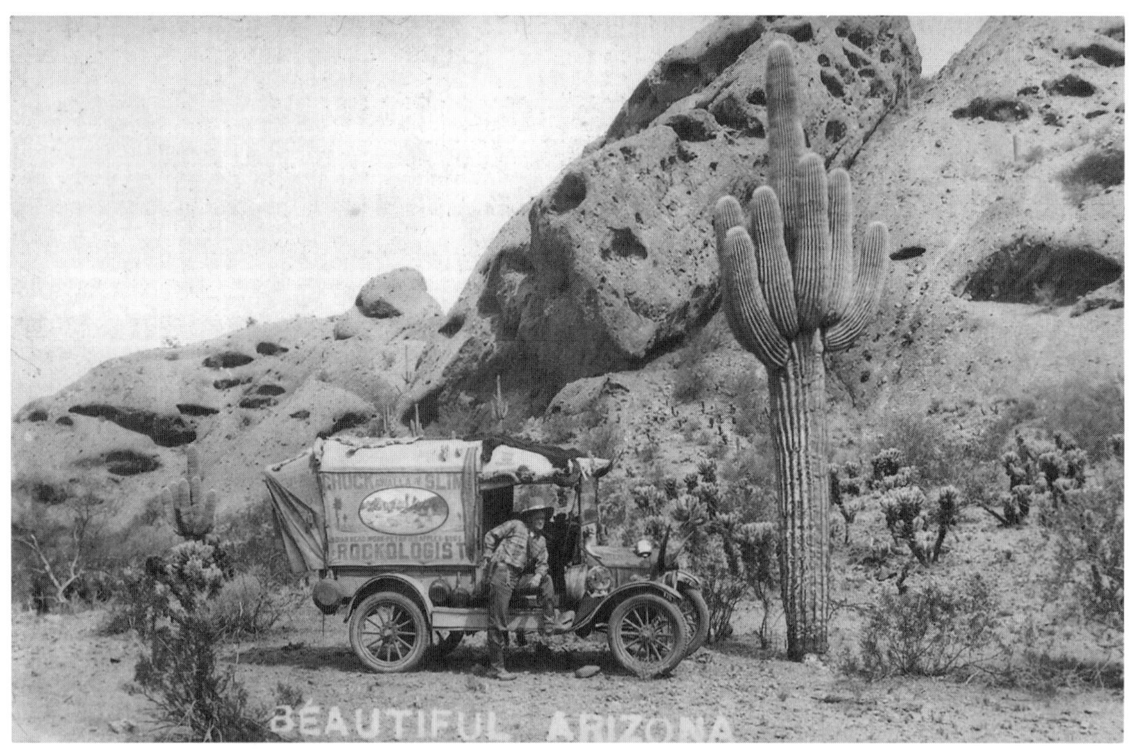

"Chuckawalla Slim, the Rockologist" at what is now Papago Park in Phoenix. Real photo postcard, photographer unknown, c. 1920. Collection of the author.

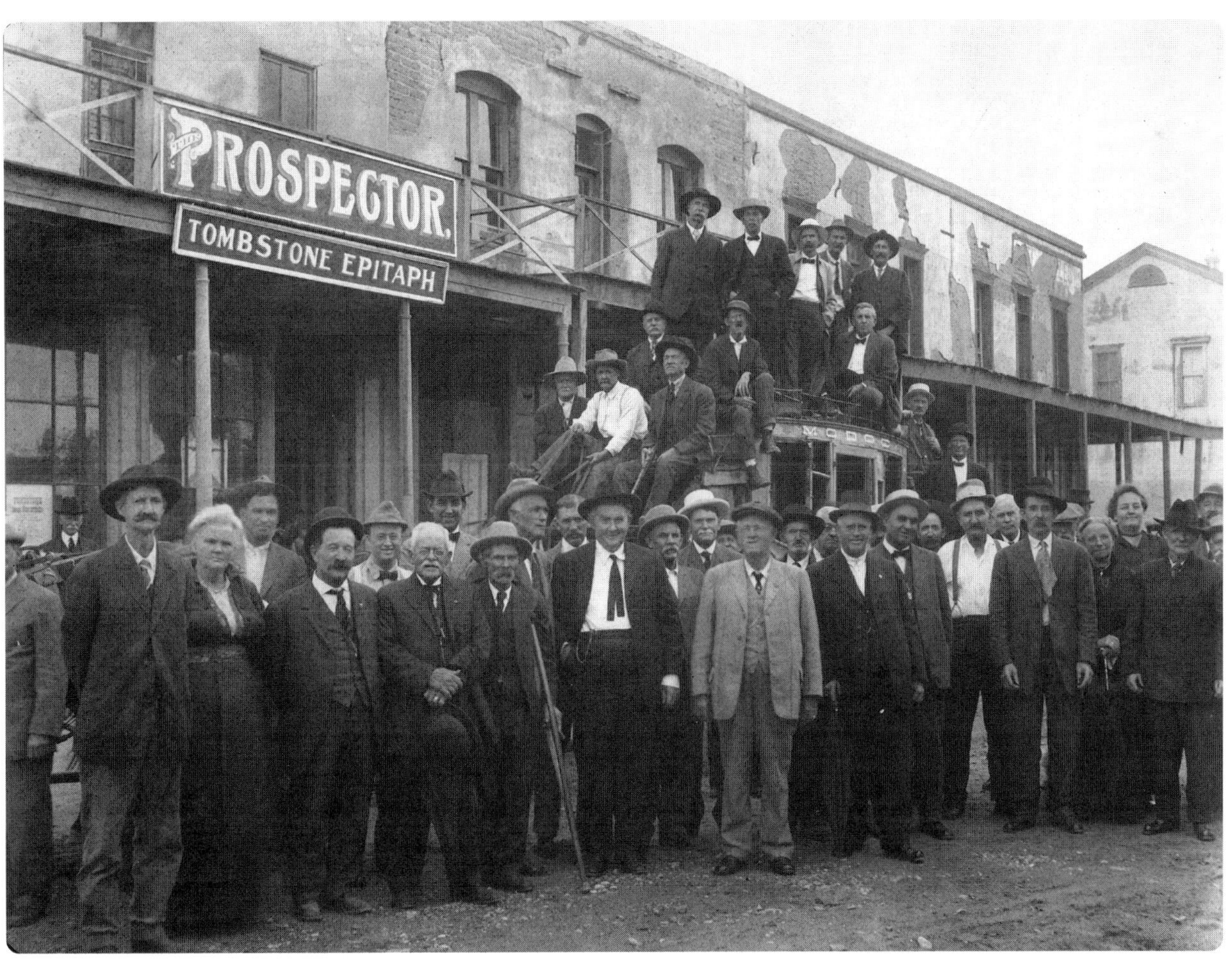

Old-timers' reunion in front of the Tombstone Prospector *(office of the* Tombstone Epitaph*). Silver print, photographer unknown. Collection of the author.*

Directory of Photographers in Arizona
1850-1920

Addis, Alfred Shea
Possibly licensed in Leavenworth, Kansas, September 1862, and with brother, May 1863. Probable partner with Koch at 425 Montgomery Street in San Francisco, licensed as photographers, February 1865. Operated a gallery in Tucson, Arizona Territory, on Myers Street south of the Palace Hotel with partner Porter (ca 1879). Bought out Porter in October, 1879. Gallery at corner of Camp & Convent Streets, Church Plaza. Moved to New Mexico, 1880 (Las Cruces, 1880s, Silver City, 1881-82, Lake Valley, 1882).
> *Arizona Daily Star,* October 17, 1879.
> Rudisill, Richard, *Photographers of the New Mexico Territory, 1854-1912,* Museum of New Mexico, 1973, p. 9.

Adkins, Wesley C.
Phoenix c. 1912. Operated at 218 ½ W. Washington with Ralph T. Harrison as Adkins & Harrison in 1913.
> *1912 Phoenix City and Salt River Valley Directory.*

Allen, Charles R.
Born 1846; died 1925. Itinerant photographer, partner of Mr. Jennings, c. 1898. Sold 450 negatives to Albert S. Reynolds c. 1899. Photographed Arizona and New Mexico with Weiner, 1889-91. Listed c. 1892-93 with partner Gommel; 1895-1900 with partner Jennings.
> Arizona Historical Society, Tucson, photographer listing.

Allen, W. H.
Lowell, Arizona Territory c. 1909-10.
> 1909-10 directory.

Altenburgh, William
Phoenix, Arizona Territory c. 1895. Operated at 243 W. Madison as Messinger & Altenburgh c. 1897.
> *Phoenix Directory for 1897 and 1898,* Phoenix Directory Company.

Ames, F. A.
Documented the Moqui Indians for the Bureau of American Ethnology, 1887-89, produced an album, "Photographs of Indian Reservation at Moqui, Arizona Territory."
> Photo credit, National Archives.

Anthony, F.
Arizona Territory. Licensed as itinerant May 15, 1907.
> Vaughn, Thomas, "A Guide to the Photographic Archives of the Bisbee Mining and Historical Museum," *The Cochise Quarterly,* Vol. 19, No. 2, Summer 1989, p. 31.

Areldson Photo
Clarkdale c. 1915-20.
> Postcard imprints.

Arizona Gallery
Tucson, Arizona Territory c. 1901. Tent gallery operated by A. M. Feldman.
> 1901 directory.

Arizona Photo Company
Phoenix c. 1915 at 27 E. Adams, Arthur E. Hackett proprietor.
> Photographic mount imprint.
> 1915 directory.

Arizona Photo Gallery
Tucson, Arizona Territory c. 1906-07. Operated at Stone and Jackson by A. M. Feldman.
> 1906-07 directories.

Arizona Photograph Company, Inc.
Organized c. 1903, in Prescott, as a partnership of Erwin Baer, Tom Bate, W. R. Humphries, A. E. Suppinger, and Percival Armitage as one of the first multifaceted photographic partnerships in Arizona, offering studio and location photogaphers, print production and marketing. Duration of the corporation unknown.

Arizona Tent Gallery
Tucson, Arizona Territory c. 1903-04. Operated at Stone and Jackson by A. M. Feldman.
> 1903 directory.

Arizona Souvenir Picture Company
Roosevelt, Arizona Territory c. 1906-11.
> Postcard imprints.

Armitage, Percival
Prescott, Arizona Territory c. 1903-06. Partner in the Arizona Photograph Company, Inc. in Prescott with Erwin Baer, Tom Bate, W. R. Humphries, and A. E. Suppinger c. 1903. Listed as Armitage Photo Company of Humboldt to c. 1915. Active in Prescott area and in Bradshaw mining districts.
> Postcard imprints.

Armitage Photo Company
Prescott, Arizona Territory c. 1906–15. Partnership of Percival Armitage, Erwin Baer, Tom Bate, W. R. Humphries, and A. E. Suppinger.

ATLANTIC PACIFIC VIEW & PORTRAIT COMPANY
(A&PV&P Co.)
Tucson, Arizona Territory c. 1902-11. Wallace B. and Joseph
C. Parker operated at Parkers, 6th & Broadway.
> 1902-11 directories.

AUSTIN, A. H.
Solomonville c. 1912-13.
> *Polk's Arizona and New Mexico Directory for 1912-13.*

AVELDSON, (?)
Jerome c. 1915. Photographed Jerome and the Montana
Hotel Fire.
> Postcard imprints.

BAER, ERWIN
Arrived in Prescott, Arizona Territory from St. Louis in
May, 1883. Operated in Prescott on Lawrence Block c. 1907-
10. Partnerships with: Mitchell until his retirement in 1885,
Hammaker, Haynes and Bate. Flagstaff gallery c. 1887-90.
Partner in the Arizona Photograph Company, Inc. in
Prescott with Percival Armitage, Tom Bate, W. R.
Humphries, and A. E. Suppinger c. 1903. In Lawler block
of Prescott 1907-08 to at least 1912.
> *1907 Arizona Business Directory,* Gazetteer Publishing
>   Company, p. 711.
> *Arizona Weekly Miner,* May 11, 1883.
> Stereograph, cabinet card, and photographic mount imprints.

BAGNASCO, POLICARPO
Tucson, Arizona Territory c. 1881. Listed as Photographer,
22 Camp Street.
> *1881 Arizona Business Directory and Gazetteer,* p. 188.

BAILEY, W.
Globe, Arizona Territory c. 1909-10. Operated Globe Photographic Co.
> 1909-10 directory.

BAKER, E. W.
Itinerant traveling from San Francisco to Williams, Arizona
Territory c. 1892. Opened tent gallery in Flagstaff in 1892.
Douglas, Arizona Territory c. 1905. Partner of Lote A. Skel-
ly (Skelley) on E Street between 9th and 10th. Also, may
have operated in Santa Fe, New Mexico c. 1888-92.
> *Polk Gazetteer.*

BALLINGER, L. A.
Bisbee, Arizona Territory. Licensed as itinerant c. 1904.
> Vaughn, Thomas, "A Guide to the Photographic
>   Archives of the Bisbee Mining and Historical Museum,"
>   *The Cochise Quarterly,* Vol. 19, No. 2, Summer 1989, p. 31.

BAN-AP PHOTO
Douglas, Arizona Territory c. 1907.
> Photographic postcard imprint.

BANNER, R.
Bisbee, Arizona Territory. Licensed as itinerant c. 1904.
> Vaughn, Thomas, "A Guide to the Photographic Archives
>   of the Bisbee Mining and Historical Museum," *The Cochise
>   Quarterly,* Vol. 19, No. 2, Summer 1989, p. 31.

BARNES, WILL CROFT
Born 1858; died 1936. Active in Ft. Apache, Arizona Territory c. 1880s. Stationed at Ft. Apache as corporal-telegrapher
then sergeant. Entered U.S. Forest Service in 1907. Traveled
extensively and photographed throughout the West.
> Barnes, Will C., *Apaches & Longhorns: The Reminiscences of Will
>   C. Barnes,* Ward Ritchie Press, Los Angeles, 1941.
> Rudisill, Richard, *Photographers of the New Mexico Territory,
>   1854-1912,* Museum of New Mexico, 1973, p. 12.

BARNETT, CHARLES
Hayden, Arizona Territory c. 1884.
> *Polk Gazetteer.*

BARNETT, CHARLES W.
Born in San Bernadino, California, September 29, 1858.
Active in Mesa, Arizona Territory. Established a gallery in
1881. In 1882 moved to Phoenix, later (about 1890) became a
partner of Rothrock 1882-94, in Tempe in 1893. To Phoenix,
1894, then retired from photography.
> Photographic mount imprint.

BARTHELMESS, CHRISTIAN
Born in Klingenberg, Bavaria, April 11, 1854; died April 10,
1906. Immigrated to U.S. in 1870s, stationed in Arizona as
bandsman/photographer at Ft. Apache, Arizona Territory
c. 1881. Traveled extensively officially and unofficially photographing throughout Arizona.
> Frink, Maurice, and Christian Barthelmess,
>   *Photographer On An Army Mule,* University of Oklahoma
>   Press, Norman, 1965.

BATE STUDIO
Phoenix, Arizona Territory, 103 S. Cortez, c. 1900–20s.
Operated by Tom H. Bate.

BATE, TOM H.
Phoenix, Arizona Territory operator for Hartwell c. 1899.
Prescott, Arizona Territory c. 1907-10. Operated in Head
Bldg. Listed in partnership with Erwin Baer until his retire-
ment in 1913. Partner in the Arizona Photograph Company,
Inc. in Prescott with Erwin Baer, Percival Armitage, W. R.

Humphries, and A. E. Suppinger c. 1903. Also operated Bate Studio at 103 S. Cortez into the 1920s.

> *1907 Arizona Business Directory,* Gazetteer Publishing
> Company, p. 711.
> 1909, 1910, 1920 directories.

BAUMAN, JULES
Prescott, Arizona Territory 1884-1900.

BEAMAN, E. O.
Beaman was a New York landscape photographer who became official photographer to the Powell Expedition in the summer of 1871, upon the recommendation of his supplier, E. & H. T. Anthony & Co. James Carleton is listed as an assistant. Beaman left the survey in January 1872, and spent some time photographing the Indians of New Mexico and Arizona before returning East. After Beaman left the expedition, his assistant and Powell's cousin, Clem Powell, took over but proved unable to photograph. He was replaced by James Fennemore of the C. R. Savage Gallery in Salt Lake City. Fennemore instructed the interested John K. Hillers in photography, Hillers became assistant, then took over as official photographer in 1873 when Fennemore quit due to illness.

> Correspondence, *Anthony's Photographic Bulletin,* New York,
> January and February, 1872.
> Lessard, Dennis, "E. O. Who?" *American Indian Art
> Magazine,* Vol. 12, No. 2, Spring 1987, pp. 52-61.
> Stereograph mount imprints.

BEARCE, E. A.
Phoenix, Arizona Territory c. 1898. Operated New York Gallery.

> *Polk Gazetteer.*

BEASLEY, A. D.
Phoenix, Arizona Territory c. 1910.

> 1910 directory.

BEATTIE, J. W.
Phoenix, Arizona Territory c. 1895-97. Operated at Fly's Gallery at 219 E. Washington in 1895, and at 409 W. Washington 1897.

> *Polk Gazetteer.*

BEATTY, MRS. C. S.
Prescott, Arizona Territory c. 1907-11. Operated gallery on Cortez St.

> *1907 Arizona Business Directory,* Gazetteer Publishing
> Company, p. 711.
> 1909-10, 1910-11 directories.

BEATTY, WILL R.
Prescott, Arizona Territory c. 1896. In Prescott, c. 1900-11.

Partner with Mrs. C. S. Beatty 1907-11.

> *Polk Gazetteer.*

BECKSTEIN, (?)
Bisbee, Arizona Territory c. 1895. Partner of Daniel A. Markey.

> See D. A. Markey.

BELL, DR. WILLIAM A.
Born in Liverpool, England, c. 1830; died in Philadelphia, January 28, 1910. Operated a gallery in Philadelphia with his brother-in-law John Keen in 1848, and his own gallery c. 1850. Later a partner of J. E. McClees and E. P. Hipple. Purchased McClees gallery in 1867. After Civil War was chief photographer for the Army Medical Museum; he photographed all of the generals and most of the battlefields. Reopened in Philadelphia c. 1869. In 1867 photographed along the 32nd parallel route of the Kansas Pacific Railway Survey across Arizona, photographing landscapes and vicinity of Camp Grant and Ft. Mohave. In 1872 Bell was the official photographer for the Wheeler survey of the Grand Canyon where he developed the idea for large panoramas. He made a panorama of the 1876 Centennial exhibition for Gutekunst using six 18″ x 22″ plates. Member of the Photographic Society of Philadelphia. Photographer on Palmer-Wright-Calhoun survey for the Union Pacific Railway, Eastern Division (Kansas-Pacific Survey) through Arizona in 1867-68. *New Tracks in North America* published in London, 1869, contained illustrations from his photos. Took over 100 negatives on 1871-72 Powell survey. Also traveled through northern Arizona in 1872, photographing the Hopi.

> Bell, William, *New Tracks in North America. A Journal of Travel
> and Adventure Whilst Engaged in the Survey for a Southern Rail
> road to the Pacific Ocean during 1867-8,* Horn and Wallace,
> Albuquerque, 1965.
> Photo citation, Smithsonian Museum of American
> History.

BELL, GEORGE V.
Bisbee, Arizona Territory c. 1905. Probable itinerant listed at Box 1980.

> Photo mount notation.

BEMIS, MRS. F. C.
Globe, Arizona Territory. Itinerant tent gallery operator c. 1885.

BERTOLACCI, G. T. E.
Yuma, Arizona Territory c. 1884.

> *Polk Gazetteer.*

BLAINE, CHARLES E.
Phoenix c. 1918-20.

> 1899 directory.

BLAINE, CHARLES S.
Phoenix, Arizona Territory. Operated at 905 W. Jefferson,
c. 1899-1900.
    1899-1900 directory.

BLEAK, ELLYE E.
Mesa c. 1915. Operated Ellsworth Studio between MacDonald and Robson.
    1915-17 directories.

BOGEN, ROBERT
Glendale c. 1919.
    1919 directory.

BOLANOS, HELIODORO
Tucson, Arizona Territory. Operated at 78 N. Stone in 1906-
07, and in Post Office building c. 1907-10.
    1907 Arizona Business Directory, Gazetteer Publishing
        Company, p. 711.
    1907-10 directories.

BONINE, ELIAS A.
Born 1843; died 1916. Active in Yuma, Arizona Territory.
Pasadena, and Los Angeles, California. Listed as photographer in Yuma, 1881. Photographs extant of studio portraits
of Native Americans, Pickett Post, Pinal, Queen Creek, Silver King and Yuma.
    1881 Arizona Business Directory and Gazetteer, p. 202.

BONINE, ROBERT K.
Tyrone, Pennsylvania. Cousin of E. A. Bonine. Marketed
photos of Yuma and Ehrenburg. Whether taken by R. K.
or exchanged with E. A. is not known.
    Stereograph mount notation.

BOOKSLY, A.
Fredonia c. 1912-13.
    Polk's Arizona and New Mexico Directory for 1912-13.

BOOTH & MILO
Douglas c. 1919. Studio on Florida near 11th.

BOOTH, ALBERT J.
Morenci, Arizona Territory c. 1911-12. Also advertised in
Yuma c. 1912-13.
    Morenci 1911-12 Directory.
    Polk's Arizona and New Mexico Directory for 1912-13.

BOROUGH, E. B.
Bisbee, Arizona Territory c. 1902. Purchased studio of Louis
A. Nemeck on south side of upper Main Street.
    Vaughn, Thomas, "A Guide to the Photographic Archives
        of the Bisbee Mining and Historical Museum," *The
        Cochise Quarterly*, Vol. 19, No. 2, Summer 1989, p. 24.

BOSTON RAILROAD PHOTO CAR
Flagstaff, Arizona Territory c. 1890s.
    Cabinet card mount notation.

BRANCH, JOHN W.
Phoenix, Arizona Territory. Operated Elite Gallery at 218
W. Washington in Phoenix c. 1909-10. Then to Hartwell
Studio 29 ½ S. 2nd c. 1912. Later operated in Tempe c. 1912-
15 at 616 Mill Ave. Then returned to Phoenix at 29 ½ S. 2nd
from 1917 to c. 1921.
    1909-10 directory.
    1912 Phoenix City and Salt River Valley Directory.

BRENNAN, M. F.
Jerome, Arizona Territory c. 1901-17.
    Photograph mount imprints.
    1907 Arizona Business Directory, Gazetteer Publishing
        Company, p. 710.
    1909-10 directory.

BRIGHT, J. A.
Wilcox, Arizona Territory c. 1890s.
    Cabinet card imprint.

BROWN, M. L.
Douglas, Arizona Territory. Operated on E Street between
8th and 9th c. 1905, then at 449 4th c. 1907-12, then 642 G
Avenue c. 1919.
    1907 Arizona Business Directory, Gazetteer Publishing
        Company, p. 710.
    1909-12 directories.
    Polk Gazetteer.

BROWN, W. CALVIN
Lieutenant in the New Mexico Territorial Militia. Photographed Johnson Canyon, Canyon Diablo, and Hopi area
c. 1885. Also, Holbrook (ca 1900) as photographer for
Atlantic & Pacific Railroad.
    Rudisill, Richard, *Photographers of the New Mexico Territory,
        1854-1912*, Museum of New Mexico, 1973, p. 16.

BROWN, WILLIAM HENRY
Born c. 1844; died in El Paso, Texas, December 19, 1886.
Active in Santa Fe, New Mexico c. 1866-86. Worked in partnership with his father Nicholas Brown until 1867. Ran a
studio in Chihuahua, Mexico 1867-69. Partnership with
George C. Bennett from 1880-82. Photographed Zuni Pueblos, Arizona Territory.
    Stereograph mount imprints.

BRUCE, C. A.
Prescott, Arizona Territory. Operated on N. Montezuma
c. 1900-12.
    1909-12 directories.

BRUUNAGE, M. J.
Tucson, Arizona Territory. Studio operator for Buehman c. 1880.

BRYANT, HENRY
Prescott c. 1920. Operated Quick Finish Kodak Co. at 218 W. Gurley.
> *Tribby's City Directory of Prescott for 1920.*

BUCK, A. J.
Traveled from Vance, Texas, to photograph Clifton, Arizona Territory in April 1897.
> Rudisill, Richard, *Photographers of the New Mexico Territory, 1854-1912,* Museum of New Mexico, 1973, p. 17.

BUEHMAN & CO. PHOTOGRAPHERS
Operated by Henry Buehman, in Tucson c. 1881, at 105 Congress.

BUEHMAN, HENRY
Born in Bremen, Germany, May 14, 1851; died in Tucson, Arizona, December 20, 1912. Emigrated to San Francisco, 1868. Worked for Bradley & Rulofson. Moved to and opened studio in Visalia, California 1869. Itinerant throughout southwest 1871-74. On June 4, 1874 purchased Tucson, Arizona Territory gallery from Adolfo and Juan Rodrigo. In December 1875 took a six week tour of Ft. Apache, Camps Bowie and Grant, and the San Carlos Reservation. 1876 photographed San Xavier. September 15, 1879 to November 1879 traveled to Camp Huachuca, Charleston, Tombstone, Ft. Bowie, Ft. Apache, Ft. Thomas. At Huachuca he took a dozen views of the camp and scenery. At Charleston, views of Tough Nut and Corbin Mills. At Tombstone, views of Tough Nut, Contention, Grand Central and other mines. Tucson c. 1881 as Buehman & Co. Photographers, 105 Congress, c. 1883-84 Buehman at 314 and 316 Congress. Partnership with F. A. Hartwell c. 1880s including galleries in Tucson and Phoenix, corner of Jefferson & Pima Streets. Buehman operated Tucson gallery at 30 W. Congress c. 1897, Post Office building. c. 1907, and 30 W. Congress c. 1909 listed as H. Buehman & Co. Photographers and Dealers in Arizona Views, Moldings and Picture Frames. Also operated Elite Studio in Post Office building c. 1911.
> *1881 Arizona Business Directory and Gazetteer,* p. 189.
> *1907 Arizona Business Directory,* Gazetteer Publishing Company, p. 711.
> 1909-10 directory.
> *Arizona Daily Star,* November 4, 1879, p. 3, cols. 1 and 2.
> *McKenney's Business Directory 1882–83,* p. 295.
> Stereograph, carte-de-visite, cabinet card and photograph mount imprints.
> *Polk's Arizona and New Mexico Directory for 1912-13.*

BULL, (?)
Prescott, Arizona Territory. Recruited from California to run Williscraft Studio c. 1875.
> See William H. Williscraft.

BURCHARD & MELVIN
Tempe, Arizona Territory c. 1892. Operated gallery on Mill Ave.
> *City of Phoenix Directory for 1892,* Bensel Directory Company.

BURCHARD, JAMES EDWARD
Flagstaff, Arizona Territory. Possible operator of the Flagstaff Art Gallery c. 1887.
> *City of Phoenix Directory for 1892,* Bensel Directory Company.

BURGE, J. C.
Prescott, Arizona Territory c. 1881. Listed on Montezuma St. Worked for Atlantic & Pacific Railroad in Prescott, June–October, 1881 and June–August, 1882. Moved to Globe in 1883, then to Grand Canyon, 1884. In partnership with Hildreth in Flagstaff, 1884, Kingman, 1885, then to New Mexico.
> *1881 Arizona Business Directory and Gazetteer,* p. 152.
> Stereograph and photograph mount imprints.

BURLAN, (?)
Arizona City (Yuma) and Clifton, Arizona Territory; also in Silver City, New Mexico, advertised with Harry W. Lucas.
> Mount imprint notation.

BURT, CHARLES S.
Area and date unknown.
> Photo credit, National Archives.

BURTIS, GEORGE
Roosevelt, Arizona Territory c. 1907-08.
> *1907 Arizona Business Directory,* Gazetteer Publishing Company, p. 711.

BURTIS, MRS. GEORGE
Roosevelt, Arizona Territory c. 1907.
> *1907 Arizona Business Directory,* Gazetteer Publishing Company, p. 711.

CALIFORNIA ART GALLERY
Globe, Arizona Territory c. 1882. Operated by Cicero Grime producing tintypes and stereographs.

CAPITAL ART GALLERY
Original photo studio in Prescott, begun by Francis A. Cook c. 1869. Subsequently used by other photographers such as Flanders, Williscraft and Mitchell over the next decades.
> Cook, F. A., "Journal of F. A. Cook," unpublished, Arizona Historical Foundation.

CARLTON, JAMES
Assisted Beaman on photographic excursion through northern Arizona in 1872. See E. O. Beaman.

CARSON, AMBROSE W.
Born in Texas, 1875. Active in Douglas, Arizona Territory c. October 1906. Photographer in Altus and Mountain View, Oklahoma, with brother H. R. Carson (1897-c. 1905) then to California prior to moving to Douglas. Operated studio with brother M. R. Carson until 1911 then purchased Irwin studio. Operated studio until c. 1915 then returned to Douglas studio with brother.
> Vaughn, Thomas, "A Guide to the Photographic Archives of the Bisbee Mining and Historical Museum," *The Cochise Quarterly*, Vol. 19, No. 2, Summer 1989, p. 25.

CARSON BROTHERS
Douglas, Arizona Territory c. 1909-10. Ambrose and Hugh Carson operated at 529 11th.
> *1909-10 Arizona Business Directory.*

CARSON, HUGH RUTH
Born in Carrol County, Arkansas, June 24, 1864; died in Prescott, Arizona, February 17, 1953. Partner in studios in Altus and Mountain View, Oklahoma with brother Ambrose Carson (1897-c. 1905). Douglas, Arizona Territory, operated Queen Studio at 529 11th c. 1907. Moved to Bisbee until c. 1919 then returned to Douglas studio. Active in Bisbee/Douglas as photographer until c. 1949.
> *1907 Arizona Business Directory*, Gazetteer Publishing Company, p. 710.
> Vaughn, Thomas, "A Guide to the Photographic Archives of the Bisbee Mining and Historical Museum," *The Cochise Quarterly*, Vol. 19, No. 2, 1989, p. 25.

CARSON'S STUDIO
Douglas c. 1917-19. Meguire Building and 927 G Avenue.

CARTER, CHARLES W.
Born in London, August 4, 1832; died in Midvale Utah, January 27, 1918. Immigrated to Salt Lake City in 1859. Worked for Savage and Ottinger 1862. Began Carter's View Emporium in 1863. Changed name to Carter's Photographic Gallery in 1866. Photographed Moqui Buttes and Brigham Young excursion to northern Arizona. Sold negative collection to the Bureau of Information of the Mormon Church in 1906.
> Stereograph mount imprint.

CATTON, C. W.
Phoenix, Arizona Territory c. 1881. Partner of George H. Rothrock. Several examples of Catton & Rothrock mounts with Catton's name abraded from mount indicates use by Rothrock after dissolution of partnership.
> Stereograph mount imprints.

CHASE, (?)
Tombstone, Arizona Territory c. 1880s. Assistant of C. S. Fly. See C. S. Fly.

CHRISTENSEN, PETER C.
Glendale c. 1915-18.
> 1915-18 directory.

CHRISTY, ISAAC MARSHALL
Phoenix, Arizona Territory c. 1887.
> 1887 directory.

CLARK, CHARLES
Traveled with C. L. White on his projectoscope tour showing motion pictures in Arizona c. 1898.

CLARK, ROBERT
Holbrook, Arizona Territory c. 1895.

CLAUSEN, C. H.
Phoenix, Arizona Territory c. 1895-97. Operated at 438 E. Monroe Street in 1895. Moved to Elite Gallery at 22 S. 3rd Ave. in 1897.
> *Phoenix Directory for 1897*, Phoenix Directory Company.

CLAUSEN, MRS. C. H.
Phoenix, Arizona Territory c. 1895-1900. Affiliated with Elite Gallery at 22 S. 3rd Ave.
> *Phoenix Directory for 1898*, Phoenix Directory Company.

CLEMENT, E. L.
From Oak Park, Illinois. Stereographed Grand Canyon c. 1890s.
> Stereograph mount imprints.

COBB, WILLIAM HENRY
Oak Creek and vicinity c. 1890s.
> Photographic mount imprint.

COHEN, JOSEPH
Phoenix c. 1914-17. Operated on 1st Ave.
> 1914 directory.

COLEMAN, (?)
Tombstone, Arizona Territory c. 1881. Listed as partner in Kemp & Coleman.
> *Polk Gazetteer.*

COLEMAN, JAMES. W.
Jerome, Arizona Territory c. 1895.
> 1895 directory.

CONE, J. T.
Williams, Arizona Territory c. 1895.
> Photo mount information.

CONKLIN, ENOCH
Stereographer for Continent Stereoscopic Company working in Arizona c. 1877 at completion of the Yuma Railroad bridge, and southern Arizona. Also marketed stereographs of Prescott area (at least one originally a D. P. Flanders image from 1874) and Tucson and Vicinity (original images by Henry Buehman).
> Conklin, Enoch, *Picturesque Arizona: Being the Result of Travels and Observations in Arizona During the Fall and Winter of 1877*, Continent Stereoscopic Company, illust., Mining Record Printing Establishment, New York, 1878.
> Stereograph and cabinet card imprints.

COOK, FRANCIS A.
Born 1832. Prescott photographer 1869-74 (in partnership with Nathan P. Pierce 1869-72), first partnership with L. W. Worth gallery probably on Cortez Street. Other partners include Richard M. Hargrave. Arrived in Prescott in 1864 (listed in census as age 32 from New York); also listed in 1870 census. Purchased camera from Gentile and began operation c. 1869. Operator of original photo studio in Prescott, the Capital Art Gallery, subsequently used by other photographers such as Flanders, Williscraft and Mitchell over the next decades. Operated in Camp Verde and Phoenix in 1872. Sold gallery to Williscraft in 1874.
> Cook, F. A., "Journal of F. A. Cook," unpublished, Arizona Historical Foundation.

COOLEY, BEN D.
Bisbee, Arizona Territory c. 1909. Produced photographic postcards of Bisbee floods. Also, Douglas, c. 1919 at 1089 F Avenue.
> Photographic postcard imprints.

COOLIDGE, DANE
Born in Natick, Massachusetts, c. 1873; died in Berkeley, California, 1940. Author, naturalist, and photographer. Photographed cowboys and ranch life in Arizona, Texas, and California c. 1907-16.
> Coolidge, Dane, *Arizona Cowboys*, E. P. Dutton, New York, 1938.
> Photographers listing, Arizona Historical Foundation.

COPELAND, (?)
Phoenix, Arizona Territory c. 1905-06. In partnership Stacey & Copeland.
> 1905-06 directory.

COREY, KATE
Born 1861; died 1958. Active in Arizona c. 1904-12. New York artist and self-taught photogapher who came to visit in 1904 and stayed to study Hopi people and culture, leaving in 1912. Produced a body of photographs and paintings.
> Wright, Barton, Marnie Gaede and Marc Gaede, *The Hopi Photographs of Kate Corey*, Chaco Press, 1986.

COSBY, O.
Fort Huachuca, Arizona Territory c. 1907-10.
> *1907 Arizona Business Directory*, Gazetteer Publishing Company, p. 710.
> 1909-10 directory.

CORY, H. T.
Arizona c. 1916.
> Photo credit, National Archives.

COTTEN, C. W.
Phoenix, Arizona Territory c. 1899-1908. Operated at Elite Gallery, 22 S. 3rd Ave. near Washington.
> City directories.

COX, (?)
Flagstaff, Arizona Territory, Partner with Stone c. 1908. Produced panoramic photographs.

COYLE, JOHN H.
Bisbee, Arizona Territory c. 1903-04. Operated on Brewery Gulch over Dunn's, opposite the Post Office. Later operated in Winkelman c. 1912-13.
> *Buck's Directory of Bisbee for 1904.*

COZBY, OLIVER
Tucson Arizona Territory c. 1912. Operated Model Photo Gallery at 102 S. Stone in 1912.

CULPS PHOTO STUDIO
Morenci, Arizona Territory c. 1909-10.
> 1909-10 directory.

CURTIS, C. D.
Williams, Arizona Territory and St. Johns c. 1894.

CURTIS, CLINTON
Itinerant photographer northern Arizona c. 1895.
> 1895 directory.

CURTIS, EDWARD SHERIFF
Born in Wisconsin, February 16, 1868; died in Los Angeles, California, October 19, 1952. Ethnologist and photographer based in Seattle, Washington. Traveled to Arizona in 1904 producing still and motion pictures of the Hopi. Returned

to Arizona in 1905 photographing the Hopi and Navajo, and the Apache and Navajo in 1906. Returned to photograph the Hopi in 1913 and take motion pictures of the Grand Canyon in 1915. Continued activity in Arizona and the Southwest from 1918-23.

> Curtis, Edward, *The North American Indian,* 20 Vols.;
> Vols. 1-5, University Press, Cambridge, Massachusetts;
> Plimpton Press, Norwood, Connecticut, 1907-30.
> Davis, Barbara, *Edward S. Curtis, The Life and Times of a Shadowcatcher,* Chronicle Books, San Francisco, 1985.

D'HEUREUSE, RUDOLPH

French survey photographer in southern Arizona c. 1863. Active in Yuma and Ft. Mohave.

> Hooper, Bruce, "Arizona Territorial Stereography 1864-1906," *Stereo World,* National Stereoscopic Association, Vol. 13, No. 1, March/April 1986, p. 4.
> Photographic Collection, Bancroft Library.

DAVENPORT, M. L.

Phoenix, Arizona Territory c. 1899. Operated Sunbeam Studio at 246 W. Washington in partnership with Fred B. Mussey.

> 1899-1900 directory.

DAVIDSON, ARTHUR H.

Morenci, Arizona Territory c. 1903-04. Publisher of "Picturesque Arizona" stereographs of Morenci, Metcalf, and vicinity.

> Stereograph mount imprint.

DEPUE, OSCAR B.

Early motion picture photographer active at the Grand Canyon and the Hopi Pueblos in 1899 and 1900. Presented motion pictures at trading post in Canyon Diablo in 1900.

> Depue, Oscar, "My First Fifty Years in Motion Pictures," *Journal of the Society of Motion Picture Engineers,* Vol. 49, December, 1947.

DETROIT PHOTOGRAPHIC COMPANY

Marketed numerous photomechanical postcards of Grand Canyon, Native Americans, Phoenix, and general Arizona subjects c. 1900-1907.

> Postcard imprints.

DICKISON, MISS E.

Wellton, Arizona Territory c. 1909-10.

> *1909-10 Arizona Directory.*

DINWIDDIE, WILLIAM

Photographed the Papago on W. J. McGee survey 1894.

> Photo credit, Smithsonian Institution.

DIX, GEORGE C.

Bisbee. Operated studio in Schmidt building c. 1916. Photographed the Bisbee Exportation in 1917 and marketed photo postcard series (including approximately 50-60 titles) of the event.

> Photographic postcard imprints.

DIXON, W. L.

Poland, Arizona Territory c. 1909-10.

> 1909-10 directory.

DODGE, KATHERINE T.

San Carlos, Arizona Territory c. 1899.

> Fleming, Paula Richardson, and Judith Luskey, *The North American Indians in Early Photographs,* Harper and Rowe, New York, 1986.

DONALDSON, M. D.

Bisbee, Arizona Territory c. 1911-12.

> 1911 directory.

DONNELL, T. M.

Phoenix, Arizona Territory c. 1903-10. Operated at 18 W. Washington in 1903. Operated Elite Gallery after C. C. Long at 218 W. Washington 1905-09. Also listed in Tempe 1907.

> *1907 Arizona Business Directory,* Gazetteer Publishing Company, p. 711.
> 1909-10 directory.

DOWE, D. W.

Bisbee, Arizona Territory c. 1897-1904. Produced "Souvenir of the Great Copper Belt In and Around Bisbee," 1904. Illustrated with photo-engravings.

> Photo credit "Souvenir of the Great Copper Belt In and Around Bisbee," 1904.

DRAKE, CHAS. L.

Wilcox, Arizona Territory c. 1909-10.

> *1909-10 Arizona Directory.*

EASTMAN, (?)

Bisbee, Arizona Territory c. 1904.

> Photo credit "Souvenir of the Great Copper Belt In and Around Bisbee," 1904.

ELECTRIC STUDIO

Phoenix c. 1919 at 37 W. Adams.

> 1919 directory.

ELITE STUDIO

Tucson c. 19 -1920. Located in Post Office building until at least 1911 then c. 1919-20 at 79 N. Stone Ave. Operated by H. H. Wilcox c. 1908, and Henry Buehman c. 1911.

ELITE STUDIOS & GALLERY
Phoenix, Arizona Territory c. 1899-1908. Listed at 22 S. 3rd Ave. near Washington in Phoenix until 1900, then at 218 W. Washington. Operators included Mr. and Mrs. C. H. Clausen (1897-1900), C. C. Long, T. M. Donnell, J. W. Branch, and C. W. Cotten.
    Photographic mount imprints.

ELKIN & ELKIN
Phoenix c. 1918. Operated by Lauren Elkin, at 1 Cactus Way. The former studio of Kunselman was previously known as Photocraft Shop.

ELKIN, LAUREN
Phoenix c. 1918. Took over the old Photocraft Shop from Kunselman, c. 1918, operating as Elkin & Elkin, 1 Cactus Way.
    1918 directory.

ELLSWORTH, ELLYE IRWIN
Mesa c. 1912-15.
    Polk's Arizona and New Mexico Directory for 1912-13.

ELLSWORTH STUDIO
Mesa c. 1915. Located between MacDonald and Robson, operated by Ellye E. Bleak.
    1915-17 directories.

EMANUEL, (?)
Prescott, Arizona Territory c. 1881.
    Photographic mount.

EMPIE, HAL D.
Born 1909. Active in Safford, Arizona Territory c. 1906. Cowboy, photographer, artist, and author. Produced photographic postcards of ranching and life in Arizona.
    Photographic postcard imprint.

EVERETT & SON, J. E.
Casa Grande, Arizona Territory c. 1888.
    Polk Gazetteer.

EVERETT'S STUDIO
Prescott, Arizona Territory c. 1895.
    1895 directory.

FARCIOT, CHARLES O.
Born in Switzerland, 1839; died in Chino Ranch, California, 1891. Active in Tombstone and Charleston, Arizona Territory 1879-80. Civil War veteran listed as clockmaker and engineer prior to arrival in Arizona. Traveled extensively while photographing central and southern Arizona beginning 1879. Photographed Camp Apache, Maricopa Wells, Pinal, Silver King, McMillenville, Globe, and mining and ethnographic subjects. Operated gallery at Pima Villages, also active in Globe, November 1879 to January 1880. Probable studio in Charleston c. 1881-83. Left Arizona for Alaska on first commercial mining expedition with Ed Schieffelin of Tombstone and party via San Francisco. Farciot's stereographs were marketed by the studio of his brother-in-law, Alexander Edouart of Edouart & Cobb, 504 Kearney St., San Francisco as "Arizona Views." The series may include as many as 150 titles.
    Arizona Silver Belt, January 24, 1880.
    Rowe, Jeremy, "Following the Frontier from Arizona to Alaska: The Photographs of Charles O. Farciot," *Stereo World,* National Stereoscopic Association, January/February 1989, Vol. 15, No. 6, pp. 6-13.
    Stereograph mount imprint.

FARQUAHAR, JULIUS THEO
Douglas, Arizona Territory c. 1902. Globe, Arizona Territory c. 1908. Operated the Globe Photographic Company at 162 W. Bailey. Produced cabinet and larger photos 1911-12.
    Polk Gazetteer.
    Polk's Arizona and New Mexico Directory for 1912-13.

FELDMAN, ALTTIER M.
Tucson, Arizona Territory. Tent gallery operator c. 1885-95.
    1902-07 Tucson directories.

FELDMAN, FREDERICK J.
Operated as itinerant traveling photographer. Listed in Tombstone, Arizona Territory c. 1880; Bisbee, Arizona Territory c. 1890; Tucson c. 1893 operating tent Arizona Gallery at 433 Congress Street, tintypist; then to El Paso, Texas, c. 1895.
    Arizona Citizen, August 4, 1893.

FENNEMORE, JAMES
Active 1870s and 1880s. Operator for C. R. Savage in Salt Lake, Fennemore replaced E. O. Beaman in 1871-72 as the photographer for the Powell expedition. Fennemore soon quit, but not before training expedition member John K. Hillers to carry on as photographer.
    See E. O. Beaman.

FETTER, W. L.
Flagstaff, Arizona Territory, c. 1888. Also Bisbee, Arizona Territory, c. 1888.
    Cabinet card imprint.
    Cochise County Register

FEWKES, DR. JESSE WALTER
Born 1850; died 1930. Chief of Bureau of American Ethnology, 1895-1923. Made prints and lantern slides of Arizona (at least one example of Erwin Baer original image as part of collection).
    Fewkes, Jesse Walter, "Archaeological Expedition to Arizona in 1895," *Seventeenth annual report of the Bureau of American Ethnology,* Government Printing Office, Washington, D.C., 1899.

FLAGSTAFF ART GALLERY
Flagstaff Arizona Territory c. 1887. Possible operator: James
Edward Burchard.

> Hooper, Bruce, "Camera on the Mogollon Rim: 19th
> Century Photography in Flagstaff, Arizona Territory,
> 1867-1916," *History of Photography*, Vol. 12, No. 2, April 1988.

FLAGSTAFF PHOTOGRAPH GALLERY
Flagstaff Arizona Territory c. 1890, James Edward Burchard
operator.

> See James Burchard.

FLANDERS, DUDLEY P.
Born in Massachusetts, 1840. Licensed as Flanders & Tuttle
photographers, Arcata, California, August 1865. Active in
Eureka, 1866, San Francisco and Grass Valley, 1867, with
branch gallery in Truckee, 1868. Arrived in Arizona from Los
Angeles about 1873, operating under partnership of Flanders
& Godfrey. Formed partnership with Henri Penlon in
November 1873, and arrived in Ft. Mohave, Arizona Territo-
ry in December. Opened a gallery in Prescott (purchased
from F. A. Cook), operated in the Prescott/Verde Valley.
Offered stereographs on "A Photographic Album of a Trip
Through Arizona by Flanders and Penlon" mount. Henri
Penlon died in Prescott February 6, 1874. Flanders moved on
to Tucson in summer of 1874. Operated out of studio of
Adolfo Rodrigo on corner of Courthouse and Maiden Lane
in Tucson, July 1874. Made excursions visiting Forts Bowie
and Apache, San Carlos, and southeastern Arizona until Sep-
tember 1874. Left Tucson on October 1874 to return to Los
Angeles via Yuma. Sailed out of Yuma on November 25, 1874.
Subsequently issued two versions of stereograph series
"Scenes in Arizona" including approximately 100 images.
Flanders' stereographs of Arizona were subsequently issued
on the mounts of Payne, Stanton, & Co. of Los Angeles,
Williscraft of Prescott, and the Continent Stereoscopic
Company (whether with permission or as pirated views is not
known, however prints appear to be from original negatives).

> Correspondence with Peter Palmquist.
> Rowe, Jeremy, "A Trip Through Arizona With Dudley
> Flanders in 1873-1874," *Stereo World*, November/
> December 1991, Vol. 18, No. 5, pp. 28-33.
> Stereograph mount imprints.

FLY & HOLFSTEAD
Fremont Street, Tucson c. 1888.

> *Polk Gazetteer.*

FLY, CAMILIUS S.
Born in Andrew County, Michigan, c. 1849; died in Tombstone, Arizona Territory, October 12, 1901. Came to Tombstone in 1879 with wife Mary and operated gallery on
Fremont Street near the O.K. Corral. Listed as Photographer & Lodgings, 312 Fremont, Tombstone. Photographed
Tombstone and vicinity producing cartes-de-visite, cabinet
cards, mounted photographs and some stereographs. Most
noted for images of the capture of Geronimo. Phoenix
gallery c. 1893-94 at 219 E. Washington. Operated gallery at
the Norton House on Upper Main Street, Bisbee c. 1989-
1901. Negatives destroyed in studio fire in 1912 and ware-
house fire in 1915.

> *McKenney's Business Directory 1882-83.*
> Photo credits, "Souvenir of Bisbee," 1904.
> Stereograph, carte–de–visite, cabinet card, and boudoir
> imprints.

FLY, MRS. MARY E.
Tombstone, Arizona Territory. Worked gallery with hus-
band Camilius prior to his death in 1901, continued as a
photographer until c. 1912. Also active in Bisbee.

> *1907 Arizona Business Directory*, Gazetteer Publishing
> Company, p. 711.
> 1909-10 directory.
> Cabinet card imprint.

FLYING GALLERY
Prescott c. 1876. Operated by William H. Williscraft.

> See Williscraft.

FONDERMAN, O.
Bisbee, Arizona Territory. Licensed as itinerant November
15, 1908.

> Vaughn, Thomas, "A Guide to the Photographic
> Archives of the Bisbee Mining and Historical Museum,"
> *The Cochise Quarterly*, Vol. 19, No. 2, Summer 1989, p. 31.

FORBES, DR. ROBERT
Photographed Arizona vegetation and agriculture c. 1900.

> Photo credit, Smithsonian Institution.

FORTIN, JOSEPH R.
Phoenix c. 1916-20. Operated at 716 Grand Ave. and 1100 E.
Van Buren.

> 1916 directory.

FRAESDORF, WILLIAM
Benson, Arizona Territory c. 1907.

> *1907 Arizona Business Directory*, Gazetteer Publishing
> Company, p. 710.

FUERMAN, HENRY
Grand Canyon, Arizona Territory c. 1911.

> Higgins, C. A, *Grand Canyon of Arizona: The Titan of
> Chasms*, Rand McNalley & Company, Chicago, 1915.

FURL, J. FRANK
Phoenix, A. T. c. 1900.

> Cabinet card imprint.

GAIGE, J. C.
Died at Camp Goodwin, Arizona Territory, July 1869. Early itinerant in New Mexico and Arizona. Returned to Santa Fe c. 1862. Licensed as photographer in Albuquerque March 1863. Contracted with quartermaster of New Mexico Military District to photograph posts in 1865. Active in Ft. Sumner, New Mexico February–March 1866. Advertised as J. C. Gaige, the photographer in *Tucson Weekly Arizonan* in May 1869.
   Cabinet card imprints.
   Rudisill, Richard, *Photographers of the New Mexico Territory, 1854-1912*, Museum of New Mexico, 1973, p. 28.

GALBRAITH, ROY L.
Mesa c. 1919. Operated at 106 W. 1st.
   1919 directory.

GARDNER, ALEXANDER
Born in Paisley, Scotland October 17, 1821; died in Washington, D.C. December 1882. Worked for Matthew Brady during the Civil War. Later worked for the Department of the Interior, Union Pacific Railway, and Union Army. With William Bell, photographed northern Arizona in vicinity of current Flagstaff and Ft. Mohave during the Union Pacific Railway's Eastern Division survey of the 35th Parallel (Kansas-Pacific Survey) in 1867.
   Katz, D. Mark, *Witness To An Era: The Life and Photographs of Alexander Gardner: The Civil War, Lincoln, and the West*, Viking Studio Books, New York, 1991.

GENTILE, CARLOS (CHARLES) G.
Born in Naples, Italy 1835; died in Chicago, Illinois 1893. Began photographic career in 1863, a year after arriving in Victoria from San Francisco. Worked in Vancouver Island and British Columbia until 1866. In 1864 took photographs of the Leach River Gold Flurry that arose after he discovered traces of gold while cleaning his photographic apparatus. Gentile left British Columbia in September 1866 after losing a box of his stereo negatives. Opened a gallery in San Francisco in 1867, then worked as an itinerant in the Southwest. Prescott photographer prior to 1869, then sold gallery to Francis A. Cook. Also listed in *Arizona Citizen*, August 19, 1871, as traveling with Governor Safford's prospecting party in the Pinal Mountains. Operated a gallery in Adamsville, Arizona Territory c. 1871. Exhibited paper prints and ambrotypes at the 8th Industrial Exhibition in California. Active in Arizona to c. 1874 before settling in Chicago. Operated the Gentile Photography Gallery in Chicago 1874-85. Possibly operated again in Prescott, summer 1875. Gained notoriety through affiliation with Dr. Carlos Montezuma, famous Native American doctor and Indian rights activist. Gentile had purchased the young Apache in 1872 from Pimas while in Adamsville and became his guardian.
   Arizona Citizen, August 19, 1871.

British Columbia Historical News, Vol. 14, (2), Winter 1980.
Carlos Montezuma Papers.
Correspondence with Peter Palmquist.
Photographic mount information.

GILGANNON, DANIEL S.
Morenci, Arizona Territory c. 1909-12.
   1909-10 directory.
   Polk's Arizona and New Mexico directory for 1912-13.

GILL, DE LANCEY W.
Born in Camden, South Carolina, July 1, 1859; died in Alexandria, Virginia, August 30, 1940. Illustrations editor for the U.S. Geological Survey and from 1899, for the Smithsonian Institution Bureau of American Ethnology. Photographer c. 1900 for W. J. McGee survey to study Papago.
   Photo credit, Smithsonian Institution.

GILLINGHAM, W. P.
Clifton, Arizona Territory. Operated tent gallery in partnership with Charles Granville Johnson c. 1888.

GLOBE PHOTOGRAPHIC CO.
Globe, Arizona Territory c. 1909-10. W. Bailey operator.
   1909-10 directory.

GOMMEL, G. EDWARD
Listed as partner of Charles R. Allen c. 1892-93, location unknown.
   Photographer listing, Arizona Historical Society, Tucson.

GONZALES, LEONARDO
Morenci c. 1917.
   Photo credit on Morenci postcard c. 1917.

GOTTLEIB, HARRY JOSEPH
Born in New York c. 1882; died 1936. Active in Tucson, Arizona Territory c. 1911-12. Also Tempe c. 1916-19 at 616 Mill Ave. superseding Jeanette Pollock.
   1917-19 directories.

GRAVES, G. A.
Bisbee, Arizona Territory. Photographed Bisbee, the C & A Smelter, Douglas, and Tombstone mines during summer 1906.
   Photo credit on Bisbee postcard c. 1906.

GREAT WESTERN VIEW COMPANY
Bisbee, Arizona Territory c. 1898. Operated by Lewis Jones and Kennat c. 1889-1900. Also Naco, Arizona Territory.
   Vaughn, Thomas, "A Guide to the Photographic Archives of the Bisbee Mining and Historical Museum," *The Cochise Quarterly*, Vol. 19, No. 2, Summer 1989, p. 25.

GREEN, W. HUGH A.
Bisbee, Arizona Territory c. 1909-10. Operated at 114 Tombstone Canyon. In Phoenix c. 1911-15 at 18 W. Washington.
1909-10 directory.
1912 Phoenix City and Salt River Valley Directory.

GREGORY, A. D.
Tucson, Arizona Territory. Studio operator for Buehman c. 1880.

GRIFFITHS, D.
Photographed Navajo reservation and vicinity c. 1903.

GRIME, CICERO
Globe, Arizona Territory in 1880-81. Listed as photographer in Globe, and as Cicero Grime Photographic Gallery in Globe City and Pinal. Operated the California Art Gallery in Globe, ex-operator of I. C. U. photograph car in California. Made tintypes and stereographs. Robbed stage and nearly hanged in 1882, sentenced to Yuma Territorial Prison.
1880-81 Polk Gazetteer.
1881 Arizona Business Directory and Gazetteer, p. 140.
Cabinet card imprint.

GUEN, HUGH
Bisbee, Arizona Territory c. 1900-10. Also Phoenix, Arizona Territory c. 1911-12.
Arizona Historical Society, Tucson, photographer listing.

GUZMAN, E. S.
Douglas c. 1919. Operated at 752 G Avenue.

HACKETT, ARTHUR E.
Phoenix c. 1914 as proprietor of the Arizona Photo Company.
1914 directory.

HACKETT, H. A.
Flagstaff, Arizona Territory c. 1900. Photographer and publisher of stereographs, and photographic postcards.
Stereograph and postcard imprints.

HADSELL, WALTER P.
Tucson, Arizona Territory. Worked as operator in Henry Buehman's studio.
See Henry Buehman.

HAMMAKER, H. C.
Prescott, Arizona Territory c. 1870s-90s. Listed in partnership with Erwin Baer.
Arizona Historical Society, Tucson, photographer listing.

HAMMAKER, H. L.
Phoenix, Arizona Territory c. 1897. Partner of F. A. Hartwell.
Business Directory of Arizona/New Mexico, Examiner

Publishing Company, Las Vegas, New Mexico, 1897. Stereo and cabinet card imprints.

HAMMER, RICHARD W.
Survey photographer for Native American Photo Company.
Photo citation, Smithsonian Museum of American History.

HANNA, FORMAN
Globe, Arizona Territory c. 1904. Pharmacist and photographer. Pictorial style producing huge body of work c. 1910-47.

HANSEN, H. B.
Douglas, Arizona Territory c. 1911-12.
Polk's Arizona and New Mexico Directory for 1912-13.

HARGRAVE, RICHARD M.
Prescott, Arizona Territory in 1872. Partner of F. A. Cook after breakup with Nathan P. Pierce.
Cook, F. A., "Journal of F. A. Cook," unpublished, Arizona Historical Foundation.

HARRIS, JOSEPH
Tucson c. 1920. Operated at 179 S. Meyer.

HARRISON, RALPH T.
Phoenix c. 1914-17. Operated in partnership with Wesley Adkins as Adkins & Harrison at 218 ½ W. Washington.
Phoenix City and Salt River Valley Directory, 1913-17.

HARTWELL & HAMMAKER
Phoenix, Arizona Territory c. 1899-1900. Operated at 29 S. 2nd Street.
Mount imprint notation.

HARTWELL, BYRON J.
Phoenix, Arizona Territory c. 1898.
1898 directory.

HARTWELL, FRANCIS A.
Born in Canada April 1852; died in Phoenix, Arizona Territory June 1908. Active in Tucson, Arizona Territory. Partner of Henry Buehman c. 1880s including galleries in Tucson and Phoenix, corner of Jefferson & Pima Streets. Phoenix, Arizona Territory c. 1889 until death in 1908. Studios listed at 29 S. 1st and on Maricopa between Washington and Jefferson. Also in partnership Hammaker in 1899-1900.
1907 Arizona Business Directory, Gazetteer Publishing Company, p. 711.
Stereograph, cabinet card, and carte-de-visite imprints.

HARTWELL, STEVEN
Glendale, Arizona Territory c. 1910.
1910 directory.

HARTWELL'S STUDIO
Phoenix, Arizona Territory c. 1912-13. John Branch listed as proprietor probably as subsequent owner.
Mount imprint notation.

HARVEY, FRED
Entrepreneur/publisher photographed the Grand Canyon and vicinity c. 1900-20.
Grand Canyon National Park and other Arizona Scenes, Fred Harvey, ed., F. Harvey, Grand Canyon, Arizona, 1920.
Harvey, Fred, *The Camera in the Southwest,* F. Harvey, Kansas City, Missouri, 1904.
Harvey, Fred, *The Great Southwest Along the Santa Fe,* F. Harvey, Kansas City, Missouri, 1914.
Harvey, Fred, *Through the Southwest: Along the Santa Fe,* F. Harvey, Kansas City, Missouri, 1906.
Higgins, C. A., *Grand Canyon of Arizona: The Titan of Chasms,* Rand McNalley & Company, Chicago, 1915.
Photographic credits.

HAWKINS, DR. (?)
Jerome postcard photographer c. 1920.
Postcard imprint.

HAWKINS PHOTOGRAPHER
Grand Canyon, Arizona Territory c. 1899.

HAYMAKER, H. L.
Phoenix, Arizona Territory. Partner of Hartwell c. 1898. Listed as Hammaker on some imprints and in business directory listings.

HAYNES, WILLIS P.
Tucson, Arizona Territory c. 1880s.
Photographic mount imprint.

HEATH, CHARLES E.
Phoenix and Tucson c. 1912-25. Listed as Heath Studios, Board of Trade building at Adams and 2nd Ave.
1913-20 directories.
Photographic mount imprint.

HEATH STUDIO
Tucson c. 1914. Operated in AUOW building, Miss Anna Hulbert manager.

HEATH STUDIOS
Phoenix c. 1913-20. Operated by Charles Heath, Board of Trade building at Adams and 2nd Ave.

HEGEMAN, ELIZABETH COMPTON
Phoenix, Arizona Territory c. 1897.
1897 directory.

HEISTER, HENRY T.
Santa Fe, New Mexico primary location. Photographed Fort Defiance, Arizona Territory and within the Navajo reservation c. 1877-78.
Stereograph mount imprint.

HEUTHEN, (?)
Tucson, Arizona Territory. Operated at 271-75 S. Meyer Street c. 1910.

HICKSON, C. L.
Yuma, Arizona Territory c. 1907-20. Operated in partnership Hickson & Quint c. 1912 .
1907 Arizona Business Directory, Gazetteer Publishing Company, p. 711.
1909-10 Arizona Business Directory.

HICKSON, J. C.
Polk's Arizona and New Mexico Directory for 1912-13.

HILDRETH, JAMES
Flagstaff, Arizona Territory c. 1884. Itinerant from Utah in partnership with Burge in June 1884 in Flagstaff gallery, then as itinerant again c. 1886. Apparently continued independently in Flagstaff after Burge left. Also listed in Bisbee, Arizona Territory c. 1888.
Photograph mount imprints.

HILL, MRS. W. H.
Bisbee, Arizona Territory c. 1910. Purchased studio from Hugh Green.
Vaughn, Thomas, "A Guide to the Photographic Archives of the Bisbee Mining and Historical Museum," *The Cochise Quarterly,* Vol. 19, No. 2, Summer 1989, p. 26.

HILLERS, JOHN K.
Born in Hanover, Germany 1843; died in Washington, D.C., 1925. Worked on J. W. Powell's second survey of the Grand Canyon. Replaced E. O. Beaman as photographer c. 1872. Worked with Powell through 1878. Also photographer on the 1879 expedition into the Southwest for the U.S. Geological Survey and later surveys for the Bureau of American Ethnology of the Smithsonian Institution as chief photographer, retiring in 1900.
Fowler, Don, *Photographed All the Best Scenery: Jack Hillers' Diary of the Powell Expeditions 1871-1875,* University of Utah Press, Salt Lake City, 1972.
Fowler, Don D., *The Western Photographs of John K. Hillers: "Myself In The Water,"* Smithsonian Institution Press, Washington, D.C., 1989.
The Powell Expeditions, 1871-1875, Don D. Fowler, ed., University of Utah Press, Salt Lake City, 1972.

HINSHAW, THOMAS E.
From Utah with Orson Huish, traveled through Arizona in 1899 making stereographs and portraits.

HOLFSTEAD
Tombstone, Arizona Territory c. 1888. Partner in Fly & Holfstead.
  Polk Gazetteer.

HOLLAND, LEON H.
Mesa c. 1915. Operated at 51 ½ MacDonald.
  1915 directory.

HOOPES, H. E.
From Medina, Pennsylvania. Traveled with A. C. Vroman in August 1903 through Arizona and New Mexico.
  See A. C. Vroman.

HORNER, HARRY H.
Tucson, Arizona Territory. Itinerant operating c. 1891.

HORTON, J.
Prescott, Arizona Territory c. 1885.
  Photographic mount.

HOUGH, WALTER
Born 1859; died 1935. Archeological researcher c. 1898. Photographer for the Gates U.S. National Museum survey, 1901.
  Hough, Walter, *Antiquities of the Upper Gila and Salt River Valleys in Arizona and New Mexico,* Government Printing Office, Washington, D.C., 1907.
  Hough, Walter, *Archaeological Field Work in Northeastern Arizona: The Museum Gates Expedition of 1901,* Government Printing Office, Washington, D.C., 1903.
  Hough, Walter, "Environmental Interrelations in Arizona," *American Anthropologist,* May, 1898.
  Hough, Walter, "Pueblo Environment," 1906, *Science,* Vol. XXIII, No. 597, pp. 865-869, June 8, 1906.
  Hough, Walter, "Sio Shalako at First Mesa," *American Anthropologist,* Vol. 19, No. 3, July/September 1917.
  Hough, Walter, *The Moki Snake Dance; A Popular Account of That Unparalleled Dramatic Pagan Ceremony of the Pueblo Indians of Tusayan, Arizona, With Incidental Mention of Their Life and Customs,* Passenger Department, Santa Fe Railroad, Chicago, 1901.

HOUSEWORTH, THOMAS
Born in New York, June 21, 1828; died in San Francisco, California, April 13, 1915. Stereo publisher and photographer, 1856-93. Photographed Yumas and Pimas as part of Arizona Indians series, also San Carlos agency subjects. Images are primarily studio portraits, whether taken in Arizona or in California studios is uncertain.

Palmquist, Peter E., *Lawrence & Houseworth / Thomas Houseworth & Co.: A Unique View of the West, 1860-1886,* National Stereoscopic Association, Columbus, Ohio, 1980.
Stereograph mount imprints.

HRDLICKA, ALES
1912 Smithsonian physical anthropologist documented Apache and Pima (1905), and Pueblo, Hopi, and Navajo (1908).
  Photographic credit, Smithsonian Institution.

HUISH, ORSON
From Utah with Thomas Hinshaw, traveled through Arizona in 1899 making stereographs and portraits.

HULBERT, MISS ANNA
Tucson c. 1914. Manager of Heath Studio in AUOW building.

HUMPHRIES, WILFRED R.
Born in England, c. 1876. Active in Prescott, Arizona Territory c. 1902, partner in the Arizona Photograph Company, Inc. in Prescott with Erwin Baer, Percival Armitage, Tom Bate and A. E. Suppinger c. 1903. Bisbee, Arizona Territory photographer from 1903. Operated Humphries Photo Company at Copper Queen Hotel in Bisbee c. 1904-05. Continued to visit Bisbee from El Paso, Texas. studio until c. 1909. Produced photographs, and photographic and printed postcards of Bisbee and Cochise County.
  Photograph mount and postcard imprints.

HUNT, ORRIS P.
Parked railroad car on siding in Bisbee, January, 1896. Advertised "The San Francisco Photograph Car" domiciled near roundhouse is doing a good business at present.
  Vaughn, Thomas, "A Guide to the Photographic Archives of the Bisbee Mining and Historical Museum," *The Cochise Quarterly,* Vol. 19, No. 2, Summer 1989, p. 31.

HUNTER, EDWARD
Flagstaff, Arizona Territory beginning c. 1887. Operator for Baer's Flagstaff gallery c. 1887. Later operated Hunter's Art Parlor in Flagstaff.
  Hooper, Bruce, "Arizona Territorial Stereography 1864-1906," Part IV, *Stereo World,* National Stereoscopic Association, Vol. 13, No. 4, September/October 1986, p. 26.

IRWIN, ELLYE
Mesa, Arizona Territory c. 1899-1920.
  1907 Arizona Business Directory, Gazetteer Publishing Company, p. 710.
  1909-10 directory.

IRWIN, JOHN
Bisbee Arizona Territory c. 1903 as partner with brothers
Marvin and William.

> Vaughn, Thomas, "A Guide to the Photographic
> Archives of the Bisbee Mining and Historical Museum,"
> *The Cochise Quarterly*, Vol. 19, No. 2, Summer 1989, p. 29.

IRWIN, MARVIN E.
Born in Lometa, Texas c. 1881; died 1961. Active in Bisbee,
Arizona Territory c. 1903, as assistant to brothers John and
William. Operated studio in Douglas c. 1912-45 at 927 G Ave.

> Vaughn, Thomas, "A Guide to the Photographic
> Archives of the Bisbee Mining and Historical Museum,"
> *The Cochise Quarterly*, Vol. 19, No. 2, Summer 1989, p. 29.

IRWIN STUDIO
Douglas, Arizona Territory. Operated by Marvin E. Irwin,
c. 1912–45. Associated with Ambrose W. Carson, 1911–15.

> Vaughn, Thomas, "A Guide to the Photographic
> Archives of the Bisbee Mining and Historical Museum,"
> *The Cochise Quarterly*, Vol. 19, No. 2, Summer 1989,
> pp. 25, 29.

IRWIN, WILLIAM EDWARD
Born in Red Oak, Missouri c. 1871; died in Douglas, Arizona, 1935. Active in Bisbee, Arizona Territory beginning c.
1904. Learned photography in Texas c. 1893, operated galleries in Chickasha, Oklahoma and Silver City, New Mexico, then to Bisbee c. 1904-22. Listed in P. O. Building,
Bisbee, c. 1905, Jacob Schmidt Bldg., Bisbee c. 1907. Jakob
(sic)- Schmidt Bldg. c. 1909. Renovated McPhearson Building as studio in 1913 and operated until 1922.

> *1905 Polk Gazetteer.*
> *1907 Arizona Business Directory*, Gazetteer Publishing
> Company, p. 710.
> 1909-10 directory.
> Photograph mount imprints.

IVES, LIEUTENANT JOSEPH CHRISTMAS
Expedition leader and photographer on Colorado River
expedition c. 1857. May have been one of the first photographers to work in Arizona.

> Ives, Joseph Christmas, *Steamboat Up the Colorado: From the
> Journal of Lieutenant Joseph Christmas Ives, United States
> Topographical Engineers, 1857-1858*, Alexander L. Crosby,
> ed., Little, Brown and Company, Boston, 1965.
> Ives, Joseph C., *United States Army Corps of Topographical
> Engineers Report Upon the Colorado River of the West, Explored
> in 1857 and 1858*, Government Printing Office,
> Washington, D.C., 1861.

JACKSON, WILLIAM HENRY
Born in Keeseville, New York, April 4, 1843; died in New
York, June 30, 1942. Photographed in Wyoming, Yellow-
stone, 1870–78, and the lost cities of the southwest in Arizona and New Mexico (Hopi pueblos) in 1875 and 1879.
Photographed in Mexico for Mexico Central Railway in
1883. Photographed Flagstaff and San Francisco Mountains
c. 1881.

> Jackson, William Henry, *The Canons of Colorado: From
> Photographs by W. H. Jackson*, Frank S. Thayer, Denver c. 1890.

JAMES, GEORGE WHARTON
Born 1858; died 1923. Anthropologist and photographer
active in Grand Canyon, Hopi pueblos, and northern Arizona c. 1895-1901 producing stereographs and prints.

> Collection of Southern California Historical Society
> and Southwest Museum, Los Angeles.
> James, George Wharton, *Arizona, The Wonderland: The History
> of its Ancient Cliff and Cave Dwellings, Ruined Pueblos, Conquest
> by the Spaniards, Jesuit and Franciscan Missions, Trail Makers and
> Indians; A Survey of its Climate, Scenic Marvels, Topography,
> Deserts, Mountains, Rivers and Valleys; A Review of its Industries;
> An Account of its Influence on Art, Literature and Science; And Some
> Reference to What it Offers of Delight to the Automobilist, Sportsman,
> Pleasure and Health Seeker*, Page Company, Boston, 1917.
> James, George Wharton, *In & Around the Grand Canyon:
> The Grand Canyon of the Colorado River in Arizona*, Little,
> Brown and Company, Boston, 1900.
> James, George Wharton, *The Grand Canyon of Arizona:
> How to See It*, Little, Brown and Company, Boston, 1910.
> James, George Wharton, *The Indians of the Painted Desert
> Region; Hopis, Navahoes, Wallapais, Havasupais*, Little, Brown
> and Company, Boston, 1903.
> Wild, Peter, *George Wharton James*, Wayne Chatterton and
> James H. Maguire, eds., Boise State University, Boise,
> 1990.

JARVIS, CHARLES
Active in Arizona c. 1896 (from photo credit, National
Archives), also listed in St. Johns, Arizona Territory c. 1907.

> *1907 Arizona Business Directory*, Gazetteer Publishing
> Company, p. 711.

JENKINS, S. P.
Central, Arizona Territory c. 1905-10.

> *1905 Polk Gazetteer.*
> *1907 Arizona Business Directory*, Gazetteer Publishing
> Company, p. 710.
> *1909-10 Arizona Directory.*

JENNINGS, (?)
Partner of Charles Allen as itinerant photographers c. 1898.
Sold 450 negatives to Albert S. Reynolds c. 1899.

> Arizona Historical Society, Tucson, photographer listing.

JENNINGS, E. M.
Prescott, Arizona Territory c. 1870s possibly as late as 1890s. Advertised "E. M. Jennings, Photographer, Prescott, Arizona. Views of the following sections of the Territory: Prescott and vicinity, all prominent mining camps, Walnut Grove Lake, Camp Verde and Vicinity, Hot Springs (Castle Creek), Flagstaff and vicinity, Natural Bridge (Tonto Basin), Apache, San Carlos and other posts, Fort Grant and vicinity, Cliff Dwellings on Beaver Creek, Walnut Canyon and Oak Creek, Tip Top and vicinity, Grand Canyon of the Colorado, Ec. Ec. (sic.) Ask for catalogue."
   Photographic mount imprints.

JENNINGS, M.
Prescott, Arizona Territory c. 1885.
   Cabinet card imprint from view of Camp Grant in 1885.

JOHNSON, CHARLES GRANVILLE
Born 1832; died 1914. Active in Colorado City (Ft. Yuma), Arizona Territory c. 1863-68. In La Paz per 1864 census. Produced Views of Arizona and the Colorado River, San Francisco, California 1868. Photograph mounts printed "The Arizonian, Entered according to act of Congress in the year 1868, in the Clerk's Office of California, by Chas. G. Johnson, Photographer, San Francisco, Cal." Also published pamphlets illustrated with images of Arizona c. 1869. Operated a tent gallery with W. P . Gillingham in Clifton c. 1888.
   Photographic mount imprints.

JOHNSON, K. M.
Tempe c. 1918. Operated at 417 Mill Ave.
   1918 directory.

JOHNSON, N. E.
Oatman, Arizona Territory c. 1910-20. Also Parker.
   Postcard and panoramic photograph imprints.

JONES, J. C.
Clifton, Arizona Territory c. 1899.
   1899 directory.

JONES, LEWIS
Bisbee, Arizona Territory c. 1898. Operated Great Western View Company in partnership with Kennat. Also listed in Naco, Arizona Territory.
   1898 directory.

JUDD, NEIL M.
Photographed northern Arizona with Scott Young in 1908-09.
   Photo citation, Smithsonian Museum of American History.

KELLEY, E. W.
Active 1890s to 1910s in Chicago, Illinois. Listed as Kelley & Chadwick Publishers, produced stereographs of Grand Canyon c. 1906.
   Stereograph mount imprint.

KELLEY, ROY F.
Miami from c. 1914-55. As Kelley Studios, employed A. J. and W. T. Mullarkey as operators.
   Photograph mount and postcard imprints.

KEMP & COLEMAN
Tombstone, Arizona Territory c. 1881. Operated gallery on Allen Street.
   1881 Arizona Business Directory and Gazetteer, p. 179.
   1881 Polk Gazetteer.

KEMP, EDWARD H.
Grand Canyon and Hopi Pueblos c. 1905. Operated in San Francisco, produced lantern slides of Snake Dance and Grand Canyon. Images published by Santa Fe Railroad.
   McLuhan, T. C., *Dream Tracks, The Railroad and the American Indian 1890-1930*, Harry N. Abrams, Inc., New York, 1985.

KENNAT, (?)
Bisbee, Arizona Territory c. 1898. Operated Great Western View Company in partnership with Jones and Lewis. Also listed in Naco, Arizona Territory.
   1898 directory.

KEY & TEISMAN
Bisbee, Arizona Territory. Licensed as itinerant November 1909.
   Vaughn, Thomas, "A Guide to the Photographic Archives of the Bisbee Mining and Historical Museum," *The Cochise Quarterly*, Vol. 19, No. 2, Summer 1989, p. 31.

KEY, W. H.
Globe, Arizona Territory c. 1907.
   1907 Arizona Business Directory, Gazetteer Publishing Company, p. 710.

KEYS PHOTO STUDIO
Benson, Arizona Territory c. 1909-10.
   1909-10 Arizona Directory.

KINNEY, (?)
Prescott, Arizona Territory c. 1870s. Listed as photographer, was hung below Grapevine Station, 1878.
   Photographers listing, Arizona Historical Foundation.

KLINE, J. W.
Roosevelt, Arizona Territory.
> 1909-10 directory.

KOLB BROTHERS
Emery and Ellsworth Kolb, active in Williams, Arizona Territory c. 1901, then South Rim of the Grand Canyon. Operated studio at the Grand Canyon producing stereographs, mounted photographs and motion pictures.
> *1907 Arizona Business Directory,* Gazetteer Publishing
> Company, p. 710.
> Kolb Brothers, *The Grand Canyon of Arizona,* Kolb Brothers,
> Grand Canyon, Arizona, 1913.
> Kolb, Ellsworth, *Through the Grand Canyon from Wyoming to
> Mexico,* Macmillan Company, New York, 1914.
> Stereograph and photographic mount imprints.

KOLB, ELLSWORTH
Williams, Arizona Territory c. 1901, then South Rim of the Grand Canyon with brother Emery. Produced stereographs of river trips through the Grand Canyon in 1906 and 1911. Made motion pictures of the Hopi Snake Dance at Walpi in 1911 and 1913.
> *1907 Arizona Business Directory,* Gazetteer Publishing
> Company, p. 710.
> Kolb, Ellsworth, *Through the Grand Canyon from Wyoming to
> Mexico,* Macmillan Company, New York, 1914.

KOLB, EMERY
Williams, Arizona Territory c. 1901, then South Rim of the Grand Canyon with brother Ellsworth. Made motion pictures of the Hopi Snake Dance at Walpi in 1911 and 1913.
> *1907 Arizona Business Directory,* Gazetteer Publishing
> Company, p. 710.
> Kolb Brothers, *The Grand Canyon of Arizona,* Kolb
> Brothers, Grand Canyon, Arizona, 1913.

KOPPLIN, WILLIAM ERNEST
Photographer for the Santa Fe Railroad working in northern Arizona c. 1912. Produced lantern slides of Hopi and Navajo, and motion pictures of Hopi Snake Dance.
> McLuhan, Teri C., *Dream Tracks, The Railroad and the American
> Indian 1890-1930,* Harry N. Abrams, Inc., New York, 1985.

KORF, ABE M.
Tempe, Arizona Territory c. 1909-10. Also Phoenix c. 1912-13. Operated at 316 W. Washington.
> 1909-10 directory.
> *1912 Phoenix City and Salt River Valley Directory.*

KOVARICK, ALBERT J.
Ft. Grant, Arizona Territory c. 1890.

KUNSELMAN, ELTON E.
Phoenix c. 1916-17. Operated the Photocraft Shop at 1 Cactus Way.
> 1915-16 directories.

LA LUNA STUDIO
Tucson c. 1917-18. Operated by I. K. Wilson at 146 Stone.

LACY, W. A.
Bisbee, Arizona Territory c. 1905. Operated on Main St. in Bisbee.
> *Polk Gazetteer.*

LANGFORD, W. L.
Douglas, Arizona Territory c. 1904. Operated in Ragtown (Douglas).
> *Buck's Directory of Bisbee Arizona for 1904.*

LARA, VICENTE
Nogales c. 1912-13.
> *Polk's Arizona and New Mexico Directory for 1912-13.*

LARSON, OLAF P.
Moscow, Idaho photographer who worked in Arizona c. 1900. Photographed Bisbee, Jerome, Nogales, Phoenix, and mining subjects.
> Stereograph mount imprints.

LONG, C. C.
Phoenix, Arizona Territory c. 1903. Operated Elite Gallery at 218 W. Washington.
> *1907 Arizona Business Directory.*

LORING, (?)
Prescott, Arizona Territory c. 1878. Listed in partnership with George Rothrock.
> See George Rothrock.

LOW(E), M. W.
Douglas, Arizona Territory c. 1904. Operated as partner with C. L. Stubbs in Queen Studio on 11th Street, Douglas. Photographed 1908 Bisbee flood. Also, Globe, Arizona Territory c. 1908-10. Operated at 161 E. Oak.
> *1904 Bisbee Directory.*
> 1909-10 directory.
> Postcard imprint.

LUBKIN CO.
Mesa, Arizona Territory c. 1907.
> *1907 Arizona Business Directory,* Gazetteer Publishing
> Company, p. 710.
> Photographic mount and postcard imprints.

LUBKIN, WALTER
Official photographer for the construction of Roosevelt
Dam c. 1907-12. Operated out of Mesa, Arizona Territory.
> *1907 Arizona Business Directory,* Gazetteer Publishing
> Company, p. 710.
> Photographic mount and postcard imprints.

LUCAS & BURLAN
Clifton, 1885. Harry W. Lucas and partner.

LUCAS, HARRY W.
Arizona City (Yuma), Arizona Territory c. 1880 then to Silver City, New Mexico. Operated in Clifton as Lucas & Burlan
in 1885, then returned to Silver City, New Mexico in 1886.
> Rudisill, Richard, *Photographers of the New Mexico Territory,*
> *1854-1912,* Museum of New Mexico, 1973, p. 40.

LUMMIS, CHARLES
Photographed Hopi ceremonials in 1891.

LURLEY, MISS LUCY
Snowflake, Arizona Territory
> *1907 Arizona Business Directory,* Gazetteer Publishing
> Company, p. 711.

LYMAN, HARVEY O.
Tempe c. 1912-13.
> *Polk's Arizona and New Mexico Directory for 1912-13.*

MACDOUGAL, DR. DANIEL T.
Photographed deserts of Arizona for the Carnegie Desert
Laboratory (per photo credit).
> MacDougal, Daniel Trembly, "Delta of the Rio
> Colorado," *Bulletin of American Geographical Society,* American
> Geographical Society, January 1906.
> MacDougal, Daniel Trembly, "North-American Deserts, 1
> 912," *Geographical Journal,* Vol. XXXIX, No. 2, February 1912.

MALONE, D. T.
Phoenix c. 1915. Photographed Phoenix, Hayden, and vicinity.
> Postcard imprints.

MARKEY, DANIEL A.
Ft. Apache, Arizona Territory in partnership with Myton
in 1885. Photographed San Carlos, Arizona Territory c. late
1880s (also listed as C. A. Merkey (sic) in photo credit).
Arrived in Bisbee as itinerant with Backstein (sic) c. 1895.
Operated own studio on Upper Main Street beginning 1895.
Listed as Markey's Studio to c. 1900.
> Cabinet card imprints.
> Vaughn, Thomas, "A Guide to the Photographic
> Archives of the Bisbee Mining and Historical Museum,"
> *The Cochise Quarterly,* Vol. 19, No. 2, Summer 1989, p. 29.

MARKS, C. W.
Morenci, Arizona Territory c. 1907. Possibly active as early
as 1895 per photo credit.
> Photographic mount imprint.
> *1907 Arizona Business Directory,* Gazetteer Publishing
> Company, p. 710.

MARMELEJO, GEORGE
Bisbee, Arizona Territory c. 1898. Operated Wigwam Photo.
> Vaughn, Thomas, "A Guide to the Photographic
> Archives of the Bisbee Mining and Historical Museum,"
> *The Cochise Quarterly,* Vol. 19, No. 2, Summer 1989, p. 29.

MARTIN, A. L.
Williams, Arizona Territory c. 1895.
> Photo mount imprint.

MARY ANN STUDIO
Winslow.
> Photo citation Smithsonian Museum of American
> History.

MASON, JANIE ELLIS
Wife of officer stationed at Ft. Apache.
> Photo credit in album and citation Smithsonian
> Museum of American History.

MATTESON, SUMNER
Born September 15, 1867; died 1920. Traveled and photographed throughout the Southwest visiting the Hopi in
1901 and 1902.
> Fleming, Paula Richardson, and Judith Luskey, *The North*
> *American Indians in Early Photographs,* Harper and Rowe,
> New York, 1986.

MAUDE, FREDERICK HAMER
Photographer from Los Angeles, friend of G. W. James.
Photographed the Grand Canyon and Hopi ceremonials on
annual trips beginning c. 1895.

MAUDLIN, WILLIAM E.
Miami c. 1912-13. Advertised as "Watchmaker, Jeweler and
Photographer."
> *Polk's Arizona and New Mexico Directory for 1912-13.*

MCCULLOCH, JASPER M.
Phoenix c. 1912-46. Operated at 9 E. Washington c. 1912,
then as McCulloch Brothers Inc. at 18 N. 2nd Ave.
> *Polk's Arizona and New Mexico Directory for 1912-13.*
> 1916 directory.

MCCULLOCH, WILLIAM PATRICK
Born 1880; died 1971. Active in Phoenix c. 1916-46 as

McCulloch Brothers Inc. at 18 N. 2nd Ave.
  1912 directory.

McKenna, William

Prescott, Arizona Territory. Possible operator of Cook's gallery in August 1874 prior to sale of studio to Williscraft. Also studio operator for Buehman in Tucson. Possibly active as late as 1877 per photo credit.
  Photographic mount imprint.

Mealey, M. W.

Phoenix, Arizona Territory c. 1897-1910. Operated Mealey's New York Studio at 213 E. Washington c. 1899-1900. Studio transitioned to J. A. Westburg. Opened another studio at 29 S. 2nd c. 1909.
  1897-1910 directories.
  Photographic mount imprints.

Mealey Studio

Phoenix, Arizona Territory c. 1908, also operated at 29 S. 2nd, Phoenix c. 1910.
  1909-10 directory.
  Photographic mount imprint.

Mealey, W. P.

Phoenix, Arizona Territory c. 1898 with M. W. Mealey.
  1898 directory.

Mearns, Edgar A.

Born 1856; died 1916. Active in Arizona per photo citation, Smithsonian Museum of American History.
  Mearns, Edgar Alexander, *Mammals of the Mexican Boundary of the United States. A Descriptive Catalogue of the Species of Mammals Occurring in that Region; With a General Summary of the Natural History, and a List of Trees,* Government Printing Office, Washington, D.C., 1907.

Melhagen, O. H.

Bisbee, Arizona Territory c. 1900.
  Cabinet card and photographic mount imprints.

Melven, (?)

Flagstaff, Arizona Territory c. 1891-95. Operated as Melven Photo.
  Photographic credit.

Melvin, (?)

Tempe, Arizona Territory c. 1892. Operated on Mill Ave. as Burchard & Melvin.
  City of Phoenix Directory for 1892, Bensel Directory Company.

Mendeleff, Cosmos

Mishongnovi and Walpi, Arizona Territory Smithsonian ethnographer and photographer visiting Hopi Pueblos in August 1885.

Meriwether, Henry B.

Globe, Arizona Territory c. 1909-13. Operated as H. B. Meriwether & Co.
  1909-10 directory.
  Polk's Arizona and New Mexico Directory for 1912-13.

Messinger & Altenburgh

Phoenix, Arizona Territory c. 1895-98. Partnership of A. F. Messinger and William Altenburgh at 243 W. Madison.

Messinger, A. F.

Phoenix, Arizona Territory c. 1899-1900. Cabinet card imprint "A. F. MESSINGER, Viewest. Scenes in Phoenix and Salt River Valley. PHOENIX, ARIZONA" at 144 E. Adams. Listed in partnership Messinger & Altenburgh at 243 W. Madison, c. 1895–98.
  1899-1900 directory.
  Cabinet card imprints.

Michael & Shillcock

Flagstaff, Arizona Territory c. 1896. Itinerants operating out of Flagstaff.
  Hooper, Bruce, "Camera on the Mogollon Rim: 19th Century Photography in Flagstaff, Arizona Territory, 1867-1916," *History of Photography,* Vol. 12, No. 2, April 1988.

Middleton, F. W.

Holbrook, Arizona Territory Purchased photographic equipment in Flagstaff 1885, produced stereographs c. 1885-90.
  Stereograph mount imprint.

Miller, Andrew

Globe, Arizona Territory c. 1886 from Silver City, New Mexico then to Bisbee c. 1897. Photographed Apache Indians. Killed by Yaqui Indians August 3, 1899 in Sonora, Mexico.
  Cabinet card and boudoir imprints.
  Photo credit, National Archives.

Miller, J. MD

Arizona Territory c. 1898. Photographed Hopi pueblos and Snake Dance c. 1898 and published views.
  Imprint on photographs.

Miller, Victor

Cinematographer for *Pathe's Weekly* photographed Hopi Snake Dance at Walpi in 1913. Arrested after attempting to escape with the exposed film (which was confiscated) without signing non-commercial release.

Milo, (?)

Douglas c. 1919. Partner in Booth & Milo, studio on Florida near 11th.

MISSION STUDIOS
Yuma c. 1915. Images extant of Agua Caliente, Arizona.
   Photographic mount and postcard imprints.

MITCHELL, DANIEL FRANCIS
Born 1844. Active in Prescott, Arizona Territory c. 1877.
Left San Francisco for Prescott in December 1877. Took
over Williscraft gallery (Capital Art Gallery, on Cortez St.
North of the Courthouse) after a trip photographing
Mohave country. *Arizona Miner*, May 31, 1878, 4-1 lists
Mitchell as having Rothrock's "Arizona Views for sale in his
Gallery." Listed as photographer, Prescott. Also listed in
partnership with Baer. Active until at least 1883.
   Arizona Enterprise, July 20, 1878.
   Arizona Miner, May 31, 1878.
   McKenney's Business Directory 1882–83, p. 279.
   Stereograph and cabinet card imprints.

MODEL PHOTO GALLERY
Tucson Arizona Territory c. 1911-12. Operated at 102 S.
Stone by F. P. Sweet 1911, and by Oliver Cozby in 1912.

MONTFORT, E.
Marketed photographs of Arizona and New Mexico
c. 1885-95.
   Rudisill, Richard, *Photographers of the New Mexico Territory,*
      1854-1912, Museum of New Mexico, 1973, p. 43.

MOON, F. W.
San Carlos, Arizona Territory c. 1870s. Photographer sta-
tioned in San Carlos per note on reverse of photo: "F. W.
Moon, photographer, Company B, 11th U.S. Infantry, San
Carlos, Arizona. Views of Military post, Indian life, etc.
Always on hand. First class work guaranteed."
   Photographic mount notation.

MOON, KARL E.
Photographer for Santa Fe Railroad. Photographed Native
Americans in Arizona and throughout the Southwest up to
c. 1930.
   Moon, Karl E., *Photographic Studies of Indians*, El Tovar
      Studio, Fred Harvey, Grand Canyon, Arizona Territory,
      1910.

MOONEY, JAMES
1885-1921 Bureau of American Ethnology, photographed
Navajo in Arizona in course of his research.
   Photographic mount notation.

MOORE, SAMUEL
Douglas c. 1912-13. Operated at 713 G Ave.
   Polk's Arizona and New Mexico Directory for 1912-13.

MORA, JOSEPH
Born 1876; died 1947. Trained as a graphic artist. Traveled
from California to Arizona in 1904. Lived on the Hopi
reservation and documented ceremonial events and portraits
of participants in photographs and watercolors 1904-06.

MORRISON, R. E.
Tucson c. 1914. Operated at 102 S. Stone.

MORTIN, J.
Prescott, Arizona Territory itinerant c. 1884.

MOSSER, WILLIAM
Phoenix, Arizona Territory c. 1898.
   Polk Gazetteer.

MULLARKEY, A. J.
Miami. Employed by Roy F. Kelley.
   Photograph mount and postcard imprints.

MULLARKEY, W. T.
Miami. Employed by Roy F. Kelley.
   Photograph mount and postcard imprints.

MUSSEY, FRED B.
Phoenix, Arizona Territory c. 1898-1935. Operated Sunbeam
Studio, Gooding Bldg. and Mussey Studio. Also partnership with M. L. Davenport c. 1900 at 246 W. Washington.
   1907 Arizona Business Directory, Gazetteer Publishing
      Company, p. 711.
   1909-10 directory.
   1912 Phoenix City and Salt River Valley Directory.
   Photographic mount imprints.

NATIVE AMERICAN PHOTO COMPANY
Operated by surveyor photographer Richard W. Hammer.

NEMECK, LOUIS A.
Bisbee, Arizona Territory c. 1898. Opened studio on south
side of Upper Main Street. Sold studio c. 1902.
   Photo credits "Souvenir of Bisbee," 1904.
   Vaughn, Thomas, "A Guide to the Photographic Archives
      of the Bisbee Mining and Historical Museum," *The
      Cochise Quarterly*, Vol. 19, No. 2, Summer 1989, p. 29.

NEPHEW, J.
Bisbee, Arizona Territory c. 1901-04.
   Cabinet card imprint.

NEUMAN, WILLIAM J.
Nogales, Arizona Territory c. 1900-13. Advertised as pho-
tographer and manager of Lyric Motion Picture Theater.
   Polk's Arizona and New Mexico Directory for 1912-13.

NEW YORK GALLERY
Phoenix, Arizona Territory c. 1898. Operated by E. A. Bearce.
Polk Gazetteer.

NEW YORK PHOTO STUDIO
Phoenix, Arizona Territory c. 1897-1910. Operated by M. W.
Mealey c. 1898.
1909-10 directory.
Photographic mount imprint.

NEW YORK STUDIO
1899-1900 directory.

NEWMAN, WILLIAM J.
Active in Nogales, 1907–10.
1907 Arizona Business Directory, Gazetteer Publishing
Company, p. 711.
1909-10 directory.

NEWPORT, F. T.
Oracle, Arizona Territory c. 1909.
1909-10 directory

NIMS, FRANKLIN A.
Born in Eldorado, Kansas. Active c. 1869. Colorado Springs
c. 1870s. Photographer with 1889-90 Brown-Stanton expe-
dition down the canyon of the Colorado.
*The Photographer and the River, 1889-90 (the Diary of F. A.
Nims)*, Dwight L. Smith, ed., Stage Coach Press,
Santa Fe, New Mexico, 1967.

O'SULLIVAN, TIMOTHY
Born in Ireland; died in Staten Island, New York, January
14, 1882. Active c. 1857-80. Apprenticed with Matthew
Brady, worked with Gardner in Brady's Washington, D.C.
gallery c. 1856. Worked with Brady as assistant during Civil
War c. 1861. Joined Gardner c. 1862 as civilian photographers
of the war. Worked numerous surveys c. 1867-74. Wheeler
Survey photographer hired in 1871. He worked through
1875. Printed Wheeler Survey negatives under contract 1875-
76. In Tucson c. 1871 (per C. Altshuler) and Camp Mohave,
then into canyon with expedition.
Correspondence with Constance Altshuler.
Horan, James David, *Timothy O'Sullivan: America's Forgotten
Photographer: The Life and Work of the Brilliant Photographer
Whose Camera Recorded the American Scene from the Battlefields
of the Civil War to the Frontiers of the West*, Bonanza Books,
New York, 1966.
Stereograph imprints.

OSBON, CALVIN
Flagstaff, Arizona Territory c. 1891-97. Active c. 1900s Santa
Rosa, San Jose, and Fresno, California. Produced stereo-
graphs and imperial cabinet cards of Flagstaff, Arizona
Territory and imperial cabinet cards of Tucson and vicinity
and Grand Canyon c. 1890s. Photographed the Grand
Canyon and Bisbee c. 1910-17.
Photo credits, National Archives.
Photographic mount imprints.

PARKER & PARKER
San Diego c. 1873-75, Yuma, Arizona Territory in 1874.
Father and son partners Joseph C. Parker and Francis A.
Parker opened gallery on Main Street in Yuma in 1874.
Arizona Sentinel, April 4, 1874.

PARKER, FRANCIS A.
Yuma, Arizona Territory c. 1874. Co-founder of gallery with
father Joseph C. Parker.

PARKER, FRANCIS A.
Arizona Sentinel, April 4, 1874.

PARKER, JOSEPH C.
Yuma, Arizona Territory c. 1874. Co-founder of gallery with
son, Francis A. Parker. Returned to California, in Los Angeles c. 1877. Returned to Arizona c. 1889 with the Atlantic &
Pacific Railroad and worked in Flagstaff and Winslow. Also
operated photographic tent in Tucson c. 1899-1901. Listed
as partner in Atlantic & Pacific Portrait Co. c. 1902-11.
1899-1908 directories.

PARKER, W. B.
Tucson, Arizona Territory c. 1903-04. Operated photo-
graphic tent with Joseph Parker. Listed as partner in
Atlantic & Pacific Portrait Co. c. 1908.

PARKER, W. D.
Tucson, Arizona Territory c. 1901. Operated photographic
tent with Joseph Parker c. 1899-1901. Possibly same as W. B.
Parker.

PARKER, W. F.
Tucson, Arizona Territory c. 1899-1900. Operated photographic tent with Joseph Parker c. 1899-1900.

PARKERS, (?)
Tucson, Arizona Territory c. 1902-11. Listed as operators of
Atlantic Pacific View and Portrait Company, 6th & Broadway, Tucson.
1907 Arizona Business Directory, Gazetteer Publishing
Company, p. 711.
1909-10 directory.

PARTRIDGE, F. J.
Tucson, Arizona Territory Studio operator for Buehman
c. 1880.

PASEVITCH, JOSEPH
Flagstaff, Arizona Territory c. 1889.
>   Hooper, Bruce, "Camera on the Mogollon Rim:
>   Nineteenth Century Photography in Flagstaff, Arizona
>   Territory, 1867-1916," *History of Photography*, Vol. 12, No. 2,
>   April-June 1988, p. 96.

PAYNE, D. R.
Bisbee, Arizona Territory c. 1892. Photographer for 1892
border survey.
>   Vaughn, Thomas, "A Guide to the Photographic
>   Archives of the Bisbee Mining and Historical Museum,"
>   *The Cochise Quarterly*, Vol. 19, No. 2, Summer 1989, p. 32.

PEABODY, HENRY GREENWOOD
Born in St. Louis, Missouri, April 27, 1855; died in Glendo-
ra, California, March 27, 1951. Photographer for the Boston
& Maine Railroad and Detroit Publishing Co. out of Boston
1880s-1900, moved to California 1900. Photographed the
Grand Canyon c. 1896; Arizona Indians c. 1906. Possible continued activity around Grand Canyon into 1930s.
>   Peabody, Henry Greenwood, *Glimpses of the Grand Canyon
>   of Arizona*, F. Harvey, Kansas City, Missouri, 1902.
>   Photo credit, National Archives.

PENLON, HENRI
Died in Prescott, Arizona Territory, February 6, 1874.
Licensed as photographer in Los Angeles, May 1865. Partner
of D. P. Flanders during trip to Arizona in 1873. Flanders &
Penlon mounts issued by Flanders for images produced
throughout enterprise in Arizona.
>   Correspondence with Peter Palmquist.
>   Stereograph imprint.

PEREIRA, JOS.
Tucson c. 1919-20. Operated Pereira Studio at 136 E. Congress.

PEREIRA STUDIO
Tucson c. 1919-20. Operated at 136 E. Congress.

PERRINE, EDWARD I.
Bisbee, Arizona Territory c. 1903. Assistant to J. H. Coyle.
>   Cabinet card imprint.
>   Vaughn, Thomas, "A Guide to the Photographic Archives
>   of the Bisbee Mining and Historical Museum," *The
>   Cochise Quarterly*, Vol. 19, No. 2, Summer 1989, p. 30.

PERRY, OLIVER H.
Jerome c. 1912-13.
>   *Polk's Arizona and New Mexico Directory for 1912-13*.

PETERSON, JOSEPH
Snowflake, Arizona Territory c. 1907.
>   *1907 Arizona Business Directory*, Gazetteer Publishing Com-
>   pany, p. 711.

PHILLIPS, FENLEY W.
Hackberry, Arizona Territory c. 1890. Photographed Grand
Canyon, Williams, and vicinity.
>   Photographic mount imprints.

PHOTOCRAFT SHOP
Phoenix c. 1915-18. Located at 1 Cactus Way, operated by G.
B. Wilbur, c. 1915; by Elton E. Kunselman, c. 1916-17. The
name was changed to Elkin & Elkin by Lauren Elkin, c. 1918.
>   1915-16, 1918 directories.

PHOTOGRAPHIC ARTIST OLD GALLERY
Prescott, Arizona Territory c. 1875. Listed as N. of Courthouse.
>   *Prescott Miner*, August 20, 1875.

PIERCE, NATHAN PARDA
Born 1830; died 1911. Active in Prescott, Arizona Territory
c. 1869-72. Partner of F. A. Cook.
>   *Arizona Miner*, January 23, 1869.

POLLOCK, JEANETTE
Tempe c. 1916.
>   1916 directory.

PORTER, (?)
Tucson, Arizona Territory c. 1879. Partner of Alfred S. Addis.
>   *Arizona Daily Star*, October 17, 1879.

PORTILLO, JESUS
Phoenix c. 1918. Operated at 417 E. Madison.
>   1918-19 directories.

POWELL, CLEMENT
Assistant photographer 1871 Powell survey, cousin of Major
Powell.
>   Photo credit, National Archives.

PRESCOTT STUDIO
Prescott c. 1919-20. Operated at 119 E. Gurley by A. J.
Jennings.
>   *Tribby's City Directory of the City of Prescott for 1919*.

PRESTON, JOHN C.
Listed in 1870 Arizona census as Photographer, age 27,
originally from Alabama. Traveling Photographer 1880s.
>   1870 Arizona census.

PRIOR, N. W.
Listed in 1870 census as artist, age 30, from Virginia in
Williamson's Valley, near Prescott.
>   1870 Arizona census.

PUTNAM & VALENTINE
Photographed the Grand Canyon c. 1910.

Higgins, C. A, *Grand Canyon of Arizona: The Titan of Chasms,* Rand McNalley & Company, Chicago, Illinois, 1915. Photo Credit.

QUEEN STUDIO
Douglas, Arizona Territory c. 1904. Operated on 11th Street as partnership of M. W. Low and C. L. Stubbs. Operated by Hugh Ruth Carson c. 1907, at 529 11th.
> *1907 Arizona Business Directory,* Gazetteer Publishing Company, p. 710.
> *Buck's Directory of Bisbee Arizona for 1904.*
> Vaughn, Thomas, "A Guide to the Photographic Archives of the Bisbee Mining and Historical Museum," *The Cochise Quarterly,* Vol. 19, No. 2, 1989, p. 25.

QUICK FINISH KODAK CO.
Prescott c. 1919. Operated at 218 W. Gurley by Henry Bryant.
> *Tribby's City Directory of the City of Prescott for 1919.*

QUINT, ROY T.
Yuma c. 1912-13. Operated in partnership Hickson & Quint.
> *Polk's Arizona and New Mexico Directory for 1912-13.*

RANDALL, A. FRANK
Wilcox, Arizona Territory and traveling itinerant c. 1883-88. Some overlap in negatives and prints from Ft. Apache area with Ben Wittick, however specific authorship uncertain. In Las Cruces, New Mexico November 1885-May 1886.
> Boudoir card mount imprints.

RANDEBAUGH, J. D.
Williams, Arizona Territory operated gallery c. 1898, selling to the Kolb brothers in 1907.

RATCLIFF, C. E.
Williams c. 1920. C. E. Ratcliff Photos and Curios, Williams, Arizona.
> Postcard imprint.

RAUDELEAGH, OLIVER B.
Williams, Arizona Territory c. 1907. Also Flagstaff.
> *1907 Arizona Business Directory,* Gazetteer Publishing Company, p. 711
> Photo citation, Smithsonian Museum of American History.

RESLER, CALVIN A.
Buckeye c. 1914.
> Postcard imprints.

REYNOLDS, ALBERT S.
Photographed Tucson area, also Bisbee and Douglas c. 1898-1901, probably as serious amateur.
> Photo credits.

RHODES, JOHN. P.
Phoenix, Arizona Territory c. 1892-1906. Operated at 213 W. Washington.
> *Business Directory of Arizona/New Mexico,* Examiner Publishing Company, Las Vegas, New Mexico, 1897.
> Photograph mount imprints.

RINCKWITZ, RICHARD L.
Glendale c. 1918.
> 1918 directory.

RING, T. A.
Tucson c. 1917. Operated at 240 E. Congress.

RISDON, O. A.
Clifton and Metcalf, Arizona Territory c. 1900-16. Operated in Bisbee c. 1912-13.
> 1909-10 directory.
> Photograph mount and postcard imprints.

RISDON'S STUDIO
Clifton and Metcalf, Arizona Territory c. 1907.
> *1907 Arizona Business Directory.*
> Postcard imprints.

RISTELHEUBER, MR.
Bisbee, Arizona Territory c. 1902. Opened studio in Barnaby Building offering stamp photographs, button jewelry, copying and enlarging.
> Cabinet card imprint.
> Vaughn, Thomas, "A Guide to the Photographic Archives of the Bisbee Mining and Historical Museum," *The Cochise Quarterly,* Vol. 19, No. 2, Summer 1989, p. 30.

RISTELHEUBER, MRS.
Bisbee, Arizona Territory c. 1902. Opened studio in Barnaby Building offering stamp photographs, button jewelry, copying and enlarging.
> Cabinet card imprint.
> Vaughn, Thomas, "A Guide to the Photographic Archives of the Bisbee Mining and Historical Museum," *The Cochise Quarterly,* Vol. 19, No. 2, Summer 1989, p. 30.

ROBINSON, H. F.
Phoenix, Arizona Territory first president of Phoenix Camera Club in 1892.

RODRIGO, ADOLFO
Visited Prescott from Los Angeles in May, 1870. Operated a gallery in Tucson in July 1874 at the corner of Courthouse and Maiden Lane Streets, worked with Flanders during his 1874 excursion to southern Arizona. Also partner of Buehman, who operated the gallery prior to buying it in 1875.
> See Henry Buehman and Dudley P. Flanders.

ROGERS, CHARLES THOMAS
Born in Maine, 1827; died 1903. Active in Portland, Maine
c. 1850-52, Gardiner, Maine c. 1853, then in St. Louis. Missouri c. 1853-55. Arrived in Arizona c. 1863. Listed in 1864
Arizona census as photographer.
> 1864 Arizona census.
> Craig, John, *Craig's Daguerreian Registry,* John S. Craig,
> Tortington, Connecticut, 1994, p. 111.

ROSE, GEORGE LYMAN
Photographed petrified forest, Holbrook, and Winslow c.
1890. Produced stereographs of the Hopi.
> Higgins, C. A, *Grand Canyon of Arizona: The Titan of Chasms,*
> Rand McNalley & Company, Chicago, Illinois, 1915.

ROSKRUGE, GEORGE
Tucson, Arizona Territory c. 1880s. Partner of Buehman in
Buehman & Co. c. 1883. Also made photographs in Arizona
as a surveyor for the U.S. Surveyor General c. 1890.
> See Henry Buehman.

ROTHROCK, GEORGE H.
Born in Jefferson City, Missouri, March 1843. Operated a
gallery in Bakersfield California c. 1870-75, and as an itinerant
from 1876-78 after arriving in Yuma with Young, and alone
after Young's death in 1876. Established a gallery in Prescott
in January 1878 on Montezuma Street. In April 1878, formed
partnership with Loring and established a studio at the News
Depot, then at Loring's Bazaar. Partnership with Charles Barnett 1882-94. Moved gallery to Tempe in 1893, Rothrock and
Barnett then retired. *Arizona Miner,* May 31, 1878, lists Mitchell
as having Rothrock's "Arizona Views for sale in his Gallery."
Listed as RATHROCK (sic) photographer, Phoenix
(*McKenney's Business Directory, 1882-83,* p. 277). Traveled to Bisbee c. 1885. After leaving photography, Rothrock became a
farmer and worked for the Arizona Canal Company.
> *Arizona Miner,* May 31, 1878, 4-1.
> *McKenney's Business Directory 1882-83,* p. 277. Stereograph,
> carte-de-visite, photographic mount imprints.

ROWNTREE, W. A.
Tucson, Arizona Territory c. 1908-13. Operated at S. Stone
& Jackson. Possibly in Bisbee c. 1916-17.
> 1909-10 directory.
> *Polk's Arizona and New Mexico Directory for 1912-13.*

ROYAL STUDIO
Douglas c. 1919. Operated at 732 G Avenue.

RUSSELL, FRANK
Photographed on the Gila Reservation 1901-02.
> Photo mount imprint.

RUSSELL, WILLIAM F.
Phoenix c. 1914-17. Operated at 35 E. Washington.
> 1916-19 directories.

RYDEN & WESTBERG
Partnership in Phoenix, Arizona Territory c. 1907.
> *1907 Arizona Business Directory,* Gazetteer Publishing
> Company, p. 711.

RYDEN, (?)
Phoenix, Arizona Territory c. 1907. Listed as partner in
Ryden & Westberg.
> *1907 Arizona Business Directory,* Gazetteer Publishing
> Company, p. 711.

SADLER, GEORGE
Phoenix, Arizona Territory Listed as official photographer
for the 1910 Phoenix Aero Meet.

SAMANO, RAYMOND
Nogales, Arizona Territory c. 1906-07.

SANDERS, (?)
Photographed Walnut Canyon c. 1889.
> Photographic mount notation.

SATO, T.
Winslow c. 1912-13.
> *Polk's Arizona and New Mexico Directory for 1912-13.*

SAVAGE, CHARLES R.
Born in Southampton, England, August 16, 1832; died in Salt
Lake City, Utah, February 3, 1909. Active in New York City
c. 1850, then Council Bluffs, Iowa c. 1858-59. Reached Salt
Lake City on August 28, 1860. Founded Pioneer Art Gallery
with Marsella Cannon. Partnership dissolved c. 1861, with
Savage carrying on in the gallery. Partnership with George M.
Ottinger 1862-70. Gallery also known as Savage's Art Bazar
and Pioneer Art Bazar. Fire destroyed gallery and negative col-
lection June 21, 1883. Worked in Arizona c. 1872, 1875, 1877-79.
> Craig, John, *Craig's Daguerreian Registry,* John S. Craig,
> Tortington, Connecticut, 1994, p. 114.
> Stereograph mount imprints.

SCHOLEY, (?)
Arizona c. 1882, location unknown.
> Arizona Historical Society, Tucson, photographer listing.

SCHROEDER, (?)
Prescott, Arizona Territory. Assistant to Williscraft in
Prescott/Camp Verde, came from California in 1876. Possi-
ble alternate spelling of Schroeter.
> See William Williscraft.

SCHROETER, (?)
Ft. Huachuca, Arizona Territory c. 1885-90s. Also active in
Bisbee and Wilcox.
   Cabinet card imprints.

SCHWEMBERGER, SIMEON
Franciscan monk working in Gallup New Mexico and Win-
dow Rock area c. 1909, also St. Michaels.
   Photographic postcard credits.

SCOTT, (?)
Assistant to Flanders in Prescott, 1874.
   See Dudley Flanders.

SEXTON, JAMES H.
Phoenix c. 1917. Operated at 604 ½ W. Van Buren.
   1917 directory.

SHAW, C. H.
Phoenix, Arizona Territory c. 1900. Advertised "Arizona
Views", 26 and 30 N. 1st Ave. dated 3/6/1900. Pho-
tographed Hopi Snake Dance c. 1901.
   Photo mount notations.

SHILLCOCK, (?)
Flagstaff, Arizona Territory c. 1896. Listed as Michael &
Shillcock, itinerants in Flagstaff c. 1896.
   Hooper, Bruce, "Camera on the Mogollon Rim: 19th
      Century Photography in Flagstaff, Arizona Territory,
      1867-1916," *History of Photography*, Vol. 12, No. 2, April 1988.

SKELLEY, LOTE ADISON
Silver City, New Mexico c. 1888-98, also Globe, Arizona
Territory c. 1896-1907.
   Photographic mount imprints.

SKELLEY, MRS. ELLEN B.
Globe, Arizona Territory c. 1907.
   1907 Arizona Business Directory, Gazette Publishing Company,
      p. 710.

SLADSKY, CHARLES
Tucson, Arizona Territory Studio operator for Buehman
c. 1880.

SMITH & PEAT
Bisbee, Arizona Territory licensed as itinerants February 14,
1907.
   Vaughn, Thomas, "A Guide to the Photographic Archives
      of the Bisbee Mining and Historical Museum," *The
      Cochise Quarterly*, Vol. 19, No. 2, Summer 1989, p. 32.

SMITH, ERWIN E.
Born in Honey Grove, Texas c. 1886; died 1947. Photographed

cattle ranch life in Texas, Arizona, Mexico and New Mexico
c. 1900s. Worked on Col. Greene's ranch near Herford, Arizona Territory, summer 1909. Produced illustrated articles for
magazines such as the *Saturday Evening Post*.
   Rudisill, Richard, *Photographers of the New Mexico Territory,
      1854-1912*, Museum of New Mexico, 1973, p. 54.
   Vaughn, Thomas, "A Guide to the Photographic Archives
      of the Bisbee Mining and Historical Museum," *The
      Cochise Quarterly*, Vol. 19, No. 2, Summer 1989, p. 32.

SMITH, KNIGHT A.
Globe, Arizona Territory c. 1909.
   1909-10 directory.

SMITH, MRS. S. D.
Snowflake c. 1912-13. Advertised "Notions and Photography."
   Polk's Arizona and New Mexico Directory for 1912-13.

ST. CLAIR, EDWARD
Flagstaff, Arizona Territory. Operated St. Clair Photogaph
Gallery c. 1887-89.
   Polk Gazetteer.

ST. CLAIR PHOTOGRAPH GALLERY
Flagstaff, Arizona Territory 1887–89. Operated by Edward
St. Clair.

STACEY & COPELAND
Phoenix, Arizona Territory c. 1905-06.
   1905-06 directory.

STACEY, C. I.
Phoenix, Arizona Territory c. 1905-06.
   1905-06 directory.

STALEY, FRANK
Phoenix, A.T. c. 1910-15 postcard photographer.
   Postcard imprint.

STEPHENS, H. R.
Phoenix, Arizona Territory c. 1911. Advertised as "The
Hartwell Old Photographic Studio," 29 S. 2nd.
   1911-1913 directories.

STEVENSON, JAMES
Traveled on Powell survey 1879.
   Photo citation, Smithsonian Museum of American History.

STEVENSON, MAXILDA COXE
Born 1850; died 1915. Wife of James Stevenson of Powell sur-
vey, first in 1879, then returned and photographed Hopi and
Zuni in 1896-1909.
   Photo citation, Smithsonian Museum of American
      History.

STONE (?)
Flagstaff, Arizona Territory. Partner in Stone & Cox c. 1908.
Produced panoramic photographs.

STONE, FRED L.
Tucson, Arizona Territory c. 1908. Operated at 512 N. Stone.

STRAND STUDIO
Phoenix c. 1919.
   1919 directory.

STUART, W. F.
Flagstaff, Arizona Territory c. 1900-05. Also El Paso 1906-23.
   Photographic mount imprints.
   Rudisill, Richard, *Photographers of the New Mexico Territory,*
     1854-1912, Museum of New Mexico, 1973, p. 56.

STUBBS, C. L.
Douglas, Arizona Territory c. 1904. Operated as partner
with M. W. Low in Queen Studio on 11th Street, Douglas.
   Buck's Directory of Bisbee Arizona for 1904.

SUFEA, FRANK
Humboldt, Arizona Territory c. 1907. Also active in Prescott
c. 1912-13. Sufea Studio imprint but location of business
unknown.
   1907 Arizona Business Directory, Gazetteer Publishing
     Company, p. 710.

SUNBEAM STUDIO
Phoenix, Arizona Territory c. 1898-1900. Partnership
between F. Mussey and M. Davenport.
   Photographic mount imprints.

SUPPINGER, A. E.
Prescott, Arizona Territory as itinerant c. 1902. Documented mining and development of the Bradshaw mountains
producing photographic and printed materials. Partner in
the Arizona Photograph Company, Inc. in Prescott with
Erwin Baer, Percival Armitage, Tom Bate and W. R.
Humphries c. 1903.

SWEET, F. P.
Tucson Arizona Territory c. 1911. Operated Model Photo
Gallery at 102 S. Stone.

SYKES, GODFREY
Tucson, Arizona Territory c. 1910.
   Postcard imprint.

TABER, ISAAC W.
Operated studio in San Francisco, California 1864-1905,
marketed Grand Canyon views (possibly purchased from or
produced by other photographers).
   Photographic mount imprints.

TARR, J. A.
Kingman, Arizona Territory c. 1907.
   1907 Arizona Business Directory, Gazetteer Publishing
     Company, p. 710.

TAYLOR, GRACIE S.
Bylas.
   Photo citation Smithsonian Museum of American
     History.

TAYLOR, JAMES A.
Bisbee, Arizona Territory c. 1905. Operated on Brewery Ave.
Also Broadway and Brewery Ave. c. 1912-13.
   1905 Polk Gazetteer.
   1907 Arizona Business Directory, Gazetteer Publishing
     Company, p. 710.
   Polk's Arizona and New Mexico Directory for 1912-13.

TEISMAN, (?)
Bisbee, Arizona Territory. Listed as partner in Tiesman &
Key, licensed as itinerants November 1909.
   Vaughn, Thomas, "A Guide to the Photographic Archives
     of the Bisbee Mining and Historical Museum," *The
     Cochise Quarterly,* Vol. 19, No. 2, Summer 1989, p. 31.

THOMAS, CHARLES
Listed as photographer in Prescott in 1864 census, age 35,
from Maine, in Territory five months at that time.
   1864 Arizona census.

THWAITES, GEORGE H.
Globe, Arizona Territory c. 1907.
   1907 Arizona Business Directory, Gazetteer Publishing
     Company, p. 710.
   Photographic mount and postcard imprints.

TIBBETTS, H. C.
Produced photographic album and lantern slides of Roo-
sevelt Dam and Apache Trail. Listed as operating out of San
Francisco.
   Photographic credits.

TIESMAN & KEY
Bisbee, Arizona Territory licensed as itinerants 1905.
   Vaughn, Thomas, "A Guide to the Photographic Archives
     of the Bisbee Mining and Historical Museum," *The
     Cochise Quarterly,* Vol. 19, No. 2, Summer 1989, p. 32.

TILLOTSON, FRANK H.
   Polk's Arizona and New Mexico Directory for 1912-13.

TROTT, ANDREW. P.
Possibly active as an ambrotypist in Boston, Massachusetts c. 1859-60s. Operated in Junction City, Kansas c. 1875. Offered stereographs of Prescott and northwestern Arizona. Whether original photographer or acquired negatives through trade or purchase is yet to be determined. Identical images appear on Flanders and Mitchell mounts.
> Craig, John, *Craig's Daguerreian Registry*, John S. Craig, Tortington, Connecticut, 1994, p. 130.
> Stereograph mount imprints.

TRUAX, (?)
Winslow, Arizona Territory c. 1910.
> Photographic mount imprint.

TUCKER, C. H.
Flagstaff, Arizona Territory area c. 1890.
> Hooper, Bruce, "Camera on the Mogollon Rim: Nineteenth Century Photography in Flagstaff, Arizona Territory, 1867-1916," *History of Photography*, Vol. 12, No. 2, April-June 1988, p. 96.

TUCSON PHOTO CO.
Tucson c. 1912-13. Operated by N. G. Wallace at 29 S. Stone.

TURLEY, MISS LUCY
Snowflake, Arizona Territory c. 1909.
> 1909-10 directory.

TURNBULL, ROBERT A.
Phoenix, Arizona Territory c. 1909-16. Operated in partnership with John F. Westburg 1909-10, as Westburg & Turnbull at 213 E. Washington.
> 1909-10 directory.
> *1912 Phoenix City and Salt River Valley Directory.*
> Photographic mount and postcard imprints.

UPDIKE, LISLE CHANDLER
Phoenix, Arizona Territory 1906-76. Operated a number of portrait studios. Traveled throughout Arizona making photographs for sale in his studios.

VALENTINE
Partner in Putnam & Valentine. Photographed the Grand Canyon c. 1910.
> Higgins, C. A, *Grand Canyon of Arizona: The Titan of Chasms*, Rand McNalley & Co., Chicago, 1915.

VAN NESS, CARL
Phoenix, Arizona Territory. Operated gallery at 168-180 E. Washington c. 1901.

VROMAN, ADAM CLARK
Born in La Salle, Illinois, April 15, 1856; died 1916. Pasadena, California bookseller and photographer. Visited Hopi Pueblos in 1895 then returned over the next 10 years to photograph Hopi of northern Arizona and New Mexico.
> *Photographer of the Southwest: Adam Clark Vroman, 1856-1916*, Ruth I. Mahood, ed., Ward Ritchie Press, Los Angeles, California, 1961.
> Powell, Lawrence Clark, *Vroman's of Pasadena*, Pasadena, California, 1953.
> Webb, William, and Robert A. Weinstein, *Dwellers at the Source: Southwestern Indian Photographs of A. C. Vroman, 1895-1904*, Grossman Publishers, New York, 1973.

WASSON, C. L.
Photographer for International Stereograph Co. active in Southern Arizona at least in 1900 and 1907.
> Stereograph mount imprint.

WATKINS, CARLETON
Born in Oneonta, New York, November 11, 1829; died in San Francisco, California, June 23, 1916. Photographed in Arizona in 1880 for Southern Pacific Railroad April 10-May 18. Images include cactus and scenics, Charleston, Arizona Territory , Tombstone, Tucson, Yuma, and vicinities. Issued stereographs on the following mounts; "Watkins New Pacific Coast Series," (nos. 4837-4831); "Watkins New Series, Yosemite and Pacific Coast, 26 Montgomery Street, and Woodward Gardens, S. F." (two titles but no numbers identified to date); and "Watkins New Series of Pacific Coast Views, 427 Montgomery Street, S. F., Photographic Views of California, Oregon, Nevada, Arizona, Lower California, and the Pacific Coast Embracing Yosemite, Big Trees, Geysers, Mount Shasta Mining, City, . . ." (nos. 4842-4922 plus several unnumbered). Also offered cabinet and boudoir format images of Arizona.
> Palmquist, Peter E., *Carleton E. Watkins, Photographer of the American West*, Amon Carter Museum, University of New Mexico Press, Albuquerque, New Mexico, 1983.
> Stereograph and cabinet card imprints.

WEBSTER, LEONARD A.
Ray c. 1912-13.
> *Polk's Arizona and New Mexico Directory for 1912-13.*

WEED ART STUDIO
Tucson c. 1920. Operated at 129 S. Stone.

WEED, WILLIAM L.
Tucson c. 1920. Operated Weed Art Studio at 129 S. Stone. Previously associated with Buehman studio.

WENFOR, GEORGE
Phoenix, Arizona Territory Operated on Jefferson St. (possibly misspelling of Wonfor).
Advertisement.

WESTBURG, JOHN F.
Phoenix, Arizona Territory c. 1907-12. Operated Westburg Studio superseding Mealey Studio at 213 E. Washington c. 1908. Also in partnerships with Ryden & Westberg c. 1907, Turnbull 1909-10, as Westburg & Turnbull, 213 E. Washington, Phoenix.
1908-10 directories.

WESTGARD, A. L.
Ehrenberg, Arizona Territory c. 1911.

WHITE, C. L.
Traveled with Charles Clark on his Projectoscope Tour showing motion pictures throughout Arizona c. 1898. Fell from a train in Holbrook, his legs were mangled and he died several days later from the injuries.

WILBUR, G. B.
Phoenix c. 1915. Operated the Photocraft Shop at 1 Cactus Way.
1915 directory.

WILCOX, GEN. TIMOTHY E.
1887-91 photographed Apaches.
Photograph credit.

WILLIAMS, R.
Pima, Arizona Territory c. 1907.
1907 Arizona Business Directory, Gazetteer Publishing Company, p. 711.

WILCOX, H. H.
Tucson, Arizona Territory c. 1908. Manager of Elite Studio.

WILLIAMS, JOHN RODERICK
Safford, Arizona Territory c. 1900-1917. Also, Globe c. 1904. Produced views of mining and Globe area including February 17, 1904 flood. No imprint but manuscript titling and credits on some mounts.
1907 Arizona Business Directory, Gazetteer Publishing Company, p. 711.
1909-10 directory.
Stereograph and cabinet card mount imprints.

WILLIAMS STUDIO
Operated by Thomas F. Williams in Phoenix c. 1916-17.

WILLIAMS, THOMAS F.
Phoenix c. 1916-17. Operated the Williams Studio at 223 E. Washington.
1916-17 directories.

WILLISCRAFT, WILLIAM HAMILTON
Prescott, Arizona Territory c. 1875. Boot and shoe maker who purchased the local gallery and hired an operator to run a photograph studio making tintypes. Purchased Cook's gallery in Prescott in 1875, opened a short time, then closed until April 1876. Used assistant, Schroeder, and on May 5, 1876 began using a traveling gallery on wheels. Moved his gallery to Camp Verde November 11, 1876. Flying Gallery notation. Also Williscraft & Company Photographer notation.
Stereograph mount imprints.

WILSON, I. K.
Tucson c. 1913-20. Operated at 146 Stone c. 1913-17, as La Luna Studio at 146 Stone c. 1917-19, and as Wilson Studio at 19 Stone Ave. c. 1919-20.

WILSON, MRS. LAWRENCE
Phoenix, Arizona Territory c. 1903-19. Operated at 5 S. 2nd in 1907-10. Also at 29 W. Jefferson c. 1912.
1907 Arizona Business Directory, Gazetteer Publishing Company, p. 711.
1909-10 directory.
1912 Phoenix City and Salt River Valley Directory.

WILSON STUDIO
Tucson c. 1919-20. Operated at 19 Stone Ave.

WITTICK, GEORGE BEN
Born in Huntington, Pennsylvania, January 1, 1845; died August 30, 1903. Served in the Army at Ft. Snelling, Minnesota c. 1861. Studio in Moline, Illinois late 1870s. Came to Santa Fe c. 1878. Partnerships with W. P. Bliss, and R. W. Russell. Partnership with R. W. Russell c. 1880-84. Moved studio to Albuquerque in March 1881. Traveled to Arizona on the A. & P. Railroad, photographing Flagstaff (c. 1884) and northern Arizona. Traveled with Matilde Coxe Stevenson on her ethnographic survey of Arizona in 1881. Some overlap in negatives and prints from Ft. Apache area with A. Frank Randall, however specific authorship uncertain. Partnership with J. C. Burge in Flagstaff c. 1885. Gallery in Gallup, New Mexico, 1884-1900.
Broder, Patricia Janis, *Shadows on Glass: The Indian World of Ben Wittick*, Rowman & Littlefield, Savage, Maryland, 1990.
Packard, Gar, and Maggy Packard, *Southwest 1880 With Ben Wittick, Pioneer Photographer of Indian and Frontier Life*, Packard Publications, Santa Fe, New Mexico, 1970.
Rudisill, Richard, *Photographers of the New Mexico Territory, 1854-1912*, Museum of New Mexico, 1973, pp. 62-63.
Stereograph and boudoir mount imprints.

WONFOR, GEORGE H.
Landscape painter from St. Louis. In Albuquerque, December 1888, partnership with W. Calvin Brown, then to Las Vegas, Chloride, then Las Cruces, New Mexico through January 1890. Tucson c. 1890 with Gallery on E. Congress St. advertised as "George H. Wonfor Artistic Photographer."
   Cabinet card imprints.

WOOD, H. E.
Nogales c. 1917. Photographer with Troop F of the 1st U. S. Cavalry.

WOOSTER, GEORGE N.
Prescott.
   Photo citation, Smithsonian Museum of American
      History.

WORTH, L. W.
Prescott, Arizona Territory c. 1869. Probable partner of F. A. Cook.
   See Francis Cook.

YOUNG, (?)
Came to Yuma, Arizona with Rothrock in 1876. They opened a tent gallery offering ambrotypes, cartes-de-visite, cabinets, and stereoviews, also in March 1876, held sciopticon exhibitions. Rothrock and Young met in Phoenix in late 1876, but Young died of pneumonia soon thereafter.
   See George Rothrock.

YOUNG, R. Y.
Operator for American Stereoscopic Co. founded in 1898. 1903-07 photographed petrified forest, Clifton, Morenci. Photographs published by American Stereoscopic Company.
   Stereograph mount imprint.

YOUNG, SCOTT M.
With Neil M. Judd, photographed northern Arizona in 1908-09.
   Photo citation, Smithsonian Museum of American
      History.

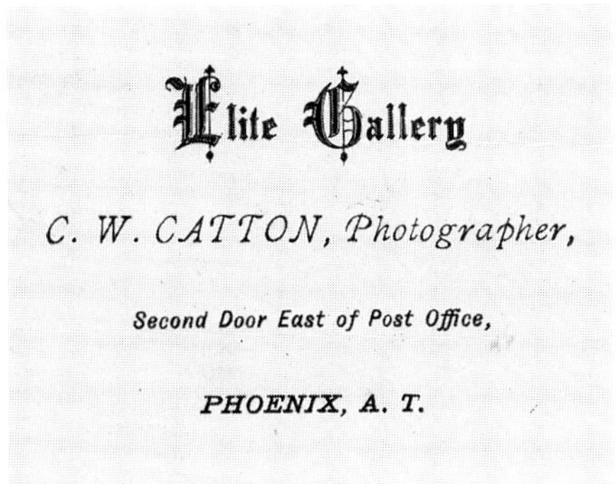

ADAMSVILLE
Gentile, Charles
(Carlos) G.

BENSON
Fraesdorf, William
Keys Photo Studio

BISBEE
Anthony, F.
Ballinger, L. A.
Banner, R.
Beckstein, (?)
Bell, George V.
Borough, E. B.
Carson, Ambrose W.
Carson, Hugh Ruth
Cooley, Ben D.
Coyle, John H.
Dix, George C.
Donaldson, M. D.
Dowe, D. W.
Eastman, (?)
Feldman, Frederick J.
Fetter, W. L.
Fly, Camilius S.
Fly, Mrs. Mary E.
Fonderman, O.
Graves, G. A.
Great Western View
Company
Green, W. Hugh A.
Guen, Hugh
Hildreth, James
Hill, Mrs. W. H.
Humphries, Wilfred R.
Hunt, Orris P.
Irwin, John
Irwin, Marvin E.
Irwin Studio
Irwin, William Edward

Jones, Lewis
Kennat, (?)
Key & Teisman
Lacy, W. A.
Larson, Olaf P.
Low, M. W.
Markey, Daniel A.
Marmelejo, George
Melhagen, O. H.
Nemeck, Louis A.
Nephew, J.
Osbon, Calvin
Payne, D. R.
Perrine, Edward I.
Queen Studio
Reynolds, Albert S.
Risdon, O. A.
Ristelheuber, Mr.
Ristelheuber, Mrs.
Smith & Peat
Stubbs, C.
Taylor, James A.
Tiesman, (?)
Tiesman & Key

BUCKEYE
Resler, Calvin A.

BYLAS
Taylor, Gracie S.

CAMP VERDE
Williscraft, William
Hamilton
Cook, Francis A.

CASA GRANDE
Everett & Son, J. E.

CENTRAL
Jenkins, S. P.

CHARLESTON
Farciot, Charles O.
Watkins, Carleton

CLARKDALE
Areldson Photo

CLIFTON
Buck, A. J.
Burlan, (?)
Gillingham, W. P.
Johnson, Charles Granville
Jones, J. C.
Lucas & Burlan
Lucas, Harry W.
Risdon, O. A.
Risdon's Studio

DOUGLAS
Baker, E. W.
Ban–Ap Photo
Booth & Milo
Brown, M. L.
Carson, Ambrose W.
Carson Brothers
Carson, Hugh Ruth
Carson's Studio
Cooley, Ben D.
Farquahar, Julius Theo
Guzman, E. S.
Hansen, H. B.
Irwin, Marvin E.
Irwin Studio
Langford, W. L.
Low(e), M. W.
Milo, (?)
Moore, Samuel
Queen Studio
Reynolds, Albert S.
Royal Studio
Stubbs, C. L.

EHRENBERG
Westgard, A. L.

FLAGSTAFF
Baer, Erwin
Baker, E. W.
Boston Railroad Photo Car
Burchard, James Edward
Burge, J. C.
Cox, (?)
Dykes, W. L.
Fetter, W. L.
Flagstaff Art Gallery
Flagstaff Photograph
Gallery
Hackett, H. A.
Hildreth, James
Hunter, Edward
Hunter's Art Parlor
Jackson, William Henry
Melven, (?)
Michael & Shillcock
Middleton, F. W.
Osbon, Calvin
Pasevitch, Joseph
Raudeleagh, Oliver B.
Shillcock, (?)
Stone, (?)
St. Clair, Edward
St. Clair Photograph
Gallery
Stone & Cox
Stuart, W. F.
Tucker, C. H.
Wittick, George Ben

FT. APACHE
Barnes, Will Croft
Barthelmess, Christian
Markey, Daniel A.
Mason, Janie Ellis

FT. GRANT
Kovarick, Albert J.

FT. HUACHUCA
Cosby, O.
Schroeter, (?)

FT. MOHAVE
Flanders, Dudley P.

FREDONIA
Booksly, A.

GLENDALE
Bogen, Robert
Christensen, Peter C.
Hartwell, Steven
Rinckwitz, Richard L.

GLOBE
Bailey, W.
Bemis, Mrs. F. C.
Burge, J. C.
California Art Gallery
Farciot, Charles O.
Farquahar, Julius Theo
Globe Photographic Co.
Grime, Cicero
Hanna, Forman
Kelley Studios
Key, W. H.
Low(e), M. W.
Meriwether, Henry B.
Miller, Andrew
Mullarkey, W. T.
Skelley, Lote Adison
Skelley, Mrs. E. B.
Smith, Knight A.
Thwaites, George H.
Williams, John Roderick

GRAND CANYON
Burge, J. C.
Curtis, Edward Sheriff
Fuerman, Henry
Hawkins Photographer
Kolb Brothers
Kolb, Ellsworth
Kolb, Emery
Peabody, Henry
    Greenwood
Putnam & Valentine

HACKBERRY
Phillips, Fenley W.

HAYDEN
Barnett, Charles

HERFORD
Smith, Erwin E.

HOLBROOK
Brown, W. Calvin
Clark, Robert
Middleton, F. W.
Rose, George Lyman

HUMBOLDT
Armitage Photo Company
Sufea, Frank

JEROME
Aveldson, (?)
Brennan, M. F.
Coleman, James W.
Hawkins, Dr. (?)
Perry, Oliver H.

KINGMAN
Burge, J. C.
Tarr, J. A.

LOWELL
Allen, W. H.

MESA
Barnett, Charles W.
Bleak, Ellye E.
Ellsworth, Ellye Irwin
Ellsworth Studio
Galbraith, Roy L.
Holland, Leon H.
Irwin, Ellye
Lubkin Co.
Lubkin, Walter

METCALF
Risdon, O. A.
Risdon's Studio

MIAMI
Kelley, Roy F.
Maudlin, William E.
Mullarkey, A. J.

Mullarkey, W. T.

MISHONGNOVI
Mendeleff, Cosmos

MOQUI
Ames, F. A.

MORENCI
Booth, A. J.
Culp's Photo Studio
Davidson, Arthur H.
Gilgannon, Daniel S.
Gonzales, Leonardo
Marks, C. W.

NACO
Great Western View
    Company
Jones, Lewis
Kennat, (?)

NOGALES
Lara, Vicente
Newman, William J.
Samano, Raymond
Wood, H. E.

OAK CREEK
Cobb, William Henry

OATMAN
Johnson, N. E.

ORACLE
Newport, F. T.

PARKER
Johnson, N. E.

PIMA VILLAGES
Farciot, Charles O.

PHOENIX
Adkins & Harrison
Adkins, Wesley C.
Altenburgh, William
Arizona Photo Company
Barnett, Charles W.
Bate Studio
Bate, Tom H.
Bearce, E. A.

Beasley, A. D.
Beattie, J. W.
Blaine, Charles E.
Blaine, Charles S.
Bleak, Ellye E.
Branch, John W.
Buehman, Henry
Catton, C. W.
Christy, Isaac Marshall
Clausen, C. H.
Clausen, Mrs. C. H.
Cohen, Joseph
Cook, Francis A.
Copeland, (?)
Cotten, C. W.
Davenport, M. L.
Donnell, T. M.
Electric Studio
Elite Gallery
Elite Studios & Gallery
Elkin & Elkin
Elkin, Lauren
Fly, Camilius S.
Fortin, Joseph R.
Furl, J. Frank
Green, W. Hugh A.
Guen, Hugh
Hackett, Arthur E.
Hammaker, H. L.
Harrison, Ralph T.
Hartwell & Hammaker
Hartwell, Byron J.
Hartwell, Francis A.
Hartwell's Studio
Haymaker, H. L.
Heath, Charles E.
Heath Studio
Hegeman, Elizabeth
    Compton
Korf, Abe M.
Kunselman, Elton E.
Long, C. C.
McCulloch, Jasper M.
McCulloch, William
    Patrick
Malone, D. T.
Mealey, M. W.
Mealey Studio
Mealey, W. P.
Messinger & Altenburgh
Messinger, A. F.
Mosser, William

Mussey, Fred B.
New York Gallery
New York Photo Studio
New York Studio
Photocraft Shop
Portillo, Jesus
Rhodes, John P.
Robinson, H. F.
Rothrock, George H.
Russell, William F.
Ryden, (?)
Ryden & Westberg
Sadler, George
Sexton, James H.
Shaw, C. H.
Stacey & Copeland
Stacy, C. I.
Staley, Frank
Stephens, H. R.
Strand Studio
Sunbeam Studio
Turnbull, Robert A.
Updike, Lisle Chandler
Van Ness, Carl
Wenfor, George
Westburg, John F.
Wilbur, G. B.
Williams Studio
Williams, Thomas F.
Wilson, Mrs. Lawrence

PIMA
Williams, R.

POLAND
Dixon, W. L.

PRESCOTT
Arizona Photograph
   Company
Armitage, Percival
Armitage Photo Company
Baer, Erwin
Bate, Tom H.
Bauman, Jules
Beatty, Mrs. C. S.
Beatty, Will R.
Bruce, C. A.
Bryant, Henry
Bull, (?)
Burge, J. C.

Capital Art Gallery
Cook, Francis A.
Emanuel, (?)
Everett's Studio
Flanders, Dudley P.
Flying Gallery
Gentile, Carlos
   (Charles) G.
Hammaker, H. C.
Hargrave, Richard M.
Horton, J.
Humphries, Wilfred R.
Jennings, E. M.
Jennings, M.
Kinney, (?)
Loring, (?)
McKenna, William
Mitchell, Daniel Francis
Mortin, J.
Penlon, Henri
Photographic Artist
   Old Gallery
Pierce, Nathan Parda
Prior, N. W.
Prescott Studio
Quick Finish Kodak Co.
Rothrock, George H.
Schroeder, (?)
Scott, (?)
Sufea, Frank
Suppinger, A. E.
Thomas, Charles
Williscraft, William
   Hamilton
Wooster, George N.
Worth, L. W.

RAY
Webster, Leonard A.

ROOSEVELT
Arizona Souvenir Picture
   Company
Burtis, George
Burtis, Mrs. George
Kline, J. W.

SAFFORD
Empie, Hal D.
Williams, John Roderick

ST. JOHNS
Curtis, C. D.
Jarvis, Charles

ST. MICHAELS
Schwemberger, Simeon

SAN CARLOS
Dodge, Katherine T.
Moon, F. W.

SNOWFLAKE
Lurley, Miss Lucy
Peterson, Joseph
Smith, Mrs. S. D.
Turley, Miss Lucy

SOLOMONVILLE
Austin, A. H.

TEMPE
Barnett, Charles W.
Branch, John W.
Burchard & Melvin
Donnell, T. M.
Gottleib, Harry Joseph
Johnson, K. M.
Korf, Abe M.
Lyman, Harvey O.
Melvin, (?)
Pollock, Jeanette
Rothrock, George H.

TOMBSTONE
Chase, (?)
Coleman, (?)
Farciot, Charles O.
Feldman, Frederick J.
Fly & Holfstead
Fly, Camilius S.
Fly, Mrs. Mary E.
Holfstead, (?)
Kemp & Coleman
Watkins, Carleton

TUCSON
Addis, Alfred Shea
Atlantic Pacific View &
   Portrait Company
   (A&PV&P Co.).
Arizona Gallery

Arizona Tent Gallery
Bagnasco, Policarpo
Bolanos, Heliodoro
Bruunage, M. J.
Buehman & Co.
   Photographers
Buehman, Henry
Cozby, Oliver
Elite Studio
Feldman, Alttier M.
Feldman, Frederick J.
Flanders, Dudley P.
Fly & Holfstead
Gaige, J. C.
Gottleib, Harry Joseph
Gregory, A. D.
Hadsell, Walter P.
Harris, Joseph
Hartwell, Francis A.
Haynes, Willis P.
Heath, Charles E.
Heath Studio
Heath Studios
Hepburn, Mrs. W. H.
Hepburn, W. H.
Heuthen, (?)
Horner, Harry H.
Hulbert, Miss Anna
La Luna Studio
McKenna, William
Model Photo Gallery
Morrison, R. E.
Parker, Joseph C.
Parker, W. B.
Parker, W. D.
Parker, W. F.
Parkers, (?)
Partridge, F. J.
Periera, Jos.
Periera Studio
Porter, (?)
Ring, T. A.
Rodrigo, Adolpho
Roskruge, George
Rountree, W. A.
Rowntree, W. A.
Sladsky, Charles
Stone, Fred L.
Sweet, F. P.
Sykes, Godfrey
Tucson Photo Co.

Wallace, N. G.
Watkins, Carleton
Weed Art Studio
Weed, William L.
Wilcox, H. H.
Wilson, I. K.
Wilson Studio
Wonfor, George H.

WALPI
Mendeleff, Cosmos

WELLTON
Dickison, Miss E.

WILCOX
Bright, J. A.

Drake, Chas. L.
Randall, A. Frank
Tillotson, Frank

WILLIAMS
Baker, E. W.
Boston Photo Car
Cone, J. T.
Curtis, C. D.
Kolb Brothers
Kolb, Ellsworth
Kolb, Emery
Martin, A. L.
Randebaugh, J. D.
Ratcliff, C. E.
Raudeleagh, Oliver B.

WINKELMAN
Coyle, John H.

WINSLOW
Mary Ann Studio
Rose, George Lyman
Parker, Joseph C.
Sato, T.
Truax, (?)

YUMA (Arizona and
    Colorado Cities)
Bertolacci, G. T. E.
Bonine, Elias A.
Booth, Albert J.
Burlan, (?)
Conklin, Enoch

D'Heureuse, Rudolph
Hickson & Quinta
Hickson, C. L.
Ives, Lieutenant
    Joseph, Christmas
Johnson, Charles
    Granville
Lucas, Harry W.
Mission Studios
Parker & Parker
Parker, Francis A.
Parker, Joseph C.
Quint, Roy T.
Rothrock, George H.
Watkins, Carleton
Young, (?)

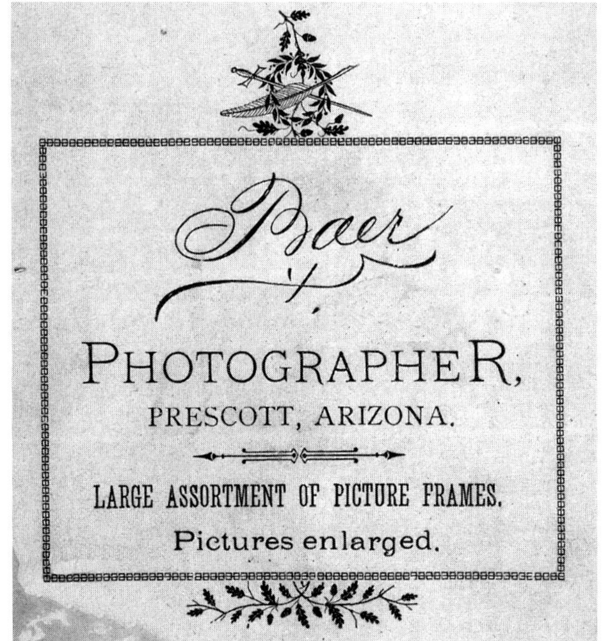

DAGUERREOTYPE

In 1839, the first practical photographic process, the daguerreotype, was introduced in France. Word of the process rapidly traveled world-wide, and by 1840, daguerreian experimentation began in America. Commercial applications of the process were soon underway, and the reign of the daguerreotype and photography had begun in America.

Over the next few years, the popularity of the daguerreotype grew at an unbelievable pace. As the process was refined and portraiture became possible, photographic studios appeared in virtually every city and town across America. Rural areas were served by itinerant photographers who advertised visits, stayed while there was business, then moved on to the next settlement. By the mid 1850s millions of portraits were being produced in America each year. Commercial applications, such as landscape, reportage, and architectural photography were also popular, but were far less common than the ubiquitous portrait, the bread and butter mainstay of most photographers.

Though the daguerreotype was extremely popular, the process had inherent limitations. First, the highly reflective surface of the plate made viewing difficult under many conditions. Second, the fact that each image was unique and could be reproduced only by re-photographing the original made sale and distribution difficult and costly.

By the late 1850s, other processes, such as the ambrotype and cartes-de-visite, began to increase in popularity, and by 1860 the daguerreotype had become a seldom made novelty. The vast majority of all daguerreotypes were made during the period from 1840 to 1860, but there has been a small, continuous following from its decline to the present. There was a brief revival in the popularity of the daguerreotype

in the 1880s, and today there is renewed interest, but despite almost 150 years of activity, the daguerreotype remains one of the more unusual photographic processes.

The process of making a daguerreotype was unbelievably complex considering its early development. The time involved in preparing a single plate could be an hour or more, making photographers' assistants essential. By the mid 1840s, the process involved the following steps:

1. The image was made on a thin sheet of copper mechanically or electrically plated with silver.
2. The plate was first prepared by hand polishing with rouge or a similar abrasive on buckskin paddles.
3. After the plate was finely polished, it was sensitized by exposing it first to iodine and then to bromine vapors in special coating boxes.
4. After sensitizing, the plate was finally placed in a holder, inserted in the camera, and exposed.
5. After the exposure was made, the image was developed by placing the plate over heated mercury, where the vapor brought out the image.
6. The final step was gilding the plate with a gold wash to increase the image contrast and provide some protection for the delicate surface of the plate.

It is no wonder that the literature of the period is filled with stories of photographers who suffered temporary, or in some cases, permanent damage from the effects of the deadly chemicals involved.

Once the plate was dried, it was packaged for presentation to the client. The usual format was to place the daguerreotype in a small hinged case, similar to the miniature portrait paintings of the era. Because the surface of the plate was so delicate, it was covered with a piece of glass for protection. To prevent the glass from touching the plate itself, a mat of decorated brass was placed between the glass and daguerreotype plate, thus framing the image as well as protecting it. To hold the glass/mat/plate "sandwich" together, a paper seal was applied, and a thin piece of embossed brass called a preserver was crimped around the edge to hold all of the pieces together. The entire grouping was then placed into a case made of pressed paper, wood, or thermoplastic.

The daguerreotype came in a number of more or less standard sizes, based on a 6½″ x 8½″ plate, called a "whole plate" or "full plate." Divisions of the whole plate were made, and the sixth plate was the most common size used in daguerreotypes, followed by ninth and quarter plates, respectively. The specific size designations for daguerreotypes are as follows:

 Full plate 6½″ x 8½″
 Half plate 4½″ x 5½″
 Quarter plate 2¾″ x 3¼″
 Sixth plate 2″ x 2½″
 Ninth plate 1½″ x 1¾″
 Sixteenth plate 1⅜″ x 1⅝″

Despite the pervasiveness of the daguerreotype, none can yet be definitively proven to have been made in Arizona. The likelihood of daguerreotypes being produced by some of the photographers who traveled across Arizona en route to and from California is great. There are a few daguerreotypes taken in New Mexico and many California images from this era. Unfortunately, traveling photographers did not usually identify their work.

AMBROTYPE

Photography kept evolving through the 1840s and 50s with inventors and entrepreneurs continually devising improved techniques and introducing new photographic processes.

One of the first to gain wide use was the ambrotype, invented in England in 1852 by Frederick Scott Archer, then refined and patented by James Cutting of Boston in 1854. Like the daguerreotype, the ambrotype was a direct positive process, with the final image being on a "plate" that had been exposed in the camera.

Ambrotypes are made by coating a glass plate with collodion, a mixture of gun cotton and ether, and a sensitizer made of silver nitrate. While the coating was still tacky, the glass plate was placed in a light tight holder, then exposed in the camera. The plate was developed in ferrous sulfate and nitric acid, fixed with potassium ferrocyanide to remove any unexposed silver, and finally washed and packaged.

The process was faster than the daguerreotype in that it did not require the exacting polishing and preparation of the plate prior to sensitizing. The ambrotype had one major limiting factor, however. The entire process, from sensitizing through fixing, had to be completed before the collodion dried and the plate lost its sensitivity. This required the photographer to make each plate immediately before exposure in the studio. Work outside of the studio required carrying the sensitizing and processing equipment as well as a dark tent, in addition to camera equipment, tripod, and finally, glass for the plates themselves.

The presentation of the ambrotype is usually very similar to the daguerreotype, using the same leather, pressed paper, or thermoplastic cases and with images produced in the same plate sizes. The processed glass plate of the ambrotype appeared as a negative until a dark backing was added. The backing caused the shadows to darken, the highlights became brighter in comparison, and the viewer saw a positive image. The dark backing took many forms: black lacquer applied to the back of the image; a blackened piece of metal or paper placed behind the plate, or using dark "ruby" glass for the plate itself.

The plate was then placed under a decorative mat, and a protective cover glass was added. The cover glass, mat, plate, and backing were then enclosed with a paper seal and an embossed metal strip, the preserver, that was crimped to hold the entire package together prior to placement in the case.

The primary visual "improvement" was that the ambrotype did not exhibit the reflective surface that made the daguerreotype difficult to view. In exchange, however, the range of tones was reduced and the resolution and image quality of the ambrotype were slightly less than was possible with the daguerreotype process. These limitations were balanced by a lower cost and the novelty of the new process, making it extremely popular until the late 1860s.

A collection of ambrotypes of Arizona subjects won awards in California in the early 1870s. In addition, many of the early Arizona photographers advertised ambrotypes as part of their repertoire. Ambrotypes are extant of a number of famous Arizona figures, such as Olive Oatman and John Clum, but these were taken outside of the state. Ambrotype portraits of Arizona pioneers exist but the frequent failure of the photographers to mark their ambrotypes makes it difficult, if not impossible, to verify whether most of portraits were made in Territorial Arizona. No ambrotypes of town views which might be identified from business signs have been verified to date, nor have ambrotypes of newsworthy events within Arizona been located.

FERROTYPE OR TINTYPE

In 1856 the ferrotype or tintype was developed by Hannibal Smith of Ohio. The tintype was also a collodion process, virtually identical to the ambrotype, but using a metal plate made of iron covered with a black japan varnish instead of glass with a dark backing. Like the daguerreotype and ambrotype, the tintype produced a unique image and required coating, exposing, and processing the plate before the collodion dried. The quality of the best early tintypes compares favorably with ambrotypes of the period, but characteristically, tintypes have an even narrower range of contrast, with veiled highlights that make tintype images appear somewhat dark and "murky."

Initially, tintypes competed with the daguerreotypes and ambrotypes, and were packaged in mat and preserver with cover glass in the same cases. The Civil War saw an explosion in popularity of the tintype which was due to two factors. The first was that the iron plates were more durable for the rigors of photography in the field, and, as a direct positive process, it did not require printing from glass negatives as did paper processes popular at the time. The second reason was that tintypes could be sent through the mail uncased without danger of breakage. This made the tintype the process of choice for exchanging photographs between soldiers and their loved ones. The

number of tintypes still extant from this period attests to the tremendous volume produced.

After the war, the tintype remained popular as a low cost photographic process. Multiple lens cameras permitted two, four or as many as thirty-six virtually identical images to be made on a single plate. The plates were then cut into individual images. Late in the 19th century, cameras and processes were developed that permitted exposure and processing in a single unit, making "instant" pictures possible. Itinerant "tintypists" were a common sight at carnivals, fairs, and tourist attractions throughout the world. The tintype process remained in active use into the 1930s. As with daguerreotypes, the tintype process has never completely disappeared and continues to have a small number of practitioners, although they are primarily produced as a novelty.

Tintypes were a popular process in Territorial Arizona. Many photographers offered tintypes and examples of both portraits and outdoor Arizona views are extant.

PAPER FORMATS

Unlike the previous processes which produce single unique images, paper processes produce a negative that can be used to make multiple copies. The ability to reproduce an image without having to recopy the original, as was required for daguerreotypes, ambrotypes and tintypes, made commercial distribution of photographs possible. As a result, photographs began to have an even greater impact on the average person's perception of places and events in the world around them.

COLLODIAN NEGATIVE

As with the ambrotype, the collodion negative was made by coating a glass plate with collodion, a syrupy mixture of gun cotton and ether sensitized with silver nitrate. The plate was placed in a light tight holder, then exposed in the camera. The exposed plate was then developed in ferrous sulfate and nitric acid, and fixed with potassium ferrocyanide to remove unexposed silver and remove sensitivity to further exposure to light. Finally, the negative was washed and dried. If many prints were to be made, the negative was often varnished to prevent scratching during handling.

Collodion negatives, like ambrotypes and tintypes, required the entire process, from sensitizing through fixing and washing, to be completed before the collodion dried and the coating was no longer water soluble.

In the studio, the photographer or his assistant were required to prepare each plate immediately before exposure, usually in a darkroom adjacent to the studio area. Away from the studio, photographers were required to carry the sensitizing and processing equipment, and a dark tent or wagon for plate preparation and developing, in addition to camera equipment, tripod, and glass plates for the negatives themselves.

The process of driving a photographic wagon to the location or carrying and setting up the equipment, composing the photograph, sensitizing the negative, making the exposure, processing the negative, and finally repacking the equipment made photography a much more complex process than can be imagined today. The hardships involved and loss due to breakage make the photographic legacy of this period an especially impressive achievement.

ALBUMEN PRINTING PAPER

Albumen paper became popular in the mid 1850s and remained popular into the 1890s when collodion and gelatin printing out papers became popular.

The albumen printing medium was generally used in conjunction with the collodion negative, and was named for the albumen (obtained from egg whites) used as a surface coating for the rag paper base of the photograph. Initially, the unsensitized, albumen-coated paper was sensitized with a silver nitrate bath, the negative placed on the sensitized paper in a printing frame and the "sandwich" then exposed to sunlight. The action of the light on the emulsion caused the paper to darken without the need for chemical development. Once the proper image density had been achieved, the print was washed, gold toned, fixed in sodium thiosulfate, then washed again, and dried. After the mid 1860s, the paper was sold pre-sensitized and its use required only exposure and processing.

Initially, albumen paper offered a matte surface. As fashion shifted and glossy image surfaces became popular, techniques such as burnishing and enameling became popular. Burnishing, which became popular in the 1860, involved adding a second albumen layer then running the photograph through a press to create a shiny surface. Enameling was a similar technique but used collodion and was only popular for a short period in the late 1860s to the mid 1870s. Many images produced in primitive studios were not burnished even though they were produced in the 1870s, so the surface sheen is not always a reliable indicator of age.

Most albumen photographs are contact prints, produced by placing the collodion negative directly on albumen paper and exposing it to sunlight until the desired image had been produced. The collodion negatives had extremely fine resolution, and as a result, the prints produced were very sharp and detailed. Albumen prints were usually mounted on card stock of varying sizes. The card mount provided an area for identification and promotion of the photographer or for notations by the owner or their descendants. Though the handwritten notations require verification, the printed identifications can provide valuable information about photographers and studio locations.

Because multiple prints could be simply and economically produced, the popularity of the albumen print exceeded that of the earlier processes. Millions of prints were produced each year for the next 40 years in formats ranging from relatively small cartes-de-visites to 20″ x 24″ mammoth plate images.

OTHER PHOTOGRAPHIC PAPER PROCESSES USED IN THE WEST

CYANOTYPES

Cyanotypes or blueprints were introduced in the 1840s but failed to gain widespread popularity until later in the 19th century. Using iron salts instead of the usual silver, cyanotypes depict the image in shades of blue and offer a matte print surface.

The process involves a simple process of coating regular paper with two solutions and letting it dry. The negative was placed on the paper and exposed to sunlight until the desired density was achieved. The final step was to wash the paper in water, then dry and mount it as desired.

The simplicity of cyanotypes, compared to albumen and other processes, made it popular for itinerant photographers and later amateurs to make photographs under primitive conditions. Though cyanotypes of expedition and survey images from the 1870s and 1880s were made, the process became popular in the 1890s and was used to produce stereographs, mounted photographs and photographic postcards well into the 20th century.

GELATIN & COLLODION PRINTING AND DEVELOPING OUT PAPERS

Gelatin and collodion printing out papers became popular in the late 1880s. Both were mass produced and pre-sensitized in both gloss and matte surfaces. They offered photographers a useful life of about a year. Like albumen printing, negatives were placed on the photographic paper and exposed to sunlight until the desired density was obtained.

Developing out, or "gaslight," papers gained popularity during the late 1890s and were frequently used for "snapshots" and became the paper of choice for most photographic postcards. The nickname for the paper came from the ability to use a gas flame to expose the paper, which was then developed to bring out the image, then fixed and dried. Gaslight papers were offered in both gloss and matte surfaces.

CARTES-DE-VISITES

Cartes-de-visite, or visiting cards, became a popular format for albumen prints in the United States beginning about 1860 and were produced until the early 20th century. The carte-de-visite was the most popular photographic format for portraiture and commercial views prior to about 1870. In addition to portraiture for families and individuals, cartes-de-visite of celebrities and political figures were mass produced and were actively collected.

Albums to house collections were popular and ranged from simple leather albums to albums with elaborately inlaid mother of pearl covers. The small size of the negative involved kept exposure times

relatively brief, and cameras for individual negatives were compact and portable. These factors, and the ability to make multiple copies for resale, made cartes-de-visite popular for documenting events and activities outside the studio despite the need for additional equipment for sensitizing and processing. During the 15 years of their major popularity, millions of cartes-de-visite and thousands of albums were produced and sold each year. Even after cabinet cards eclipsed the carte-de-visite in popularity during the mid 1870s, albums usually included pages cut for holding cartes-de-visite. Several Arizona photographers produced cartes-de-visite until just before statehood in 1912.

Typically, the carte-de-visite is an albumen print roughly $2\frac{1}{4}''$ x $3\frac{3}{4}''$ which is mounted on $2\frac{1}{2}''$ x $4''$ card stock. Collodion negatives were taken either singly or as multiple images on a single larger plate in multi-lens cameras. The photographer trimmed the finished prints, coated them with adhesive, placed them on the mount, then set them aside to dry.

Early cards used thin, square cornered, white or buff mounts. By the 1870s, colored mounts had become popular. The range of mount colors available included tan, yellow, blue, lavender, red, and brown. Later card stock tended to be thicker, often with colored or gold borders.

Early cartes-de-visite often had simple graphics identifying the photographer either below the mounted photo or on the back of the mount. Just as mount colors became more flamboyant, the identifying imprints tended to become became more elaborate later in the century. An exception is the simple rubber stamp identifications occasionally used by itinerant or traveling photographers.

Unfortunately, many early photographers did not mark their cartes-de-visite. Arizona imprints identified to date include C. S. Fly, George Rothrock, and Henry Buehman.

CABINET CARDS

Beginning about 1867 a larger format albumen print became popular—the cabinet card. Like the cartes-de-visite, the cabinet card was an albumen print made from a collodion negative and remained in use through the turn of the century. Typically, the cabinet card is an albumen print 3¾″ x 5½″ mounted on 4¼″ x 6½″ card stock.

Cabinet cards were used for portraiture as well as work outside the studio. Collecting and displaying cabinet cards and compiling family groupings were popular pastimes. Albums of family photographs or of notable figures became fixtures in parlors across the nation. Beginning around 1870, retouching techniques became widespread, providing the photographer the ability to eliminate facial flaws and further increase the popularity of portraits in this format.

Like cartes-de-visite, early mounts were thin, white or buff card stock. Again, colors, such as tan, yellow, blue, lavender, red, and brown became popular. Later card stock tended to be thicker, and embossed imprints and borders became popular. Elaborate graphics became stylish during the 1870s and continued to grow in complexity into the 20th century. In addition to albumen paper, cabinet cards were produced using other photographic papers including collodio-chloride, carbon, cyanotype, gelatin chloride, and bromide.

The cabinet card was an extremely popular format and thousands of Arizona cabinet card images exist. The imprints and mount identifications are good sources of information about the photographers and studio locations, but, unfortunately, as with other formats, many cabinet cards were unmarked.

STEREOGRAPHS

One of the most popular photographic formats of the 19th and early 20th century was the stereograph (also called stereoview or stereopticon). In the days before halftone illustrations in print media such as magazines, and before the development of motion pictures and television, stereographs provided access to images of the world, its personalities and events, which could be viewed from the comfort of one's parlor. Stereographs were produced and distributed in virtually every 19th century photographic process and format. Examples exist of stereo daguerreotypes, ambrotypes, tintypes, albumen prints and cyanotypes, as well as stereographs produced in early photomechanical processes such as lithography and woodburytype. Stereographs were produced by the millions

world-wide, and were marketed, collected and viewed with a passion that can only be imagined today.

Stereographs used the principle of binocular vision to permit the viewer to perceive three-dimensional depth from two two-dimensional images. Human eyes have a separation between left and right of just over two inches, giving each eye a view of the world from a slightly different angle of perspective. If two photographs are made from similarly separated perspectives, and are viewed in a manner in which the left eye sees only the left eye perspective, and the right eye sees only the right perspective, the viewer perceives a single, three dimensional image.

Though stereoscopic drawings preceded the invention of photography, commercial applications of stereoscopic representation of visual images were limited due to the lack of a convenient viewer. The first major breakthrough in the design of a viewing device came in 1850 when Sir William Brewster invented a viewing box with adjustable lenses, the lenticular stereoscope. The more familiar hand held stereoscope that graced hundreds of thousands of 19th century parlors was introduced by Oliver Wendell Holmes in 1859.

Development of a simple viewing device was one key factor that led to the explosion in popularity of the stereograph. Invention of a simple method of producing high quality images in quantities suitable for distribution was anohter factor. Earlier photographic processes such as daguerreotypes, ambrotypes, and ferrotypes produced unique images that could only be reproduced by recopying the original. The collodion process made it possible to produce negatives that could be printed on albumen printing out paper and reproduced by the thousands. The ability to make multiple prints from a single negative made the collodion negative and albumen print the mainstay of photography for the next forty years.

The stereo process, with its small negative size, relatively short exposure times, and large potential market, was one photography format which could be employed profitably away from the convenience of the studio. Stereographs were produced by trimming, aligning, and mounting the two images on a card mount. Since the images were made as contact prints without enlargement, they tend to carry significant detail and thus considerable information as cultural artifact.

Most stereographs marketed prior to the mid 1880s were produced as albumen prints mounted on card stock. The mounts were initially flat, square cornered, and buff, white or ivory in color. By the mid 1860s, colored mounts became popular and stereographs came with yellow, red, green, lavender, orange and blue mounts. The typical mount sizes were 7″ wide and 3½″ high holding two 3″ x 3½″ prints. Later, larger mounts 4″, 4½″ and 5″ high became popular, each maintaining the standard 7″ width.

Beginning about 1890, curved mounts were found to enhance the stereo effect and became popular among many of the larger publishers. Within a short time, the 7″ x 3½″ gray or buff curved mounts replaced the colored flat mounts and became the standard presentation for stereographs until their popularity declined in the 1930s.

As new photographic processes became practical, each was applied to the production of stereographs. By the mid 1880s, collodion negatives began to give way to more convenient dry plate negatives which freed the photographer from the need to carry dark tent and sensitizing chemicals into the field. At the same time, several new photographic printing processes were gradually replacing albumen prints as the media of choice. Since stereo images were contact printed and not enlarged, virtually all printing out processes were applied to producing stereographs. Commercial photographers and publishers used primarily the silver bromide processes, but smaller studios and amateurs used other processes such as gelatin and collodion printing out papers as they became popular.

The range of subjects depicted in 19th century stereographs is truly astounding. The potential market for stereographs was tremendous, and the competition between photographers and publishers for marketable images was fierce. Stereographs were acquired during travels, or purchased to study or explore new and unusual places or historic events without an actual visit, and were often exchanged between friends and relatives as remembrances.

Virtually every parlor or sitting room throughout America had a stereoscope and a stack of favorite views to entertain family and friends.

Enterprising photographers with their stereo cameras documented the battles and personalities of the Civil War, accompanied expeditions throughout the West, and made photographs of major social, political and cultural events available at a cost of about a dime per view.

Photographers often exchanged stereographs and actively acquired negatives of marketable subjects from other sources to enhance their offerings. Many were purchased or traded knowingly; however, in the days prior to practical copyright protection, copying and selling popular images without permission was common.

The popularity of the stereograph began to decline as the 19th century ended. Halftone reproduction began to make printed reproduction of photographs possible, and the need for visual information was filled more economically by newspapers and magazines. Also, motion pictures brought images to the large screen and made group viewing a popular phenomenon. The stereograph maintained its place in the parlors of America, but the market for new images began to drop significantly.

Several publishers, such as Underwood and Underwood and Keystone, responded to the shrinking market for stereographs by developing a new marketing strategy. Printed information on the reverse of the view was expanded and stereographs became educational materials. Sets of fifty, one hundred, or more, were packaged together in appropriately titled boxes. These series offered the viewer tours of India, Egypt, the Grand Canyon, Around the World, or almost anywhere. Others offered lessons on subjects including public service workers, botanical subjects, anatomy, etc.

In addition to the photographs themselves, stereographs often contained printed information regarding the photographer or publisher, as well as captions and titles describing the subjects depicted in the photographs. In addition, stereograph owners often made additional notations in the blank spaces on rear of the mount. The combination of photographic and printed information makes stereographs a valuable, often overlooked historic resource.

Arizona forts, towns, mining camps, desert landscapes and Native Americans were popular subjects of stereographs. In addition to the stereographs produced by photographers based in Arizona, stereographers from across America visited Arizona to produce images for commercial sale. In my research to date, I have identified over 2800 individual titles of Arizona stereographs. Projections of total numbers based on examples available to date indicate over 10,000 individual titles produced.

PHOTOGRAPHIC POSTCARDS

The rise in the popularity of the postcard paralleled a time of rapid and exciting growth in Arizona. Often, the only remains of the company camps and towns of the early 20th century are the photographic postcards that were sent to friends and investors, or slipped into an album as a reminder of life in the distant West.

Photographic postcards became common just after the turn of the century as a result of a several developments. Increasing sophistication of film, camera and paper all made photography simpler and more available to the public. The advent of flexible roll film and the new $3\frac{1}{4}''$ x $5\frac{1}{2}''$ photographic format led to the creation of amateur photographic equipment which was both simple and portable. The sensitivity of film increased to the point where it was possible to handhold the camera for daylight photography rather than requiring a tripod. With a tripod it was possible to make interior photographs without skylights or artificial light. Even night photography became an option. Finally, flexible roll film permitted multiple exposures without the burden of carrying individual film holders and bulky equipment.

Beginning in 1902, Eastman Kodak and other manufacturers marketed postcard format photographic paper that was sensitive enough to print under artificial light. This simplified the process of printing photographic negatives and further encouraged both amateur and commercial production of photographic postcards. By 1906, the postal service was providing daily delivery of letters, postcards, and

newspapers throughout most of the country. As a result, photographic postcards were produced by amateur and professional photographers by the thousands to satisfy the demands of a growing market.

Another factor that effected the popularity of the photo postcard was a change in postal regulations. In 1898 the Post Office created a program for Rural Free Delivery (RFD) to provide daily mail service to the remotest parts of America. At the same time, postage was reduced to encouraged the use of postcards, which coincided with the new $3\frac{1}{4}''$ x $5\frac{1}{2}''$ photographic format. Within a few years, interest in postcards exploded worldwide, with Americans sending over 800,000,000 postcards in 1910 alone.

As Arizona continued its evolution to statehood during the period from 1900–1912, postcard cameras documented the events in a priceless visual record. Events like the Territorial Fairs and small town parades, views of developing downtown business districts, railway accidents, mining activity, and images of daily enterprise were all available as photographic postcards to send to friends around the world.

As with stereographs during the period twenty years earlier, most Arizona photographers operating before 1920 offered photographic postcards as a commercial adjunct to their business. In addition, many drugstores, news stands, curio shops and hotels offered photographic postcards to their customers as souvenirs. As a result, there are tens of thousands of Arizona postcards extant which document a period of extraordinary growth and development.

DATING CARD MOUNTED PHOTOGRAPHS BY FORMAT AND MOUNT INFORMATION

Card mounted photographs can generally be dated by format and mount type. Notations on the mounts may provide additional information about the image, but should always be verified by other sources if possible.

Printed mount notations such as photographer's identification and title are fairly reliable, but can still provide false information. Handwritten notations are the most suspect, often being added long after the image was made by persons with only secondary knowledge. Some weight can be given to apparent period notation—in fountain pen or pencil—as opposed to ball point, but the information should be compared with other clues such as format, mount style, period of operation for identified photographers, "logic" related to events occurring near the time indicated, etc.

Dating by mount type and style provides another rough indicator for identifying images. The caveat is that many photographers, particularly in more remote areas, failed to keep up with photographic fashion and used old mounts until their stocks were exhausted.

An additional concern stems from the recent increase in interest and demand for historic photographs. The increasing activity in the photographic market has caused some forgeries to appear. In addition to simply adding incorrect notations about subject or location on the mount, more sophisticated efforts to mislead have appeared in recent years. False attributions for photographers such as Henry Buehman and Adam C. Vroman have been placed on images with rubber stamps to identify them as Arizona or Western photographs and improve marketability. Some of these images have even found their way into institutional collections to be used to "prove" the correctness of other forgeries in the marketplace.

Images have also been removed and remounted on more interesting mounts to increase value. Photographic postcards have been falsified by rubber stamping logos and stamp boxes onto vintage and contemporary photographs to make them appear to be historic images. Photographs of military subjects taken at re-enactments have also been portrayed— and sold—as vintage images. Unfortunately, as time goes on, and competition and value effect the market, the number and creativity of forgers will increase. The best protection is knowledge, either your own, or that of an expert.

Given this preface, the following information is provided to assist in verification of dating using information based on the type and style of the photographic mount.

CARD MOUNTED PHOTO DESIGNATION BY SIZE

Cigarette Card	2¾″ x 2¾″	1885-95, 1909-17
Stereograph	3½″ x 7″ to 5″x 7″	1850s to 1950s
Cartes–de–visite	2½″ x 4″	1850s to 1900s
Kodak circular images	4¼″ x 5¼″	1880s to 1890s
Boudoir	5½″ x 8½″	1880s
Swiss mount	6½″ x 2⅘″	1890s
Cabinet card	6 ½″ x 4½″	1866-1900s
Imperial mount	7″ x 10″	1890s
Promenade card	7½″ x 4″	1890s
Paris card	9¾″ x 6¾″	1890s
Panel card	13″ x 7½″	1890s

STEREOGRAPH DATING (3½″ x 7″)

Photographic images
    Flat mount
        Square corner—1857-70
            White, cream or gray—1857-63
            Shades of yellow—1861-70
            Red, green, blue, or lavender—1866-70
        Rounded corner, Standard size—1868-90
        Larger sizes (5″x 7″)—1873-90
    Curved mount
        Buff—1879-1910
        Gray—1892-1950
        Black—1902-60
Printed images
    Black and white, or colored halftones—1898-1930

CARTES-DE-VISITES (2½″ x 4″)

In use from approximately 1860 into the 1890.
    Thin stock (.4 mm) with square corners—to c. 1870.
    .5mm stock with square or rounded corners
        —c. 1870-1875.
    .6mm stock with square or rounded corners
        —c. 1873-1884.
    .7mm stock with square or rounded corners
        —c. 1879-1890s.

Revenue stamps were used on card mounted photographs produced between September 1, 1864 and August 1, 1866, most frequently on cartes-de-visites.

CABINET CARDS (6½″ x 4½″)

Variety of colors from—c. 1860s to c. 1910
Maroon or dark green—c. 1880s.
Gold border—pre-1885.
Scalloped edges—after mid-1880.
Impressed border and lettering—after c. 1890.

POSTCARDS

Postcards can include original photographs and copy images which can predate the card by almost 70 years. Guidelines for determining a range of dates for photographic postcard images can rely on several elements:

If postally used, the postmark indicated the latest possible date for the image.

Unused cards, or those sent in an envelope and without postmark, can use the stamp box printing to provide information about the earliest possible date for the image.

Images can include dating information printed in the image itself.

Undivided back (typically pre-1907) vs. divided back.

STAMP BOX IDENTIFICATION

ARGO (Defender Photo Supply Company)—c. 1905

ARISTO, above eagle logo—c. 1906

ARTURA, in fleur-de-lis—c. 1906

AZO (Kodak):

    with corner diamonds—c. 1907

    with corner triangle pointing up—c. 1906

    with corner triangle pointing up and down —after 1918

    with corner square—after 1926

CYKO:

    in solid script—(ANSCO)—c. 1904

    in open script—(ANSCO)—c. 1906

DEFENDER—c. 1910–20

DEFENDER, with diamond inside box—after 1920

KRUXO, with corner cloverleaf—c. 1907

NOKO—c. 1907

PMO—c. 1907

SOLIO—c. 1903

VELOX (Kodak):

    in general—1902–1931

    with corner triangle—c. 1906

    with corner diamonds—c. 1907

    with corner square—c. 1907

BIBLIOGRAPHY

1881 Arizona Business Directory and Gazetteer.

1880-81 Polk Gazetteer.

1905 Polk Gazetteer.

1907 Arizona Business Directory, Gazetteer Publishing Company.

Altshuler, Constance Wynn, *Chains of Command: Arizona and the Army, 1856-1875,* Arizona Historical Society, Tucson, 1981.

Anthony's Photographic Bulletin, New York, January and February, 1872.

Arizona Champion.

Arizona Citizen.

Arizona Daily Citizen.

Arizona Daily Star.

Arizona Enterprise.

Arizona Miner.

Arizona Republican.

Arizona Sentinel.

Arizona Silver Belt.

Arizona Weekly Miner.

Arizona Weekly Star.

Babbitt, James, R., "Surveyors Along the 35th Parallel: Alexander Gardner's Photographs of Northern Arizona, 1867-1868," *Journal of Arizona History,* Autumn, 1981.

Barnes, Will C., *Apaches & Longhorns: The Reminiscences of Will C. Barnes,* Ward Ritchie Press, Los Angeles, 1941.

Barnes, Will C., revised and enlarged by Byrd Granger, *Arizona Place Names,* University of Arizona Press, Tucson, 1985.

Beaman, E. O., "Among the Aztecs, Colorado River," *Anthony's Photographic Bulletin,* New York, November, 1872.

Bell, William, *New Tracks in North America. A Journal of Travel and Adventure Whilst Engaged in the Survey for a Southern Railroad to the Pacific Ocean during 1867-8,* Horn and Wallace, Albuquerque, 1965.

British Columbia Historical News, Vol. 14, (2), Winter, 1980.

Broder, Patricia Janis, *Shadows on Glass: The Indian World of Ben Wittick,* Rowman & Littlefield, Savage, Maryland, 1990.

Buck's Directory of Bisbee for 1904.

Buck's Directory of Phoenix and the Salt River Valley for 1909.

Business Directory of Arizona/New Mexico, Examiner Publishing Company, Las Vegas, New Mexico, 1897.

Census of the United States (Tenth), U.S. Bureau of Census, 1880.

Census of the Territory of Arizona, 1864.

Census of the Territory of Arizona, 1870.

Cesarini, Roland J., "Ben Wittick: Adventurer with a Camera," *Journal of American History,* Summer, 1961.

City of Phoenix Directory for 1892, Bensel Directory Company.

Clifton Clarion.

Coke, Van Deren, *Photography in New Mexico from the Daguerreotype to the Present,* University of New Mexico Press, Albuquerque, 1979.

Conklin, Enoch, *Picturesque Arizona: Being the Result of Travels and Observations in Arizona During the Fall and Winter of 1877,* Continent Stereoscopic Company, illust., Mining Record Printing Establishment, 1878.

Cook, F. A., "Journal of F. A. Cook," unpublished, Arizona Historical Foundation.

Coolidge, Dane, *Arizona Cowboys,* E. P. Dutton, New York, 1938.

Cooper, Evelyn, "The Buehmans of Tucson: A Family Tradition in Arizona Photography," *Journal of Arizona History,* Vol. 30, Autumn, 1989.

Cooper, Evelyn, "C. S. Fly of Arizona," *History of Photography: An International Quarterly,* Vol. 13, January-March, 1989.

Cooper, Evelyn, "Etched with Light: A Survey History of Photography in the Territory of Arizona," unpublished manuscript, doctoral dissertation, Arizona State University, Tempe, 1993.

Craig, John, *Craig's Daguerreian Registry,* John S. Craig, Tortington, Connecticut, 1994.

Curtis, Edward, *The North American Indian,* 20 Vols.; Vols. 1-5, University Press, Cambridge, Massachusetts; Plimpton Press, Norwood, Connecticut, 1907-30.

Cozzens, Samuel, *Explorations & Adventures in Arizona & New Mexico,* Castle Books Sales, Inc., Secaucus, New Jersey, 1988.

Cozzens, Samuel, *The Marvelous Country,* Ross and Haines, Inc., Minneapolis, 1967.

Darrah, William Culp, *Stereo Views, A History of Stereographs in America and their Collection,* William C. Darrah, Gettysburg, Pennsylvania, 1964.

Darrah, William Culp, *The World of Stereographs,* William C. Darrah, Gettysburg, Pennsylvania, 1977.

Davis, Barbara, *Edward S. Curtis, The Life and Times of a Shadowcatcher,* Chronicle Books, San Francisco, 1985.

Depue, Oscar, "My First Fifty Years in Motion Pictures," *Journal of the Society of Motion Picture Engineers,* Vol. 49, December, 1947.

Douglas City Directory, Douglas Directory Company, 1917, 1919.

Farish, Thomas Edwin, *History of Arizona*, Filmer Brothers Electrotype Company, Phoenix, 1915.

Fewkes, Jesse Walter, "Archaeological Expedition to Arizona in 1895," *Seventeenth Annual report of the Bureau of American Ethnology*, Government Printing Office, Washington, D.C., 1899.

Fleming, Paula Richardson, and Judith Luskey, *The North American Indians in Early Photographs*, Harper and Rowe, New York, 1986.

Fowler, Don, *Photographed All the Best Scenery: Jack Hillers' Diary of the Powell Expeditions 1871-1875*, University of Utah Press, Salt Lake City, 1972.

Fowler, Don, *The Western Photographs of John K. Hillers: "Myself In The Water,"* Smithsonian Institution Press, Washington, D.C., 1989.

Frink, Maurice, and Christian Barthelmess, *Photographer On An Army Mule*, University of Oklahoma Press, Norman, 1965.

Grand Canyon National Park and other Arizona Scenes, Fred Harvey, ed., F. Harvey, Grand Canyon, Arizona, 1920.

Graybill, Florence Curtis, and Victor Boesen, *Edward Sheriff Curtis: Visions of a Vanishing Race*, Houghton Mifflin Company, Boston, 1976.

Harvey, Fred, *The Camera in the Southwest*, F. Harvey, Kansas City, Missouri, 1904.

Harvey, Fred, *The Great Southwest Along the Santa Fe*, F. Harvey, Kansas City, Missouri, 1914.

Harvey, Fred, *Through the Southwest: Along the Santa Fe*, F. Harvey, Kansas City, Missouri, 1906.

Hatch, Heather, "A Glorious Legacy," *Journal of Arizona History*, Vol. 28, Winter, 1987.

Higgins, C. A., *Grand Canyon of Arizona: The Titan of Chasms*, Rand McNalley & Company, Chicago, 1915.

Hodge, Hiram, *1877 - Arizona As It Was*, Rio Grande Press, Inc., Chicago, 1965.

Hooper, Bruce, "Arizona Territorial Stereography 1864-1906," Parts I–IV, *Stereo World*, National Stereoscopic Association, Vol. 13, Nos. 1, 3, 4, March/April, July/August, September/October, 1986.

Hooper, Bruce, "Camera on the Mogollon Rim: 19th Century Photography in Flagstaff, Arizona Territory, 1867-1916," *History of Photography*, Vol. 12, No. 2, April, 1988.

Hooper, Bruce, "High Water on Pinal Creek—Roderick Williams' Stereos of the Globe, Arizona Flood of 1904," *Stereo World*, National Stereoscopic Association, Vol. 19, No. 5, November/December, 1992.

Hooper, Bruce, "Joseph C. Parker in Northern Arizona," *History of Photography*, April–June, 1987.

Hooper, Bruce, "McKinley in Arizona: The Underwood & Underwood Record of a Presidential Tour 90 Years Ago," *Stereo World*, National Stereoscopic Association, Vol. 18, No. 2, May/June, 1991.

Horan, James David, *Timothy O'Sullivan: America's forgotten Photographer: The Life and Work of the Brilliant Photographer Whose Camera Recorded the American Scene from the Battlefields of the Civil War to the Frontiers of the West*, Bonanza Books, New York, 1966.

Hough, Walter, *Archaeological Field Work in Northeastern Arizona: The Museum Gates Expedition of 1901*, Government Printing Office, Washington, D.C., 1903.

Hough, Walter, *Antiquities of the Upper Gila and Salt River Valleys in Arizona and New Mexico*, Government Printing Office, Washington, D.C., 1907.

Hough, Walter, "Environmental Interrelations in Arizona," *American Anthropologist*, May, 1898.

Hough, Walter, *The Moki Snake Dance; A Popular Account of That Unparalleled Dramatic Pagan Ceremony of the Pueblo Indians of Tusayan, Arizona, With Incidental Mention of Their Life and Customs*, Passenger Department, Santa Fe Railroad, Chicago, 1901.

Hough, Walter, "Pueblo Environment, 1906," *Science*, Vol. XXIII, No. 597, June 1906.

Hough, Walter, "Sio Shalako at First Mesa," *American Anthropologist*, Vol. 19, No. 3, July/September 1917.

Houlihan, Patrick and Betsy Houlihan, *Lummis in the Pueblos*, Northland Press, Flagstaff, 1986.

Iverson, Peter, *Carlos Montezuma and the Changing World of American Indians*, University of New Mexico Press, Albuquerque, 1982.

Ives, Joseph C., *Steamboat Up the Colorado; From the Journal of Lieutenant Joseph Christmas Ives, United States Topographical Engineers, 1857-1858*, Alexander L. Crosby, ed., Little, Brown and Company, Boston, 1965.

Ives, Joseph C., *United States Army Corps of Topographical Engineers Report Upon the Colorado River of the West, Explored in 1857 and 1858*, Government Printing Office, Washington, D.C., 1861.

Jackson, William Henry, *The Canons of Colorado: From Photographs by W. H. Jackson*, Frank S. Thayer, Denver c. 1890.

James, George Wharton, *Arizona, The Wonderland: The History of its Ancient Cliff and Cave Dwellings, Ruined Pueblos, Conquest by the Spaniards, Jesuit and Franciscan Missions, Trail Makers and Indians; A Survey of its Climate, Scenic Marvels, Topography, Deserts, Mountains, Rivers and Valleys; A Review of its Industries; An Account of its Influence on Art, Literature and Science; And Some Reference to What it Offers of Delight to the*

Automobilist, Sportsman, Pleasure and Health Seeker, Page Company, Boston, 1917.

James, George Wharton, *In & Around the Grand Canyon: The Grand Canyon of the Colorado River in Arizona,* Little, Brown and Company, Boston, 1900.

James, George Wharton, *The Indians of the Painted Desert Region: Hopis, Navahoes, Wallapais, Havasupais,* Little, Brown and Company, Boston, 1903.

James, George Wharton, *The Grand Canyon of Arizona: How to See It,* Little, Brown and Company, Boston, 1910.

Katz, D. Mark, *Witness To An Era: The Life and Photographs of Alexander Gardner: The Civil War, Lincoln, and The West,* Viking Studio Books, New York, 1991.

Kolb Brothers, *The Grand Canyon of Arizona,* Kolb Brothers, Grand Canyon, Arizona, 1913.

Kolb, Ellsworth, *Through the Grand Canyon From Wyoming to Mexico,* Macmillan Company, New York, 1914.

Lessard, Dennis, "E. O. Who?" *American Indian Art Magazine,* Vol. 12, No. 2, Spring 1987.

Long, Paul, *Big Eyes: The Southwestern Photographs of Simeon Schwemberger, 1902-1908,* University of New Mexico Press, Albuquerque, 1992.

Lyon, Luke, *History of the Prohibition of Photography of Southwestern Indian Ceremonies, presented at Researching Dance through Film and Video,* Smithsonian Institution, Washington, D.C., 1986.

MacDougal, Daniel Trembly, "Delta of the Rio Colorado, 1906," *Bulletin of American Geographical Society,* American Geographical Society, January 1906.

MacDougal, Daniel Trembly, "North-American Deserts, 1912," *Geographical Journal,* Vol. XXXIX, No. 2, February 1912.

Mautz, Carl, *Checklist of Western Photographers: A Reference Workbook,* Folk Image Publishing, Brownsville, California, 1976.

McClintock, James, *Arizona,* Clarke Publishing Company, Chicago, 1916.

McLuhan, T. C., *Dream Tracks, The Railroad and the American Indian 1890-1930,* Harry N. Abrams, Inc., New York, 1985.

McKenney's Business Directory, 1882–83.

Mearns, Edgar Alexander, *Mammals of the Mexican Boundary of the United States. A Descriptive Catalogue of the Species of Mammals Occurring in that Region; With a General Summary of the Natural History, and a List of Trees,* Government Printing Office, Washington, D.C., 1907.

Metzger, Joan, "Albert Sutton Reynolds: Ordinary Man, Extraordinary Photographs," *Journal of Arizona History,* Vol. 28, Winter 1987.

Moon, Karl E., *Photographic Studies of Indians,* El Tovar Studio, Fred Harvey, Grand Canyon, Arizona Territory, 1910.

Morenci 1911-12 Directory.

Myrick, David, *Railroads of Arizona,* Howell North Books, San Diego, 1975, 1980, 1983.

Newhall, Beaumont, "Early Western Photographers," *Arizona Highways,* Vol. 22, May, 1946.

Packard, Gar, and Maggy Packard, *Southwest 1880 With Ben Wittick, Pioneer Photographer of Indian and Frontier Life,* Packard Publications, Santa Fe, 1970.

Palmquist, Peter E., *Carleton E. Watkins, Photographer of the American West,* Amon Carter Museum, University of New Mexico Press, Albuquerque, 1983.

Palmquist, Peter E., "'It Is As Hot As H——,' Carleton E. Watkins' Photographic Excursion Through Southern Arizona," *Journal of Arizona History,* Vol. 28, Winter, 1987.

Palmquist, Peter E., *Lawrence & Houseworth/Thomas Houseworth & Co.: A Unique View of the West, 1860-1886,* National Stereoscopic Association, Columbus, Ohio, 1980.

Peabody, Henry Greenwood, *Glimpses of the Grand Canyon of Arizona,* F. Harvey, Kansas City, Missouri, 1902.

Peplow, Edward, *History of Arizona,* Lewis Historical Publishing Company, Inc., New York, 1958.

Phoenix City Directory for 1895, Arizona Directory Company, Phoenix, 1895.

Phoenix City Directory for 1897, Arizona Directory Company, Phoenix, 1897.

Phoenix City Directory for 1899-1900, Arizona Directory Company, Phoenix, 1899.

Phoenix City and Salt River Valley Directory, 1912.

Phoenix City and Salt River Valley Directory, 1913-17.

Phoenix Daily Herald

Phoenix Directory for 1897 and 1898, Phoenix Directory Company.

The Photographer and the River 1889-90 (the Diary of F. A. Nims), Smith, Dwight, ed., Stage Coach Press, Santa Fe, 1967. *Polk's Arizona and New Mexico Directory for 1912-13.*

Photographer of the Southwest: Adam Clark Vroman, 1856-1916, Ruth I. Mahood, ed., Ward Ritchie Press, Los Angeles, California, 1961.

Powell, Lawrence Clark, *Vroman's of Pasadena,* Pasadena, California, 1953.

The Powell Expeditions, 1871-1875, Don Fowler, ed., University of Utah Press, Salt Lake City, 1972.

Prescott Miner

Rowe, Jeremy, "A Trip Through Arizona With Dudley Flanders in 1873-1874," *Stereo World,* National Stereoscopic Association, Vol. 18, No. 5, November/December, 1991.

Rowe, Jeremy, "Arizona Views By Charles O. Farciot," *Journal of Arizona History,* Vol. 28, No. 4, December, 1987.

Rowe, Jeremy, "Copper Creek: Photographic Post Cards of Arizona," *Journal of the West,* Sunflower University Press, Vol. XXVIII, No. 1, January, 1989.

Rowe, Jeremy, "Following the Frontier from Arizona to Alaska: The Photographs of Charles O. Farciot," *Stereo World,* National Stereoscopic Association, Vol. 15, No. 6, January/February, 1989.

Rowe, Jeremy, "The Man-Birds Fly in Phoenix," *Journal of Arizona History,* Autumn, 1994.

Rowe, Jeremy, "Stereographs and Stereoscopic Photography," *Visual Literacy Review,* Vol. 19, No. 1, January, 1990.

Rudisill, Richard, *Photographers of the New Mexico Territory, 1854-1912,* Museum of New Mexico, 1973.

Sawyer, Mark, *Forman Hanna: Pictorial Photographer of the Southwest,* University of Arizona Press, Tucson, 1985.

Serven, J. E., "C. S. Fly: Tombstone, A. T.," *Arizona Highways,* February, 1970.

Simmons, George and Virginia, "First Photographers of the Grand Canyon," *American West,* July/August, 1977.

Skinner, A. P., *A. P. Skinner's Phoenix City Directory for 1903,* A. P. Skinner, Phoenix, 1903.

Skinner, A. P., *A. P. Skinner's Phoenix City and Maricopa County Directory for 1905-1906,* Phoenix Printing Company, Phoenix, 1903.

Sloan, Richard, *History of Arizona,* Record Publishing Company, Phoenix, 1930.

Sobieszek, Robert, "Alexander Gardner's Photographs Along the 35th Parallel," *Image,* June, 1971.

Spude, Robert, "Shadow Catchers: A Portrait of Arizona's Pioneer Photographers, 1863-1893," *Journal of Arizona History,* Vol. 30, Autumn, 1989.

Thrapp, Dan, *The Conquest of Apacheria,* University of Oklahoma Press, Norman, 1967.

Tombstone Epitaph

Tribby's City Directory of the City of Prescott for 1919.

Tribby's City Directory of Prescott for 1920.

Trimble, Marshall, *Arizona: A Cavalcade of History,* Treasure Chest Publications, Tucson, 1989.

Tucson Citizen

Tucson Daily Citizen

Tucson Directories, 1902-07.

Vanderwood, Paul and Frank Samponaro, *Border Fury: A Picture Postcard Record of Mexico's Revolution and U.S. Preparedness, 1910-1917,* University of New Mexico Press, Albuquerque, 1988.

Vaughn, Thomas, "A Guide to the Photographic Archives of the Bisbee Mining and Historical Museum," *The Cochise Quarterly,* Vol. 19, No. 2, Summer, 1989.

Webb, William, and Robert A. Weinstein, *Dwellers at the Source: Southwestern Indian Photographs of A. C. Vroman, 1895-1904,* Grossman Publishers, New York, 1973.

Welling, William, *Collectors' Guide to Nineteenth-Century Photographs,* Macmillan Company, New York, 1976.

Welling, William, *Photography in America: The Formative Years, 1839-1900,* Crowell, New York, 1978.

Wild, Peter, *George Wharton James,* Wayne Chatterton and James H. Maguire, eds., Boise State University, Boise, 1990.

Woody, Clara and Milton Schwartz, *Globe Arizona: Early Times in a Little World of Copper and Cattle,* Arizona Historical Society, Tucson, 1977.

Wright, Barton, Marnie Gaede and Marc Gaede, *The Hopi Photographs of Kate Corey,* Chaco Press, 1986.

Younger, Erin, "Changing Images: A Century of Photography on the Hopi Reservation (1880-1980)," *Hopi Photographers, Hopi Images,* University of Arizona Press, Tucson, 1983.

OTHER SOURCES:

Altshuler, Constance Wynn, correspondence with the author.

Biographical files, Arizona Historical Foundation (Sachs Collection).

Biographical files, Arizona Historical Society.

Biographical files, Bill Jay Research Files.

Hall, George, correspondence with the author.

Palmquist, Peter, correspondence with the author.

Photographic research and publication of images from personal collection.

Sachs Collection, Arizona Historical Foundation, Hayden Library, Arizona State University.

Index